Organizational Surveys

The Diagnosis and Betterment of Organizations Through Their Members

Organizational Surveys

The Diagnosis and Betterment of Organizations Through Their Members

Frank J. Smith
College of William and Mary

2003

LAWRENCE ERLBAUM ASSOCIATES, PUBLISHERS
Mahwah, New Jersey   London

Copyright © 2003 by Lawrence Erlbaum Associates, Inc.
All rights reserved. No part of this book may be reproduced in any
form, by photostat, microform, retrieval system, or any other
means, without prior written permission of the publisher.

Lawrence Erlbaum Associates, Inc., Publishers
10 Industrial Avenue
Mahwah, NJ 07430

Cover design by Kathryn Houghtaling Lacey

Library of Congress Cataloging-in-Publication Data

Smith, Frank J., 1927-
Organizational surveys : the diagnosis and betterment of organizations through their members / Frank J. Smith.
    p. cm. – (Applied psychology series)
    Includes bibliographical references and index.
ISBN 0-8058-4384-1 (alk. paper)
1. Employee attitude surveys. 2. Organizational effectivenes—
    Evaluation. I. Title II. Series in applied psychology.

HF5549.5.A83 S65 2003
658.3'007'23—dc21   2002029470
                                                            CIP

Books published by Lawrence Erlbaum Associates are printed on
acid- free paper, and their bindings are chosen for strength and dura-
bility.

Printed in the United States of America
10 9 8 7 6 5 4 3 2 1

To Edgar B. Stern, Jr., visionary,
who always had the courage to ask
and the wisdom to act.

Series in Applied Psychology
Edwin A. Fleishman, George Mason University,
Jeanette N. Cleveland, Pennsylvania State University
Series Editors

Manuel London
How People Evaluate Others in Organizations

Manuel London
Job Feedback: Giving, Seeking, and Using Feedback for Performance Improvement, Second Edition

Manuel London
Leadership Development: Paths to Self-Insight and Professional Growth

Robert F. Morrison and Jerome Adams
Contemporary Career Development Issues

Michael D. Mumford, Garnett Stokes, and William A. Owens
Patterns of Life History: The Ecology of Human Individuality

Kevin R. Murphy
Validity Generalization: A Critical View

Kevin R. Murphy and Frank E. Saal
Psychology in Organizations: Integrating Science and Practice

Erich P. Prien, Jeffery S. Shippmann, and Kristin O. Prien
Individual Assessment as Practiced in Industry and Consulting

Ned Rosen
Teamwork and the Bottom Line: Groups Make a Difference

Heinz Schuler, James L. Farr, and Mike Smith
Personnel Selection and Assessment: Individual and Organizational Perspectives

John W. Senders and Neville P. Moray
Human Error: Cause, Prediction, and Reduction

Frank J. Smith
Organizational Surveys: The Diagnosis and Betterment of Organizations Through Their Members

Contents

Series Foreword

Series Editors

Edwin A. Fleishman
George Mason University

Jeanette N. Cleveland
Pennsylvania State University

There is a compelling need for innovative approaches to the solution of many pressing problems involving human relationships in today's society. Such approaches are more likely to be successful when they are based on sound research and applications. This Series in Applied Psychology offers publications that emphasize state-of-the-art research and its applications to important issues of human behavior in a variety of societal settings. The objective is to bridge both academic and applied interests.

Surveys conducted within organizations have become an important aspect of human resource management and organizational functioning. These surveys provide management with information about the organization that can provide a basis for informed and competent decision making and organizational development and change. Surveys can provide feedback to organizational members and have a critical role in assessing employee attitudes, training needs, diagnosing organizational situations, and motivating organization members. Thus, surveys constitute an important research tool in developing and maintaining effective organizations. The most effective surveys are those based on sound research procedures and grounded in knowledge drawn from research in industrial psychology and organizational behavior.

The present book, *Organizational Surveys: The Diagnosis and Betterment of Organizations Through Their Members*, by Frank Smith offers a unique perspective on organizational surveys by a recognized leader in this field. Dr. Smith draws on 40 years of experience in formulating, directing, and interpreting organizational surveys. He served as Director of Organizational Studies at Sears Roebuck and Company for 21 years and, after that, as President of Organizational Studies, Inc.

The program developed at Sears is regarded as a model of how organizational surveys can be conducted and used to enhance organizational development, with benefits to employees and to management. The fact that the Sears program has endured for more than 40 years, and has led to hundreds of applications, is a tribute to the success of the program Dr. Smith and his colleagues developed.

In this book, Smith does not focus on specific methodological issues, such as details of questionnaire construction, sampling, and highly technical aspects of conducting surveys, which are covered nicely elsewhere (see e.g., Dr. Smith's book with R. Dunham, *Organizational Surveys: Internal Assessment of Organizational Health*, which includes methodology and survey construction). Rather, he has chosen to emphasize the *experience* of developing, carrying out, and interpreting surveys on a wide variety of organizational issues in a very diverse set of organizations. The reader will learn a lot about life in organizations and what it feels like to deal with organizational issues, and how the data provided by appropriately formulated and designed surveys can lead to the "betterment of organizations through their members".

It should be noted that, in addition to developing sound sets of questionnaires, the Sears program placed particular stress on interviewing, and this is reflected in this book. It will be seen that these interviews proved to have considerable explanatory value in the interpretation and impact of survey results.

After presenting some fundamentals of organizational survey research and development, the author provides specific "cases" of survey applications in organizations, with illustrations of actual reports of survey results to top management. Each case is presented with its historical context in the organization and with a discussion of the aftermath and consequence of the study. These cases illustrate a variety of organizational problems and settings for which survey data turned out to be remarkably useful. An especially useful feature is the book's description of the follow-up impact of surveys and of the sometime unexpected consequences of the survey's administration and findings.

The book is appropriate for human resource managers and professionals, as well as students, teachers, consultants, and practitioners in the field of organizational behavior who want to learn more about this important area of research and application.

Foreword

I first met the author of this book at an Illinois Psychological Association meeting when we were both members of a symposium, "Attitude surveys in large organizations." At the beginning of the session the audience outnumbered the symposium members eight to five. The eight audience members included four nuns, all in the first row. After the first paper the four nuns arose as one to leave. One of them said apologetically that they were in the wrong session; they wanted to be in the session on sex in therapeutic relations. Of the remaining four audience members, two left after the second paper and one left a bit later. One avid fan of job attitude surveys sat in the back row and refused to leave voluntarily or be driven away by our pointed comments. We presented our papers to an audience of one. After the symposium, we retired to the nearest bar to complain about the lack of perspicacity of the psychologists who were in attendance at the meeting. Perhaps because we survived the embarrassment of this traumatic first meeting, Frank Smith and I began a series of collaborative efforts that lasted for the next 40 years. I served as a consultant to his department. Frank served as an occasional (and unpaid) consultant to our students, a research collaborator with some of them, and as an occasional PhD committee member.

During most of this 40-year period, Frank was director of the Sears Employee Attitude Survey Department. This book is the result of Frank's experience directing the internal attitude survey program and later as a consultant to organizations. The book reflects his intellectual curiosity and willingness to devote time and effort to aspects of his program and job-attitude research well removed from a narrow focus on his specific set of scales and their use with Sears employees.

Our collaboration seemed to be mutually beneficial. For my part, I learned much about how to apply my own basic research on job attitudes to important questions about employee-attitude programs. The Sears program that Frank developed and directed was a model of how such a program should be conducted within an organization from the developmental work on the measurement of job attitudes, to the tri-annual timing and the administration of the survey itself, and to the feedback of the survey results to the management and the employees at Sears. Frank and the Employee Attitude Department functioned as an unofficial but effective ombudsman for the employees in getting complaints heard and concerns aired and addressed. The Department was also a contributor to personnel decisions made within Sears regarding managerial succession and store management when job attitudes of employees became a part of the evaluation of store managers. Frank managed to serve both masters from the base of information about employees' attitudes throughout the organization. One of the important and enduring lessons I took away from the Sears program was that Frank never allowed the program to be used in ad hoc, "fire-fighting" efforts. The data from the annual surveys of one third of the Sears employees formed an extremely useful database, but special administrations of the survey were not perverted to use in union fighting or in attempts to remove a particular manager. The trust engendered in the employees by this and other, similar, decisions by Frank contributed much to the success of the job attitude survey program.

The 5 years from 1995–2000 were marked by intense competition among organizations to attract high-quality human resources (HR), as well as continuing efforts to retain the talented personnel organizations already had on their roles. During this time, I have heard a number of presentations by HR managers from Fortune 500 companies who have discovered the usefulness of the information contained in scores from employees' job-attitude surveys, have seen the benefits of feedback of job attitudes to both managers and the employees, and have realized the necessity for basing their programs on high-quality measurement of employees' evaluations of their jobs. After each of these presentations, I was struck by how little has changed in most of today's organizations, and how much the more successful programs being described today resemble the program Frank devised during his years at Sears. It was clear to me that HR managers would learn much from an examination of the Sears program. The knowledge and experience distilled in this book might save current and future HR managers much time and effort in the development and implementation of effective employee attitude programs.

I have learned much from Frank Smith during the years of our colleague-ship. The publication of this book makes much of what he learned available to a wider audience of today's HR professionals and managers, as well as students and teachers of organizational behavior.

—*Charles Hulin*
University of Illinois

Preface

This book is about experiences with a survey program that has guided management decisions and actions in a wide array of industrial settings. I did give serious thought to calling it Confessions of a One Method Man, for during the last 40 years, surveys have been the focus of my approach to organizational studies. After more sober thought, and realizing that this one method has involved me in almost every aspect of organizational psychology as well as organizational life, I chose a less defensive title.

The 40 years were divided into two almost equal periods—20 years within corporate life at Sears, Roebuck and Company and 20 years as an outside consultant (although I continued to administer the Sears program for another 10 years after leaving the company). The experiences related here come from both periods and in them are lessons gained from very successful efforts, as well as from failures; from major survey projects, as well as one-shot efforts; some from long ago and some from only yesterday. Whatever their vintage, one common goal of the surveys reported has been to provide managers with a reliable idea of what their employees were thinking.

In preparing this book, I have tried to keep in mind a criticism of an earlier survey text that Randy Dunham and I wrote 20 years ago. It was said the book lacked "personal experiences." Of course, at the time my whole experience had been within Sears and could not be published—for ethical reasons as well as for my own job security. So, while seething over this criticism for 20 years, I did manage to gain some outside experience along with an OK from Sears to publish.

Several experiences reported here occurred some time ago and their delayed reporting is out of respect for both the institutions and people involved, but as can be seen in the other cases of recent vintage, most of the issues raised are as current today as they were then.

In some chapters I have included a good deal of detail to allow the readers to judge the results and interpretations for themselves. In others I have summarized the survey results and research findings in order to focus on their impact. In most cases I have let the reports speak for themselves. Except for those involving Sears, I have not identified the organization studied. In the Sears case, any attempt to disguise it would have been a sham. Even here, however, the identities of individuals have been omitted or disguised for ethical considerations as well as the likelihood that some of the more dubious characters are still alive and may remain serious gun owners.

I should add for today's reader that my association with Sears occurred during some of its most halcyon years. It was then by far number one in the industry and was a leader in progressive human relations policies and practices.

It was most of all a fun place to work. Its people had a curious resilience that often turned setbacks into games. One example:

> When the new Renton, Washington, store opened, its gala celebration was marred by a particular union informational picket.
>
> He remained there for years.
>
> To a company that was almost pathologically concerned about unions, this could have been alarming. To the employees who had no interest in unions, for the most part, he was just another person trying to make a living. They not only befriended the picket but accepted him as one of their own. He in turn became a pretty good customer! He would always put down his sign before entering the store at the end of his shift. On frequent rainy days, he was actually seen directing traffic, helping people find their cars, and carrying some of their packages.
>
> On its fifth anniversary, the store held a grand celebration. The picket was invited as a guest and was given a special 5-year service pin! (For a more elaborate example of the climate in Sears, see "An Evening With Leonardo" Appendix C.)

From my professional point of view, Sears provided a huge, diverse, and international laboratory consisting of factories, laboratories, stores, warehouses, and an array of technical and administration functions. Unfortunately, a fairly long-standing policy in my department prevented much of our work from being published, but once this prohibition was lifted, a number of our studies did appear in various publications. In an effort to remain professionally respectable while it was in effect, I got around the "no-publication policy" by having academic friends and hordes of graduate students conduct studies, which were published by them or became dissertations. I think it only fair that these same students, now long employed, buy a copy of this book.

There is one further point about the Sears experiences. In meetings with some counterparts in other companies, I have learned that the relationships my predecessors and I enjoyed with Sears top management were in many ways unique. We had a direct line to top management and were frequently involved as advisors on company policies and planning. Admittedly, although our advice was as often ignored as accepted, we always had total support for what we did. Although my own "boss" did refer to me as his "hair shirt," I took this as a compliment, recognizing that, on many occasions, no better service could have been rendered. At the very top levels a somewhat more generous perception of our role was expressed and even the most remote of CEOs, 10 in all during my time, were quite open to our findings—even the very bad news delivered with the bark on. I like to think, and have always claimed, that we earned their support, although it is possible they simply saw us as a source of information with no axe to grind.

(I suppose it may be of passing interest that shortly after my 20 + 10-year relationship ended, the company went into something of a decline. Although I, of course, never saw or claimed any causal connection, a surprising number of people have!)

Looking back at all my experiences and not just those reported here, gives rise to mixed feelings. Did the survey program do any good? Could it have been done better? Did it do any harm? The answers I think are "Yes," "Hell yes," and "Maybe." Certainly, to the method's credit, scores of organizations benefitted, hundreds of managers became better leaders, and thousands of employees had their careers and workplaces improved. As to what was left wanting, even the inexperienced reader will see that had results been reported more meaningfully and implemented with greater skill, improvements may have been more enduring and demonstrable. Any harm that may have occurred was limited, for the most part, to few individuals. I don't know of any organizational damage. No doubt a few managers found it painful to find out what their employees really thought of them, but many others, almost all in my experience, claimed they profited by such feedback and gained a good deal of insight from it. Less than a handful had careers attenuated by survey reports, which in every case revealed examples of gross leadership behavior or unacceptable practices.

In the end, my chief regret is that some surveys had either less impact than was expected or produced positive changes that were less than enduring. At their very least, however, the results of this one method, lasting or not, did uncover a great deal of talent hidden in organization "closets," made the work life of many employees more rewarding and enjoyable, and left the health of many organizations better than it was found.

This volume is divided into three major sections. Part I includes a brief history of the particular survey approach cited throughout the book and lays the groundwork on which any sound survey program rests. The intent is to provide managers, students, and other interested readers with an understanding of the different functions served by surveys and an appreciation of the different stages involved in survey program development and implementation. Also included is a nontechnical discussion of the tools of survey work: the questionnaire and the interview. This should provide a working understanding of their design requirements as well as their organizational implications. Finally, a section is devoted to some survey pitfalls and to questions often raised by managers regarding survey administration and implementation.

Part II summarizes four studies that illustrate research efforts that have helped establish the validity of the survey instruments described in this book. These are nontechnical discussions, but do refer the interested reader to related published work.

Part III consists of examples of actual survey projects and cases. These are taken from a broad array of organizational settings and are intended to demonstrate the kinds of information surveys can provide. In some cases, the surveys have been used to give management an objective description of a situation, to initiate or facilitate change, and even to defend organizations in legal proceedings. Where possible, emphasis is placed on the necessary and profitable link surveys have with conceptual and applied research.

The book should be of interest to managers who want to know what surveys can offer their organizations or who want a basis for judging programs they may be developing or considering; instructors or students of organizations who want a slice of organizational life or an understanding of what goes into building a competent survey approach; and survey practitioners who may want to examine, or even be amused by, the efforts made here.

ACKNOWLEDGMENTS

The help and encouragement of friends and colleagues is sincerely recognized. Certainly first on the list is Professor Edwin A. Fleishman, whose patience, sound advice, and editorial help were indispensable.

Dr. Jack Martin made many helpful suggestions on an earlier version of the book. I wish I could blame him for any errors in the present work, but I can't.

Thanks to Karen Foley, resident genius of the Data Lab Corporation, who resurrected data thought to be lost, and was always ready to do the impossible. Thanks also to Sandra Hollett, my Canadian colleague, who alerted me to the customer service data reported in chapter 5.

Two long-term colleagues, Professors Chuck Hulin and Lyman Porter, both solid professionals, both steadfast friends, and both mediocre fortune tellers, for more than 40 years, never failed to help educate the author.

From within the Sears organization, thanks to Con Massey, Bill Sanders, and Charlie Bacon, Senior Vice-President, who lifted the ban on publication and provided unfettered support. Thanks also to Bill Ashley and Kathy Bell who carried out much of the survey follow up. A host of coworkers from happy days: Willa Lee, Cheryl Johnson, Barry Rabin, and Janice Kolbaska who made a group into a team also deserve my thanks.

Special thanks to Marie Caulford CPS for deciphering skills and for putting the manuscript in order.

Grateful acknowledgment is also given to Scott Foresman and Company for permission to adapt Appendix A and the passage: p.119–120, from *Organizational Surveys: Internal Assessment of Organizational Health* (Dunham and Smith 1979).

Part I

Introduction: Survey Functions, Tools, and Development

This section introduces the subject of employee surveys with a brief reference to some of the pioneering work carried out in this field within Sears Roebuck. This is followed by a somewhat fuller account of later developments made possible by electronic data processing.

Beyond this brief history, an attempt is made to acquaint readers with the many ways organizations have come to use surveys. The functions served by surveys are detailed in chapter 1.

In chapter 2, a nontechnical discussion of the steps involved in developing a valid survey program are described in order to acquaint readers with a general understanding of the process and to show its close and necessary relationship with behavioral research.

Chapter 3 is a discussion of the tools of survey work questionnaires and interviews as they were developed and used within Sears and later applied there and elsewhere.

Chapter 4 points out some significant but avoidable survey pitfalls to which managers should be alerted. The chapter also provides a reassuring discussion of common questions about the survey process.

1

Functions of Organizational Survey Programs

Since the rather unsteady and unstructured introduction of attitude surveys in the 1930s, they have increasingly helped managers gain perspectives on many facets of organizational life. The expanded use of surveys has been an evolutionary process, born of practical experience and strengthened by behavioral research in and of organizations. As a result, some fairly sophisticated instruments and techniques are now available to address more and more complicated situations. In this process, surveys have come to serve a number of functions that are the primary focus of this chapter.

The presentation of the book is given through the lens of a current, long-established program, originally designed for use in all divisions of a very large company, Sears, Roebuck & Co., but soon extended to serve several hundred other organizations. As such, it also served as a model for programs in other institutions (e.g., Los Alamos National Laboratory, IBM, Johnson Controls, Union Carbide).

HISTORY AND CONTEXT OF THE SURVEY PROGRAM

The Sears survey program has had a long and protean history. Although its very early development is not detailed here, a short account of its very beginnings may be helpful. In briefest terms, the program was founded with the best of intentions, almost destroyed by some of the worst, and reborn by some of the most enlightened. It began almost by accident when a senior manager, famous for his legendary "people oriented" style, became the company president. Wanting some means of retaining his contact with employees, he commissioned a staff assistant to "figure out

3

some way to find out what was going on out there" (Worthy, 1982, personal communication). The staff assistant contacted a pioneer in public opinion polling (David Houser) and in short order the survey program became a reality. It was a very unstructured vehicle and made no claim to psychometric respectability and was limited to the company's mail-order plants. It did, however, serve its intended purpose for more than a decade. Its most unlikely beginning in the midst of the Great Depression (circa 1936) makes it the oldest continuous industrial survey program. An excellent and comprehensive account of its very early history (1938–1960) can be found in Jacoby (1986).

It may be of interest that the early survey's potential influence on productivity and labor relations was not initially considered, (Worthy, 1988, personal communication). That soon changed in the post World War II period. As confirmed by Jacoby (1986), the early survey eventually was used by outside labor consultants as a union prevention tool—in some cases as a weapon! Needless to say this nearly destroyed the program's credibility among employees and managers. Had it not been for the professionalism of those who actually developed that very early program, it may have died. According to Jacoby,

> as this study will show, the research spawned by the program made significant contributions to a number of academic disciplines, notably motivation theory, attitude survey methodology, and organizational theory. Although the research contributed to the company's objectives of improving labor relations, that was not always its intended purpose. The researchers who participated in the program were not mere servants of power. They had their own intellectual agendas. (p. 603)

As the company became a huge, diversified, and rapidly expanding international concern, the role of the survey program was greatly expanded. Any vestige of its union-fighting role was effectively quashed by an enlightened management action and the insistence of professionals who later became involved with the program. Their actions (circa 1950) completely separated the survey organization from that of labor relations. From then on, the survey program operated independently.

With the availability of electronic data processing, the program received considerable company support in an effort to place it on a sound professional basis and make it a company-wide service. It is this later so-called "modern" era (1960–2000) that is the subject of this book.

Because of the company's size, cultural variations, and diverse operations, the later survey program had to meet a number of ever-changing situational and procedural demands. For example, the program had to start developing a uniform measure of employee attitudes to be used over a reasonable time and across many work situations. At the same time it had to develop a means for tapping various site-specific opinions expressed in different languages by people at different organizational levels. As such, the program began an evolutionary process through which many different organizational functions were served.

THE PURPOSES OF SURVEYS IN ORGANIZATIONS

Almost all survey functions share a common objective, that of providing management at various levels with a picture of an organization from which informed decisions can be made and competent interventions can be mounted.

Some of the purposes to be served by a properly constructed survey in an organization were anticipated very early by Vitelies (1953). He cited four purposes, chiefly aimed at employee welfare concerns: (a) learn how much importance workers attach to different aspects of work, (b) assess levels of satisfaction and morale, (c) identify influences on satisfaction and morale, and (d) extend motivational therapy. In a 1947 address to the American Management Association, Worthy looked at surveys in a more expanded role, where the aim was understanding the whole organization. According to Worthy, "Surveys have as their scope the functioning of the organization as a whole and the entire pattern of formal and informal relationships which comprise it." Later Smith (1962) and Dunham & Smith (1979) described seven separate functions.

Still later, Higgs and Ashworth (1996), and Kraut (1996) provided a comprehensive list of survey functions ranging from the general to the very specific. The following 10 functions lean on their list and extend it a bit. They are:

1. Diagnosing organizational situations
2. Providing a feedback loop
3. Predicting organizational outcomes
4. Surfacing organizational strengths and weaknesses
5. Monitoring and trending organizational change
6. Facilitating management decisions
7. Providing training structure
8. Providing platforms for organizational research
9. Reifying corporate values
10. Documenting corporate experience

In the following discussion, each of these functions is described in some detail.

Diagnosing Organizational Situations

Almost all surveys are diagnostic either by intent or simply as a result of the process itself. In many instances the aim is not much more than letting management know what is happening among people in the organization. This is no small chore, nor is it without value to the executives, especially those at the top. Consider, for example, the plight of President Wilson expressed before the National Press Club (1916); paraphrased here: "The people of the United States are thinking for themselves. You do not know, and what's worse, since the responsibility is mine, I do not know what they are thinking about. I have the most imperfect means of finding out, and yet I have to act as if I knew." This is not to suggest that President Wilson needed a national survey, but his statement does contrast with the situation of the more modern CEO, described in chapter 14, who by means of a survey, was able to find out what the employees were thinking and was able to act on it.

Assessing current attitudes is all part of the diagnostic function as is the measure of an organization's strengths and weaknesses, its goal paths and the barriers to them—all as seen by its members. Several examples of surveys, which were at least initially designed as purely diagnostic efforts are given in chapters 11 and 10. Chapter 17, which is devoted to a decade of safety surveys conducted between 1985 and 1996, is also an example of the diagnostic effort.

Providing a Feedback Loop

Somewhat related to the diagnostic function is the notion of a survey as a direct backward channel to top management. It is a channel that automatically completes the management–employee loop; one that often creates a basis for an ongoing dialogue between the two levels. In large organizations, this function can be especially effective in providing *"a communication system which gets around the filtering of negative reports often seen in organizations"* (Kraut, 1996, p. 8).

Given the "isolation" of the top executive, an unfiltered yet balanced account of "what is going on out there" can be a unique source of knowledge—be it reassuring or disturbing. The survey series reported in chapter 15 had this feedback function as one of its aims.

Predicting Organizational Outcomes

Most organizations would welcome a means by which employee reactions to management decisions could be anticipated, or by which specific organizational outcomes such as turnover, absenteeism, labor negotiations, and customer acceptance could be predicted. In many companies surveys have been used to provide just this kind of information and have often alerted managers to the likely result of their actions. Chapters 5 through 8 provide examples of research that helped establish predictive links between employee attitudes and certain organizational outcomes. Chapter 18 describes an applied example of a prediction, based solely on questionnaire data, of how employees would react to a contemplated organizational change.

Surfacing Organizational Strengths and Weaknesses

Surveys for many years, have been effective in pinpointing problem areas and, through indepth approaches, have often uncovered their probable causes. An example of this function was clearly shown in a series of surveys conducted in a large-scale coal-mining operation. It brought to the surface the extent and depth of the problems whose intensity was only vaguely sensed by management. In doing so it set the stage for a successful intervention based on employee and managerial participation (chap. 9, this volume).

In a similar vein, a survey of a TV and radio station reported in chapter 16 revealed the reality of what turned out to be a "pseudo problem" and in doing so was able to persuade management to abandon a drastic, and likely dysfunctional action it was considering. Chapter 15 includes an example of how a survey identified critically important talents that were largely hidden from management's purview.

Monitoring and Trending Organizational Change

Change is so ubiquitous in organizational life, its effects are often neither anticipated nor immediately recognized. In organizations with ongoing survey programs, the monitoring of such effects has become a conventional practice. Similarly, where reliable survey measures are available, trends in the acceptance of many policies and practices can be readily plotted. Chapter 15 also includes an example of survey monitoring in a 19-year study conducted in two ski resort operations, elements of which preceded and followed a major change in its location and management.

Facilitating Management Decisions

Probably all top management decisions are made with some sense of trepidation. Questions of how they will be received and the extent to which their hoped for effects will be realized are common. As suggested, properly designed and executed surveys can often give reasonably precise answers to such questions. They can always measure postdecision reactions and often can anticipate them. What is frequently overlooked, however, is the role surveys can play in *facilitating* the acceptance of management decisions. In unique situations they may even determine the decision itself. An instance of the latter can be seen in chapter 19, in which the use of survey results all but decided the choice of a new CEO. Chapter 13 relates how survey results influenced both the choice of a compensation plan and facilitated its acceptance.

Providing Training Structure

Identifying the training needs of employees is probably one of the oldest functions provided by surveys. One unusual extension of this function, however, is given in chapter 20. It depicts a situation in which supervisory training needs were not only identified, but the survey findings themselves served as the actual content of a subsequent training exercise.

Providing Platforms for Organizational Research

On many occasions surveys have been vehicles for carrying out newly designed research studies or for testing results of previous work. Both are spawned by academic interests and by inhouse organizational needs. Sometimes they are carefully planned although perhaps, more often than admitted, they are accidental. Chapter 7 is an example of the former, an 18-month longitudinal study of organizational commitment, whereas chapter 13 includes an example of the fortuitous use of a set of attitude scales that were included in a survey solely for the purpose of helping a graduate student obtain data for a dissertation. These same scales later came to guide a very successful organizational intervention.

Reifying Corporate Values

An extremely important yet often unrecognized function of a survey is its reinforcement of a corporate value. As noted by Kraut (1996) and Smith (1962), the very process of asking about the reality of a corporate value (i.e., whether it is observed or reinforced in practice) serves to communicate that value. Moreover, the extent to which a survey quantifies a corporate value, especially those relating to the treatment of employees, establishes a kind of managerial discipline regarding it. Plato's aphorism, "what is honored in a country will be fostered there" seems apropos. However, in most organizations, that which is honored had best be measured if it is to receive managerial and employee attention. An excellent example of this is seen in the work of Schneider (1990), who has shown that customer satisfaction is most likely to occur in situations where this value is clearly emphasized and measured by management at all levels in the organization.

> The gap between values that are simply stated and those that are practical (measured) can be seen in one blatant but not atypical example. In a pre-survey interview with the CEO of a very large concern, the notion was voiced repeatedly that the company firmly believed that its "gains and pains" were to be evenly shared across the whole organization. This was so forcibly stated that several survey items were created to measure its credibility among employees. Shortly before administration of the survey, however, the company's Vice President of Human Resources insisted on the removal of the items. The company was about to lay off a number of lower-level people and these items, it was felt, would prove embarrassing.

Documenting Corporate Experience

This last function was recognized in the documentation provided by survey data in a federal discrimination trial, but there are undoubtedly similar examples. An account of this use is given in chapter 21. Briefly, survey data collected 10 years earlier, became the only documented contemporaneous evidence of employee job interests at the time of the original charge of discrimination. Of course these data proved very useful when the case eventually came to trial 10 years later. The case involved rather high stakes (almost a billion-dollar liability) and without the documented evidence provided by the survey, the company's successful defense would have been hindered.

CONCLUDING NOTE

The discussion of the functions served by surveys is intended to acquaint readers with the many ways managers and their organizations have used and implemented survey results. In the survey experiences reported later, workplace examples of how each function has played out are presented.

The reader will undoubtedly note that many of the survey experiences presented later tend to concentrate on fairly serious problems. This focus is appropriate in that such issues usually require much time and effort, are sometimes difficult for management to accept, and often have major organizational implications. An unfortunate inference drawn from this orientation, however, is that surveys are only concerned with fault-finding—that they only deal with organizational issues that have gone awry. Such an inference is not only unfortunate, it misses the point. Although any well designed survey approach, be it based on questionnaires, interviews, or both, will certainly identify problem areas, its major thrust must be on revealing the essential elements of an *organization's health*. If this were not the case, any serious attempt to correct existing problems would not be possible.

To a manager, the process by which the elements of organizational health are discovered and manipulated can be challenging, rewarding, and fun: *challenging*, in deciding what, and what not, to act on, which priorities must be set, and what consequences can be expected; *rewarding*, in seeing the hoped-for acceptance of an organizational intervention; *fun*, in gaining that "aha" experience in which the tacit influence of ones own behavior (or that of others) has on the organization is discovered. The whole process often identifies leadership practices that work best or are most appreciated, the day-to-day ways in which people interact successfully, and even the organizational effect of the ever present "character" who seems to find a way to "stir things up" and in so doing helps energize a work group or larger family of employees.

2

Stages of Survey Program Development

Although the early surveys in the industry had a "boot-strap" quality that relied almost totally on common sense notions and very practical experience, their constant growth and increasing sophistication has profited greatly from the flow of research and conceptual studies of organizational behavior. So it is with the survey program discussed here. Although this program's early development was, of course, highly dependent on the studies and attitude-scaling techniques available at the time, some as early as 1964, the modern reader can be assured these techniques are still current and much of the conceptual and empirical research on which the program was based is still quite relevant. This chapter outlines some of the studies that influenced three broad stages of survey development, namely, the *Design, Interpretive,* and the *Follow-up* stages. Additional research, directed at maintaining the reliability and validity of the program, is discussed in later chapters.

THE DESIGN STAGE

As indicated earlier, given the very rapid growth and expansion of Sears across North and South America, senior management decided the survey program might be most helpful if re-established on a permanent and regularly scheduled corporate-wide basis. It was, in fact, set up to survey one third of the entire company every year. This allowed for timely monitoring and follow-up action but avoided being overly intrusive. To these ends, the program was completely overhauled and adopted a dual path approach—one aimed at attaining a set of core scales that would provide a consistent, stable, and psychometrically sound measure of job satisfaction, and the other aimed at identifying the likely but ever changing influences on it. The idea was to create a basic and workable "cause and effect" system of analysis in which job satisfaction would be measured by a set of *core scales*, while its likely causes would be determined by an accompanying inventory of descriptive items. This analysis would, of course, be reinforced by the free written comments of survey participants and, on occasion, by the results of interviews.

Core Scales

Although the actual steps involved in developing the core scales are given in chapter 3, a brief account of their formatting may be of interest. The format of each core item was largely determined by extensive trials and interviews with employees and, to a lesser extent, by organizational "political" concerns. This latter point may need an explanation for it is a part of organizational life that, along with technical demands, has to be considered in survey development. In this instance, the issue involved a challenge, voiced by a few (but vocal) managers regarding the ambiguity of certain questionnaire items. Their specific targets were item statements that required an *agree* or *disagree* response (the so-called *Likert* item.) Their question was: does a *disagree* response imply an opposite opinion or does it mean that the item statement was incorrect? A well known example relates to the item: "all politicians are a little dishonest." It was discovered that a large percentage of those who disagreed did so because they felt "all politicians were *very dishonest!*"

Rather than allow this admittedly minor concern to become a point of debate, all the items in the *core scales* were designed with bipolar responses in which both positive and negative positions on an issue would be stated. For example: The work I do:

1. Greatly encourages extra effort
2. Encourages extra effort
3. Makes little difference
4. Discourages extra effort
5. Greatly discourages extra effort

Although this format requires more space, it not only muted a "political" concern but, by a later analysis, was actually shown to be a robust method of attitude measurement (Dunham & Smith, 1979). Once the format of items in each core scale was determined, the scales were subjected to a series of trials and statistical analysis (described in chap. 3)

The noncore items were written in more-or-less neutral terms and are hereafter revered to as *descriptive items*. As indicated these were intended to accompany the *core scales* but only as a means of identifying presence or absence of certain workplace conditions. Their creation rested less on psychometric considerations than on extensive employee interviews.

The creation of both core and noncore items rested on the then available body of research and theoretical speculations regarding job satisfaction, leadership practices, and work-related need satisfaction. Some of these now well known works are briefly noted here.

One obvious and very early need-satisfaction theory was that proposed by Maslow (1958). Not intended as a theory of work motivation, it never-the-less gained wide acceptance in the industry and that in turn encouraged its inclusion in both survey questionnaires and interviews. Although Maslow's proposed hierarchical arrangement of needs (ranging from survival to self-actualization) was neither accepted nor tested by the survey, individual questions regarding need satisfaction did continually serve to identify the important and dominant work-related motives of various employee groups. For example, a survey of a nursing school in the1980s discovered a strong motivational need for improved social interactions (chap. 11); a series of studies in coal mines (circa 1981–1986) revealed the conflicting social needs of miners—the need to conform to group pressures versus the need to resist group coercion (chap. 9); a study of a research institute (1990), pointed to a conflict between work-related ego needs of one group of scientists and the self-actualizing needs of another (chap. 10); and a long series of surveys (1989–2000) in the petrochemical industry clearly identified the importance of safety needs and their influence on and by employee motivation and morale (chap. 17).

Another source of questionnaire content came from the "*Participative School*" (Likert, 1967; McGregor, 1960). Its stress on employee participation in management decisions had a dual appeal. First, it was in keeping with the Sears management philosophy and the decentralized structure of its expanding retail operations. In addition, the company's participative *Profit Sharing* plan been seen in effect for many years, and even to this day, company training manuals have stressed participative supervision.

The clinical-like reasoning of McGregor (1960) also seemed compelling and was supported by field research (Marrow, Bowers, and Seashore 1967). One of McGregor's (1944) very early suggestions that, "equating" the parent-child relationship with that of the supervisor–subordinate, struck a very resonant chord within the Sears retail operations. It tended to fall on deaf ears among managers in the more routine and time controlled systems found on the company's catalog order function. Here McGregor's *Theory X* style actually seemed preferred, while in the retail organization his *Theory Y* style was the norm! These differences, of course, had to be considered in questionnaire construction.

The motivational theory posed by Herzberg, Mausner, and Snyderman (1959), and Herzberg (1965; 1968) was also an early influence on survey item content. Although no effort was made to include or even consider Herzberg's methodology, his conclusions, however arrived at, seemed eminently relevant. As a result a whole questionnaire category (Work Appeal) focused on items relating to what Herzberg referred to as *intrinsic factors*.

Another significant source of survey content was the Ohio State Studies of leadership, which identified and defined two independent factors of leadership, namely, Initiation of *Structure* and *Consideration*, (Fleishman, 1953; Stogdill & Coons, 1957). These dimensions were extremely valuable in constructing appropriate questionnaire items and in interpreting interview protocols. As subsequent studies indicated relationships between the Ohio State scales and certain organizational outcomes, survey items were refined and their interpretations were offered with greater confidence (Fleishman, 1998; Fleishman & Harris, 1962; Fleishman, Harris, & Burt, 1955; Peters, 1962).

Similarly, the studies of Mowday, Steers, and Porter (1979) dealing with *organizational commitment*, were very helpful in refining that very elusive construct, especially during those consecutive time periods in which the concept of organizational commitment became an almost irrelevant consideration for both employees and employers. In one such period, potential management trainees were so bombarded with lucrative job offers that the idea of employee identification with a company was not even discussed. Later, as those same companies began wholesale lay-offs of managers and long-time service people, commitment became a topic of derision. Chapter 7 summarizes a longitudinal study by Porter, Smith, and Crampton (1976) dealing with issues of organizational commitment and its relationship to turnover among management trainees.

INTERPRETIVE STAGE

The reason for relying on the work of psychometricians and academic researchers is the economy of measurement the former provide and the confidence the latter lend to survey interpretation. The psychometricians, by establishing the standards for attitude measurement, provided meaningful and reproducible methods that are part of any properly mounted program. The works of other academic researchers in the field of organizational behavior have enhanced the meaning of such measures by providing insights into their organizational implications and their current interpretation.

One current example of this later contribution can be seen in a stream of research that accompanied the dramatic shift to a service orientation among large segments of American industry. It was one thing to "guarantee satisfaction or your money back," but to provide the kind of customer service demanded by today's client required a whole new interpretation of customer satisfaction as well as a new view of both internal and external customer expectations. Studies such as those of Schneider and Bowen (1985), Tornow and Wiley (1996), Rogg, Schmidt, Shul, and Schmitt (2001), along with a host of others, have greatly contributed to the current interpretation of customer satisfaction and the influences on it. Chapter 5 discusses this issue in some detail.

It should also be recognized that the insights provided by behavioral research have had both elaborating and discerning effects. Herzberg, for example, greatly expanded the interpretation of work motivation and some of his speculations have enriched its description. At the same time, many of the exaggerated claims growing out of his work and the job enrichment movement, which it helped spawn, were greatly modified and brought down to earth by more penetrating research, such as that of, and Dunnette, Campbell, and Hakel (1967), Hulin (1971), and Ondrach (1974).

Another example of the influence academic research has had on survey interpretation is again that of the Ohio State studies of leadership. The two dimensions of leadership these studies identified, *consideration* and *initiation of structure*, were relied on in many surveys and certainly in the program that is the focus of this book. Moreover, as research on these two scales showed a relationship between the *consideration* scale and employee grievances, as well as with several measures of organizational withdrawal behavior (Fleishman & Harris, 1962), these findings refined the scale's interpretation and any subsequent predictions of its likely effects. At the same time, questions were raised by the Ohio State researchers themselves as well as others such as Kerr, Schriesheim, Murphy, and Stogdill (1974), which have lent a sense of caution to interpretation. For example, the likely existence of a curvilinear relationship between managers' scores on *consideration* and *structure* scales with grievances and turnover in their work groups was noted by Fleishman and Harris (1962) and raised again by Fleishman (1998). It suggests there may be a point beyond which increased considerate or reduced structuring behavior on the part of supervisors may have little additional effect on the performance of their work groups. If so, interpretation of the survey results based on these scales would have to be tempered. Perhaps just this kind of moderation was intended in a question from a very practical minded plant manager, "When is too much consideration too much?"

FOLLOW-UP STAGE

Once survey data have been interpreted, follow-up action can be initiated. This is a two-phase process consisting of feedback and action planning.

Feedback of Results

The first step in almost all survey follow-up is the feedback of results to participants. Be it brief or extended, feedback must above all be an honest summary and should be given by the highest appropriate level of management. More important, it should generate an energy (feeling of excitement) regarding any implied change and should give it a sense of its direction (Nadler, 1977).

Note: One of the most extensive feedback efforts known to the author occurred in the Los Alamos National Laboratory. After a brief overall summary of survey results, management extended the process by using the organization's monthly newsletter. Each issue was devoted to the results of one of the eight categories included in the survey. This helped maintain a continuous focus on the survey and its organizational effects.

Action Planning

The Second phase of survey follow-up usually involves the implementation of the organizational changes that had been alluded to in the feedback phase. Sometimes, this action involves an obvious and tangible move such as repairing a damaged piece of equipment, and so on. More often, it involves the whole organization and requires the cooperative action of management and employees.

Because the implementation of organizational change is increasingly guided by the conceptual and empirical findings of behavioral science, a few examples of this influence are offered here. At the outset, it should be recognized that organizational change—even that suggested by employees—will likely produce a great deal of anxiety. The management of anxiety is, therefore, an integral part of the follow-up process.

An example of a conceptually guided follow-up action aimed at the management change-induced anxiety has been put forward by Schein (1993). He has suggested that the initial concern created by the threat of an organizational change can be overcome, paradoxically, by the creation of an even stronger anxiety arising from the *failure* to change. It is a process in which employees learn that the failure to change will be more-anxiety provoking than that created by change itself.

Ironically, an unplanned approximation of this process occurred some years ago when Sears management suddenly announced its stores would be open on Sunday. Although this change was actually prompted by the strongly voiced requests of store managers and commission salespeople, it produced a very shock-like response among a majority of employees who feared their religious practices, family interactions, and nonwork related activities would be negatively affected. Although this widespread concern was somewhat allayed by newsletters, survey feedback, and even word-of-mouth interactions, the real acceptance of the decision came from the many straight-forward discussions with managers who made it clear that the change was not only inevitable, but was absolutely necessary for *store survival*. In these meetings, the consequences of *not changing* (not opening on Sunday) were realistically stressed (rise of competition, likely cut-backs, loss of earnings, etc.) According to later survey interviews, employees quickly learned to accept the change and in time its benefits were clearly recognized.

Quite a different example of research guided follow-up occurred almost accidently in a survey of Sears' management people. In it, a number of survey items designed for one purpose were recognized as the approximate elements of a well known expectancy theory of work motivation (Vroom, 1964). That is, some of the items explored career goal expectancies, whereas others tapped the perceived likelihood that different career paths would lead to these goals, and still others asked about the importance attached to such goals. As discussed in chapter 13, Vroom's theoretical structure was helpful in tying these survey elements together and in guiding a set of follow-up actions, which helped establish career path progressions for people in both line and professional jobs, and later led to an indepth management performance review program.

Another example of theory-based follow-up made use of the "job characteristics model of work motivation" provided by Hackman and Oldham (1975). Their model holds that work motivation is influenced by certain job characteristics and by the degree of autonomy and responsibility a job affords. An account of this particular follow-up action based on their work is also given in chapter 13.

As indicated in chapter 1, surveys very frequently indicate a need for some type of training. This can be simply a need for better communication skills, or for acquiring new or novel technical knowledge. Most often, it involves a need for better interpersonal skills especially at the supervisory level. So it is that survey follow-up action may involve some form of "human relations" training. Here the influence of research has been both encouraging and daunting. One of the earliest and influential studies by Fleishman (1953) clearly points out the importance of contextual factors as moderating the effectiveness of human relations training. The most critical of these factors was termed *managerial leadership climate*, referring to the leadership behavior and attitudes exhibited by each supervisor back in his or her own work place. A second influence was the personal predisposition among supervisors to incorporate any training induced changes in their own leadership behavior. Taken together, these two factors strongly suggested that any enduring change in supervisory leadership brought about by training would most likely occur when it was reinforced by the "leadership climate" experienced "back on the job," and when the implied change in role behavior was personally acceptable to participants.

The identification of these two influences has been so frequently confirmed by subsequent studies and training exercises that they have become nearly axiomatic considerations in the human relations training field. As one example, chapter 20 portrays a series of training exercises that seriously considered both factors. Because the training program was initiated by a top management request, this implied and almost guaranteed an improved "management leadership climate" in which the hoped for changes in supervisory behavior would be reinforced. At the same time, it had to be recognize that the training would be carried out among groups of seasoned supervisors whose autocratic leadership style, conditioned over years, would seem all but invincible.

A final example of research-guided follow-up can perhaps be best seen in a brief but reasonably well documented anecdote. It involved work in a large department of a distribution center, which was run by an "in-the-flesh Theory X manager" (McGregor, 1960). In this case, the postsurvey recommendations were based on the work of Fiedler (1967), an early and current proponent of the *the contingency* approach to leadership.

Briefly, Fiedler maintained that certain situational factors (contingencies) influence, if not control, the effectiveness of leadership. These factors are: work group climate, task structure, and leader position power. Fiedler further stated that certain combinations of these three factors act to determine whether a "task oriented" or "relationship oriented" style of leadership will be most effective. Later, Fiedler (1994) went so far as to suggest that their leadership styles are relatively fixed and that rather than training people to play one role or another, it would be more effective to place people in situations that best fits their already developed styles.

In the current example, the job was highly routine and repetitive, dissatisfaction was prevalent, and conflicts between younger and older employees were constant. The work was supervised by a relatively new management trainee who relied heavily on a Department Manager for direction. In such a situation, Fiedler's theory would suggest a relationship-oriented (considerate) style of leadership, but given the Department Manager's own coercive leadership style, there was little likelihood of reinforcement for a considerate style. In fact, the Department Manager's first reaction to the survey results, which were at about the sixth centile, was to direct his subordinate to take a tougher stance and apply more pressure to his group.

Armed with a chart based on Fiedler's theory, and an only slightly exaggerated account of its validity, a young survey practitioner was able to persuade the Department Manager to allow his subordinate supervisor to play a considerate role and to be supportive of his efforts. As a later inquiry showed, the manager could not quite bring himself to actually encourage or reinforce this style of leadership, but did "the next best thing"—he left the supervisor alone. In this, he at least neutralized the "leadership climate" that his subordinate would experience.

In the present case, Fiedler's theory bumped up against reality. The young supervisor had not established any preferred leadership style and the "morale" situation in his work group was almost desperate. In view of this, it was simply decided to make the best of a difficult situation and to "bet" on the young supervisor succeeding. He did, to an extent. A follow-up survey came 9 months later and indicated a modest but significant change. Attitudes toward leadership rose from the 6th to the 29th centile—hardly a miracle but a very noticeable improvement.

SUMMARY

This chapter showed the dependence of effective survey development on behavioral research. By way of demonstrating the practical nature of this continual interplay, the survey-research links were presented in the context of the early development of a single survey program—its design, interpretive, and follow-up stages. It should be clear, however, that this linkage is not unique to the program described here. It is, in fact, a *sine qua non* of any serious survey construction.

In utilizing this research linkage, almost all organizational surveys take on a "shot gun" format in which many targets are addressed. The present program was no exception. That it was not simply a "scatter shot" affair, however, rested first on the careful construction of its *core scales* by means of which separate, distinct categories of work-related attitudes were measured. In this, the contributions of psychometric research were indispensable. Second, the valid interpretation of each scale's meaning and its predictive validity rested on the work of a host of researchers, who continue to define what is, and what motivates effective organizational behavior.

3

Survey Tools

There are hundreds of established survey programs in the United States. Some are conducted by consulting firms, some are sideline projects for academics, and still others are administered by professionals within large organizations. It may be of interest to potential survey clients that in some cases, companies coordinate results across industries in order to gain specific external comparisons. One such effort is the Mayflower Group, (which the author cofounded with Dick Dunnington of IBM and Jack Stanek, a consultant). That consortium now has more than 40 members. For a very good account of its present workings, see S. Johnson, (1996).

Whatever their origin or purpose, all survey approaches share a common technology: structured questionnaires and or some form of individual or group interviews. What they do not share, however, is an observance of agreed-on professional guidelines. At one extreme are professionals who carefully follow these standards, whereas at the other are out-and-out charlatans who seemingly have never heard of them!

Although any discussion of so broad and varied a field as this would not only be unmanageable but unhelpful, the present chapter does attempt to provide a potential survey user with a working understanding of the two survey tools and some of the standards observed in their development. This discussion is presented in the context of operating survey programs in which both tools are a part, and its emphasis is on survey approaches intended to serve for an extended period. What it attempts to convey are simply some of the things managers may want to know and consider in evaluating or implementing a survey program.

THE QUESTIONNAIRE

Most of the standards used in evaluating a survey questionnaire can be stated in a series of questions that a manager or potential survey client might consider. To be effective, the design of questionnaires should reasonably satisfy these questions:

1. Does the questionnaire cover the issues needed to diagnose the strengths and weaknesses of an organization? (Precanned instruments often have little relevance to specific or localized situations.)
2. Are the issues covered distinct and separate from one another? (Overlap in meaning among attitude scales can be confusing and gives the impression of being redundant.)
3. Has the reliability or consistency of its scores been adequately demonstrated? (Scores, which fluctuate over time for no reason, are not only inadequate but can give very misleading interpretations.)
4. Are there tested theoretical or empirical reasons to believe the proposed questionnaire, or related versions, will yield valid results? (Survey results should relate to or actually predict important organizational outcomes.)
5. Has the questionnaire at the very least, been pretested in populations similar to that proposed?
6. Does its content lend itself to translation into other languages? (The over use of culturally bound expressions or parochial jargon can be very misleading when cast in other languages.)
7. Can its results be reasonably interpreted cross-culturally? (Variations in results obtained in differing cultural settings should, where possible, reflect differences in actual behavior or attitude rather than language.)

The Questionnaire in a Survey Program Context

In modern organizations, a survey program is almost always required to devise questionnaires and interview techniques that meet the above requirements in widely different settings. This involves people with different job skills and responsibilities and often, in very different kinds of environments. In very large organizations, the variations present within its own boundaries may in fact be as wide as those found across hundreds of smaller firms. Moreover, both relatively small companies and those of global dimensions, increasingly involve foreign cultures and certainly foreign languages. (In Canada for example, some 22 languages are commonly spoken aside from French and English, which by law must be accommodated.)

The construction of a questionnaires to meet these varying demands poses seemingly contradictory requirements: To measure job satisfaction over time and across many job situations, a single instrument seems called for, but to have questionnaire items that resonate with needs of people in widely varying circumstances, many different or tailored versions are required.

The instrument discussed here was originally designed for use in the many diverse businesses of the Sears organization. It is presented *as only one possible approach* to these seemingly contradictory demands. The instrument used multiversion sets of questionnaires in which the first part of each version contained the same set of carefully crafted items (grouped into eight *core scales*) intended as the sole general measure of job satisfaction in almost any job situation. The second part of each questionnaire version contained a set of *descriptive items* that varied from one version to another depending on the situation and were tailored to the needs of all employees in each particular setting.

As indices of job satisfaction, the items in the *core scales* were written in an evaluative tone. They asked respondents whether they were satisfied, motivated, or influenced by such factors as the supervision received, the rewards given, the work itself, and so on. In contrast, the descriptive items were written in a neutral tone and simply asked whether or not certain conditions existed, were safe, were helpful, and so on.

Some examples follow:

Evaluative items: Ask respondents: Are people motivated by, satisfied with, or personally engaged by a particular aspect of the work situation.
   The example my co-workers set

A. greatly encourages me to do my best.
B. encourages me to do my best.
C. neither encourages nor discourages me to do my best.
D. discourages me from doing my best.
E. greatly discourages me from doing my best.

   To what extent are you getting ahead in this company?

A. I am making a great deal of progress
B. I am making some progress.
C. I have mixed feelings about my progress in this company.
D. I am making little progress in this company.
E. I am making no progress in this company.

Descriptive items: Ask respondents: Does this condition exist; not whether it is liked or disliked?

A. My manager and I work together as a team (supervisory people).
B. I have influence on the selection of employees in my unit (supervisory people).
C. We are given notice of price changes (retail).
D. The layout of our department makes it difficult to give good customer service (retail).
E. Our dock and storage people work at cross purposes (distribution).
F. The lift trucks are well maintained (distribution).
G. Our service trucks are properly equipped (technical services).
H. We are given advance training on new appliances (technical services).
I. I have been shown how to handle chemical products used in our office machines (administration).
J. The design of our work station prevents serious ergonomic injuries (administration).
K. All of our machines have adequate safety guards (manufacturing).
L. First aid supplies are always available (manufacturing).
M. What we are told in safety meetings makes sense in the real world of doing our jobs (oil production).
N. When errors are made here, management is more interested in finding the cause rather than finding someone to blame (oil production).
O. Emergency facilities that include decontamination, showers, masks, and radiation protection are readily available (laboratories).
P. Our system in this department prevents the contamination of samples (laboratories).

One further distinction between *core* and *descriptive items* concerned the used comparative norms. Items in the *core scales* were constructed to yield a uniform set of responses that readily allowed for the establishment of norms. This allowed the scaled scores for one group of respondents to be compared to those of others. (To most management people who "live and die" by comparing results, this was an especially important consideration.) Normative comparisons also influence the interpretation of survey results by indicating which scores were in or outside of expected parameters. *Descriptive items* on the other hand, had no basis for comparison. Because they were site specific and subject to change, their interpretation was essentially determined by their effects. For example, should a significant number of supervisors, in response to a descriptive item, indicate: "they *did not* have influence on the selection of their subordinates," this response would be considered a subject for action only if it was associated with an expression of dissatisfaction by this supervisory group. In other words, responses to *descriptive items* were judged by their apparent effect on job satisfaction as measured by the *core sales*.

To repeat: In their final form, all questionnaire versions contained the same set of core scales, which measured job satisfaction across all sites, but each version also included its own set of site specific descriptive items intended to tap local influences on job satisfaction.

Because the core scales were to be the sole measure of job satisfaction and were intended to endure over a reasonable period of time, a good deal of attention was given to their construction. The steps taken in developing the IOR scales are summarized in the following section. References to some of its related published research are given in Appendix A. Now known as the Index of Organizational Reactions (IOR), the following eight scales have been accepted as a workable measure of job satisfaction.

- Leadership and Direction
- Work Appeal
- Work Demands
- Coworkers
- Physical Work Conditions
- Financial Rewards
- Career Future
- Company Identification (later, Organizational Commitment)

The hope was that the IOR would prove sufficiently stable and general to allow its use in almost any work situation. That expectation has been generally realized in subsequent applications in which IOR results proved meaningful and helpful to managers in different work and cultural settings (see chap. 19, this volume). Its predictive value has also been demonstrated in different situations (see chaps. 5, 6, and 7).

The idea of using one general measure of job satisfaction across different jobs was first put to a "test" in an unusual classroom situation in which all 36 students were Jesuit priests. On what might be termed a *slow metaphysics* day, the author asked them to describe their "jobs" using the eight IOR scales. It may come as a surprise to some readers that with one exception, scores on the eight scales were in the low to middle range. The exception, "Company Identification" produced near perfect scores!

Although only anecdotal, this was taken as encouraging and suggested the IOR was on the right track.

Development of the Core Scales (IOR)

This brief account of scale development is presented here, based on the author's long and varied dealings with different levels of management. That experience strongly suggests that even a cursory understanding of what is involved in building survey instruments can prove helpful, for it provides managers with a sense of confidence in a survey's intent, structure, and validity. It also helps answer three often raised questions by uninformed survey recipients: What is it, why is it put together this way, and how does it work? At the same time the reader should be aware that the actual technical steps involved in attitude scale construction constitute a tedious and pains-taking process that is mainly of interest to professionals who are engaged in the actual scale construction. The following summary of the IOR's scale development, therefore, is not intended as a managerial "how to do it" manual. It is rather an attempt to acquaint the general reader with under- standing of what is involved in creating valid and reliable instruments. For those who would like a more technical documented account, the published research on the IOR is provided in Appendix A.

1. *The scales should be reliable and should give consistent results.* This step is usually the most tedious. In the case of the IOR, more than 300 survey questions were collected as potential questionnaire items. These were then edited and pared down to 15 for each of the eight proposed scales. This was followed by numerous trial runs in which the questions were administered to different employee groups. The purpose of the trials was to determine which items belonged in a given scale and which could be eliminated or modified to better fit it. This involved a number of statistical analyses in which the inter-relationships, or correlations among questions was determined. This led to a tentative assignment of questions into separate categories. Correlations were then computed between the scores of each question and its category total score. This analysis helped identify those questionnaire items which "held together" within a given category and reliably measured it. After three such trials, approximately 60 items were selected as the probable measures of the eight proposed scales. In another series of trials, these were reduced to 42 items.

2. *Scales should be independent of one another.* Although all items within a given scale should be closely related in meaning, the scales themselves should be as clearly different from one another as possible to avoid apparent or actual duplication. A statistical technique (factor analysis) is used to determine whether correlations among total category scores are sufficiently low to treat the categories as separate measures.

3a. *Scales should measure what they are intended to measure—what might be called "intentional validity".* For example, different methods of measuring the same issue, such as "satisfaction with pay," should produce similar scores.

3b. *Scales should not inadvertently measure what they are not supposed to measure—what might be thought of a "distinctive validity."* For example, a measure of "pay satisfaction" should not reflect or indirectly measure some other issues as well, such as, satisfaction with "physical working conditions." In the IOR development, both this and the preceding scale requirement were tested by comparing all eight-scale results with three other established methods of measuring similar categories of job satisfaction.

4. *Scale scores should relate to measures of work behavior—should have predictive validity.* Ideally, scores on a given scale should predict (or at least correlate with) various aspects of work performance, or productivity. This kind of validity was shown for the IOR in studies of its relationship to customer satisfaction, employee absenteeism, and even unionization activity.

5. *Scales should be adaptable to use in foreign languages.* This usually involves detailed statistical analyses and field comparisons of parent language and translated versions of each scale. To meet this requirement the IOR scales were translated by one individual and then back translated into the parent language by another person. This process was repeated several times to reduce ambiguity. An analysis of these results produced an equivalent Spanish version that was much later confirmed by studies among Spanish and English speaking populations. A fuller discussion of the difficulties involved in adapting survey instruments can be found in Ryan, Chan, Ployhart, and Slade, (1999). See also, Riordan and Vandenberg (1994).

6. Beyond noting the validity and reliability of attitude measures, managers may also want to consider the degree to which they have been accepted within industry and, more important, among professionals in the field. The IOR has, since the 1970s, been completed by over 3 million of Sears' employees and just under that number in other organizations. It has also been used in a number of academic dissertations and professional studies. A list of its known academic use is given in the reference section of this volume.

Treatment of Descriptive Items

As indicated earlier, the Descriptive (non-Core) items were treated far less rigorously than those in the *core scales*. Because they were intended to reflect only the current conditions in the workplace, they were seen as subject to frequent change. They were consequently constructed or selected on the basis of clarity, relevance, and current face validity. This process relied heavily on the continuous stream of employee comments, which revealed the current developments in different work situations and functions. These

descriptive items helped identify conditions that either enhanced or dampened job satisfaction but were not intended to measure it.

This interplay of the evaluatively worded core scales and the more neutrally phrased descriptive items made for a rough, but workable, "cause and
effect" analysis of job satisfaction. When buttressed by employees' written
comments and interview data, the combination became a reasonably robust
method of organizational diagnosis. Examples of the "cause and effect" interpretations are given in several later chapters. Chapter 21, in particular,
does so in some detail.

Interim Summary

It is hoped that an understanding of the developmental steps just outlined
will help managers and students evaluate *any* survey approach. Although
the examples noted referred to one particular program, they apply quite
generally and should be viewed as such. Beyond that, it is also hoped that
these examples will add to the reader's confidence in the use of survey instruments in organizational life.

THE INTERVIEW

It may surprise readers, who think of surveys only as questionnaires, that interviews are also an important part of many survey programs. Often, they
are used as exploratory vehicles for constructing questionnaire items, but in
other cases they are integral parts of the actual survey process. Indeed, in
many cases surveys are carried out entirely by means of interviews. This is illustrated in examples given later in this book.

Unlike questionnaires, which by their very structure are static and quantitative measures of attitudes, the interview provides a more dynamic means
for sensing affect or feelings. When both tools are combined, a more indepth
analysis of an organization's climate can be obtained.

Because the particular interview techniques discussed here, and used
throughout studies reported in later chapters, can yield some very rich information and insights into organizational workings, these techniques are discussed in some detail. For the "how-to-do-it" oriented reader, an interview-
training manual is included in Appendix B. Beyond the issues of mechanics
however, the use of interviews in Sears and elsewhere had some extremely
important organizational implications and had a definite impact on management development. Perhaps, above all, it taught a great many managers
how to listen, not an unworthy skill. For these reasons, the present discussion

is extended to make these unique organizational contributions clear to managers and other organizational observers.

> A manager's ability to listen was especially stressed by Iococa, former CEO of Chrysler Corporation: "I only wish I could find an institute that teaches people how to listen. After all, good managers have to listen at least as much as they need to talk. Too many people fail to realize that real communication goes in both directions" Lee Iococa (1984, p. 5)

The interview program developed at Sears relied on a *nondirective interview approach*. Its roots were in the employee-counseling program, which grew out of the now classic Western Electric Hawthorne Studies (Rothlisberger & Dickson, 1939) and in the still current client-centered therapy founded by Carl Rogers (1951). Although sharing many of the techniques used by these pioneering approaches, the Sears program was neither a "ventilation device," as in the employee-counseling program, nor did it have the Rogerian therapeutic intent. Instead, its sole purpose was to collect information that would influence *constructive changes in managerial behavior or company practices*.

Non-directive Rationale

The chief virtue of the nondirective approach is that it is *nondirective*. It is an "agenda-free" method of exploring employee feelings about their work situations. Although a more structured approach can be less time consuming, it can also suffer from a directional bias; one which leads employees to suspect a hidden agenda or to discuss only the subjects of interest to the interviewer. In contrast, the nondirective approach attempts to discover what is important *to the employee*.

Nondirective interviewing requires, and is almost totally dependent on, intelligent listening. Although the actual techniques involved are presented in Appendix B, the overall approach rests on establishing an accepting climate in which an employee feels free to express opinions and feelings under a guarantee of *absolute anonymity*. The interviewer responds only to encourage clarification of what was said. No attempt to lead, challenge, or contradict is allowed.

Interviewer Selection

From its inception, interviews were used rather widely as an integral part of the survey program in Sears. For economic reasons, the company came to use its own employees (usually new managers) as interviewers and for reasons discussed shortly, this had an unexpectedly positive impact on both the company and the participants.

Although in many organizations survey interviewing is done by outside professionals, the expense involved all but precluded such an approach in the very large-scale program established in Sears (thus, its use of newly appointed managers). The reader may easily appreciate the value of simply exposing managers, early in their careers, to some of the problems and challenges experienced by employees. What was not so obvious, however, was the impact and developmental value of this experience when carried out in a disciplined quasiprofessional manner.

Interviewer Training

Because the kind of active listening required by the nondirective approach does not come naturally to young managers who are anxious to solve problems and to demonstrate knowledge, listening of this type has to be learned. In so doing, many of their otherwise admirable problem-solving tendencies had to be unlearned or at least set aside temporarily. By way of background, in Sears and among other clients, interviewers were selected to be members of an interview team based on test scores, evaluations by their managers, and general educational background. They were then trained by professionals who usually accompanied them on field assignments. Among other things, training required them to demonstrate (usually through role-playing) an adequate grasp of nondirective techniques, and although not intended to produce experts, the training was sufficiently intense to result in a reasonable level of competence. It included detailed audio and video taped demonstrations of techniques in various kinds of situations along with numerous opportunities for each trainee to demonstrate a command of these mechanics in role-playing exercises.

Because this new role requiring active listening does not fit the natural bent of most young managers, a great deal of training was devoted to developing a kind of "sophisticated naïveté," the ability to grasp what is being said while remaining open to its emotional nuances or shades of meaning. This requires an ability to resist a natural tendency to make assumptions about what is being said or to overreach for its implications. For example, an employee may express what *appears to be* a common complaint (jokingly referred to as #13). In such instances there is the tendency to assume that this has all been heard before, and as the interviewer's "eyes roll over," the essence of the complaint is often missed. This perceptual error of leveling details to fit a preconceived notion is therefore one of the points purposely driven home in interview training demonstrations.

In addition, a good deal of time was devoted to the role trainers were to play in the field unit to which they would be assigned. The assignment was almost always in a unit far distant from their home organization to further assure objectivity. Because they were to be "guests" of a local manager, they would not be allowed to play any kind of managerial role and had to refrain from answering questions, giving advice, or attempting any kind of problem-solving. Although this was awkward for most young managers who normally would find such opportunities hard to resist, in the nondirective role few mistakes prove more damaging. Even a mundane example makes this point. Because employees often see interviewers as members of management, they frequently take the opportunity to ask questions about company policies, benefits, or procedures. However, by answering such questions, an interviewer may miss the chance to explore the reasons for their being asked in the first place. For example,

- Has the employee asked his or her own manager? If not, why?
- Does the question imply a possible misunderstanding or mishandling of the issue raised?
- Do employees know who to go to for answers?
- Are they reluctant to do so and if so, why?

By responding directly to such questions the interviewer not only forecloses such probing but, worse, shifts the employee dependency away from local management, the very contradiction of a survey's intention.

Also included in interviewer training was instruction and practice in integrating interview findings into a meaningful group-based summary, which also protected the anonymity of individual employees. In this regard, and as further protection against even the inadvertent identification of an employee, interviewers were trained to report on "group results" only. They were instructed, for example, to avoid the use of precise percentages, which might accidentally identify particular respondents. Instead they were taught to use more general statements such as one third, one half, a majority, an overwhelming number, and so on.

Interview summaries would be presented to the manager of the unit surveyed. In Sears, these unit managers were either senior executives or, in the case of smaller units, were run by promising candidates for senior positions—a kind of corporate "combat infantry badge." In either case, reporting to this level was a real challenge for most young interviewers and in some instances, memorable.

Based on the results from a great many surveys, the kind and level of training given seemed more than adequate. With a few unforgettable exceptions, the training was taken very seriously by highly motivated people. Most saw their participation and performance as not only a learning experience but as an important career step. As a result, they were more than eager to perform well. (In one of the unforgettable cases, an interviewer somehow got the idea that his production was an ultimate goal; he interviewed 32 people in one morning! He, of course, learned nothing and left his subjects wondering what had just happened!)

Personal and Organizational Impact

The introduction of inhouse people as interviewers led to some very beneficial, largely unanticipated results. Although management recognized that survey participation could be helpful to their young subordinates, they were surprised at the depth of its impression and how lasting it could be. It soon became clear that the developmental impact of the experience on both the participant and the organization often equaled or actually outweighed the value of the information collected.

The Personal Level Impact.   Survey participation by employee interviewers was repeatedly reported by them as personally valuable and eye opening. (This was most obviously seen within Sears due to the continued contact with former interviewers, but was also reported in other client companies.) Being selected to participate, learning the skills required, and actually applying them had a lasting effect on participants; because they were the future executives of their companies, the effect was all the more amplified. Put simply, the experience was seen as both *special* and *insightful*.

The survey experience was *special* in that nondirective skills were found to generalize beyond just the isolated survey situation. Former interviewers reported effective use of such skills:

- with coworkers (very frequently),
- with spouses (often),
- with children (occasionally),
- and (alas) with superiors (hardly at all).

Over the years, participants reported that, through active listening, they had learned to see problems from different viewpoints, and that problems of subordinates were often clarified or became better understood by nondirective probing. A few, and only a few, went on to become near experts. Several of these reported that by restating and reflecting back the rambling and emotionally laden complaints of subordinates, a healthy insight was achieved and often generated its own solution.

The experience was also *insightful* in that participants realized many of the complaints heard about supervisors, work conditions, rewards, and so on could easily have been made by their own subordinates or coworkers back home. This insight was sometimes painful when, for perhaps the first time, they sensed the intensity of resentment that could be caused by a supervisory "slight," a sarcastic remark, or even a casual joke made at an employee's expense.

Of perhaps even greater significance was the frequent transfer of learning to one's home base. Because interviewers were purposely placed in work settings similar to their own (engineers interviewed technical people, retail people interviewed sales, and support people and factory people talked to manufacturing counterparts), what they learned was seen as readily transferable and applicable to their back-home environment.

In all, the survey experience proved to be a very effective way of teaching young managers the *art of listening,* and participation in it became a significant management development device. Needless to say, it was often a sought-after assignment.

The Organizational Level Impact. Information collected by questionnaires and interviews had a palpable effect on local management and brought about tangible changes in the workplace: more effective communication, improved working conditions, and most important, positive changes in leader behavior.

At the corporate level, survey-generated data helped bring about major changes in organizational structure, even at the highest executive levels (examples are discussed in chap. 13). It also assisted in the modification of existing policies and in introducing new ones. Some tangible examples included: changes in employee health insurance such as catastrophe coverage, a paid up life insurance coverage at retirement, a retirement program that went beyond the Profit Sharing Plan, and an improved merchandise discount plan. In other client organizations, changes in laboratory designs were introduced, dual ladder compensation plans for professional and line managers were implemented, and a large number of safety and environmental protections were introduced or corrected, as were improvements in work station layouts.

The usefulness of survey-generated data also led top management to increase the use of surveys of its decision-making. Over time, top management's reliance on information from the ongoing survey program led to requests for literally hundreds of special survey-oriented studies of various issues. Again, some examples from various client organization: a longitudinal study of management trainee recruitment (see chap. 7); studies of engineer-recognition programs, safety of oil rigs and platforms; management training needs; interest among females in traditionally male jobs; the acceptance of equal opportunity and diversity programs; the likely acceptance of a 4-day, 40-hour week among truck drivers; proposed changes in managerial compensation, and the identification of special needs and aspirations of part-time employees. Within Sears, one of these studies was used as significant evidence in a major Federal court case (see chap. 21).

A Residual Effect. An extremely important effect of survey participation was seen clearly within Sears where there was an opportunity to observe its influence over a long period. This effect was simply the enhanced use of surveys by participants in their later executive roles. Through their early experience with the approach, most participants came to see the value of the information gathered and that it was collected in a professional manner, treated confidentially, and reported honestly. Perhaps as a result, one of the first actions many managers took on being promoted to a new department or location was a request for a survey of it. This not only speaks to the integrity and acceptance of any program, but suggests that both can best be established through the early participation of managers.

4

Survey Pitfalls
and Managerial Questions

For survey clients who are new to the survey process, an awareness of possible pitfalls and frequently raised objections may prove helpful. Some of the more common ones are touched on here, along with what is hoped are reassuring explanations and advice on handling them. This attempt to alert and prepare the potential user of a survey is based on the experience of practicing professionals in the field. The discussion provides some answers and should assure survey sponsors that most objections can be legitimately answered and most pitfalls can be avoided.

SURVEY PITFALLS

The following list of potential difficulties is not exhaustive, but focuses on a few potentially serious issues. In order to avoid discussion of problems caused by incompetent survey construction, this list assumes the survey program under consideration has been properly designed. It also omits examples of gross unprofessionalism, such as the violation of promised confidentiality. Avoidance of these issues is a matter of managerial judgements in the survey and surveyor selection process.

Report Delays

One pitfall that even the most well constructed survey can encounter is the delayed delivery of results to management. Whether caused by mechanical processing problems or by lengthy interpretation of results, delays are frustrating to clients and participants. Although this problem has and will continue to dissipate as more sophisticated data processing systems emerge and as computerized administration of questionnaires become more common, there is still a problem of delay caused by interpretation of results. Although it should be recognized that interpretive delays are a special problem in programs that make broad use of employee interviews and written comments, the trade-off in interpretive richness should be also recognized.

In all cases, the severity of any delay-related problem can be greatly moderated when clients and survey respondents are given an accurate estimate of the survey's turnaround time. The pitfall is especially irksome when a surveyor purposely underestimates this interval in order to sell a program to management.

Client Preparation.   Surveys are likely to create problems when they are administered without preparatory explanations to the managers and others who may be impacted by the results. An incident described in chapter 15 provides a case and point and should serve to alert survey clients to the importance of an up-front explanation of a survey and its process.

Issues Sensitivity

A fairly rare pitfall, often overlooked by all but corporate lawyers, concerns the possibility that a survey may uncover problems, which are quite sensitive or potentially damaging to a company. This cuts both ways, for the problem exists whether or not it is uncovered by a survey. If it is revealed by a survey, corrective action can be taken. If it is not surfaced by this means, it may remain dangerously submerged. A detailed example of a two-edged concern is given in chapter 21, where survey data collected many years prior to a trial turned out to strongly corroborate the company's position. Had they not been supportive, however, the process of pretrial discovery may have led to their use by the plaintiff.

The avoidance of this pitfall usually relies on the survey follow-up action taken by an organization. Even in instances in which surveys have turned up information that may seem damaging, prompt and constructive action aimed at its correction can prove very effective in enhancing the company's defense. This too was demonstrated in the case described in chapter 21. In it, survey data on the company's well-developed affirmative action program were favorably viewed by the court as a constructive attempt to correct problems, including those raised in previous surveys.

Reporting Sequencing

The sequence in which survey results are reported back to management can be a potential problem. This usually occurs when a manager whose unit or department has been surveyed is bypassed in the process of reporting back results. As a consequence, a higher level person receives the report before the manager does. Although this can simply prove awkward it can also lead to deep resentment, the very opposite effect of that intended by any survey.

Avoiding this problem comes from observing a fairly standard rule: Unless the reporting sequence is otherwise understood, reports should *first* go the manager of the surveyed unit (store, plant, or department) and later to higher management. This rule has been strictly enforced in many companies. On several occasions within Sears, a response to an officer's request for a unit report was delayed until the unit manager had received it.

Translation and Cultural Challenges

Faced with a global economy and the presence of people with limited English skills, many companies have a compelling need for reliable foreign language surveys. *This challenge is not simply a matter of translation.* Its resolution involves a number of considerations, and in most situations different language versions should be carefully developed and tested. The interested reader may find the account of how this process works and how it resulted in a workable Spanish language version of the Index of Organizational Reactions (IOR) in Katerburg, Smith, and Hoy (1977). The subsequent verification of the IOR's reliability among Spanish speaking subjects is found in McCabe, Dalessio, and Sasaki (1989).

Managers and other potential survey clients should be aware that translation of an instrument can be substantially aided by the careful attention to its parent language version. Some questions managers may want to ask in evaluating translations are:

- Has jargon or transient phrases been avoided? Cloudy metaphors can lead translators to overreach in search of meaning.

> A favorite example of translation problems—probably apocryphal —makes this point. It involves a now dated survey item, which in English read, "Does your boss pass the buck?" In a German translation, it became "Does your supervisor deal in black-market dollars?"

- Are the phrases used within an industry understood across cultures?

For example, the oil industry phrase, "up-stream or down-stream" may seem to an outsider as meaningful only in a given national or cultural context, but it has actually become generally understood in the oil industry worldwide and as such serves as a basis for every meaningful survey question. (On the other hand, the phrase "up the creek," which is not limited to the oil industry, should probably be avoided.)

The concept of *cultural accommodation* should also be considered in foreign language questionnaire construction. For example, in establishing its sites in most foreign locations, the oil industry introduced a new work vocabulary. Challenging as it may have been, native employees had only to learn and add these new terms to their existing knowledge. Survey translations were able to make use of the new terms once they were in place. On the other hand, some industries introduced systems that *supplanted* those already existing within a culture. In these instances native employees had to unlearn the old language and concepts while absorbing the new. Here survey translations had to avoid adding to the confusion. For example, when Sears entered the Latin American market, the whole idea of placing merchandise where customers could "see it, feel it, and steal it" was quite foreign to the typical retail employee. So was the concept of *satisfaction guaranteed or your money back!* In fact, these concepts actually contradicted traditional Latin American retail practices and had to overcome a fair amount of resistance. When surveys were introduced, care had to be taken to observe the change.

Observational Interference

Surveys can, on rare occasions, create a pitfall by interfering with the situation they are intended to observe. The most obvious example of this might be a survey conducted during a labor relations dispute. In such cases, the survey could be looked on as interfering with a union effort to organize employees. It may, in fact, be illegal! This subject is discussed in the second part of this chapter.

Another actual example of this potential pitfall is discussed in chapter 19, which describes a situation in which a survey was used to help decide who, among several candidates, would be most acceptable to employees as their new CEO. Unless great care is taken in such a case, survey integrity could easily be distorted by political maneuvering of employees and candidates alike.

Because situations like this do occur from time to time, a procedure followed *in avoiding* it is explained in chapter 19.

SURVEY LENGTH

A questionnaire that is *too long* will often raise objections from managers as well as from survey respondents. Appropriate length is therefore an axiomatic condition of questionnaire construction. *Appropriate, however, does not mean short!* In fact, a questionnaire lacking sufficient length can also be a pitfall by its being ineffective, noninterpretable, or resented. Although each of these considerations is discussed here, the essential point is that questionnaire length is a practical rather than an absolute standard. There is wide variation in questionnaire length, for both good and poor reasons. Potential survey users should be aware that expanding a questionnaire for the purpose of clarity and completeness is usually well justified. Reducing it simply for sales or cosmetic appeal is not.

The length of the questionnaire rests primarily on three conditions: practical time constraints, complexity of content, and, above all, the interest of participants.

Time Constraints

The amount of time available is usually obvious. In surveys (if they can be called surveys) of customers in hotels and restaurants, brevity is a must. Respondents have neither the time for nor the interest in such forms, and real complaints are usually delivered in person or in letters. Phone surveys must also be brief in order to retain respondent interest and patience. In many surveys administered through personal computers, the assumed need for brevity can also result in a serious loss of meaning and effectiveness.

An obvious time constraint on questionnaire length is the respondent's work schedule. In some cases this is an absolute limiting condition, but often there are alternatives: administering the survey in separate parts at different times, rearranging shifts, and in a surprising number of cases overtime pay has been authorized when surveys were conducted before or after shifts.

In making a decision on questionnaire length, a manager or other survey user should ask are:

1. Is the subject of the survey important enough to justify the survey's length?
2. Are the issues in the survey covered adequately?
3. Will respondents be able to make sense of the responses?
4. Can time be made available to respond to it?
5. Is the subject(s) covered by the survey of enough interest *to respondents* to have them respond realistically?

Complexity of Subject

An often overlooked consequence of surveys that are either too brief or overly simple is the resentment they cause among employees who sense management is not taking them or their concerns seriously. As one example, a 15-item survey covering 7 different categories of job satisfaction yielded very ambiguous results and elicited a number of critical comments:

- "How can I truthfully answer a single question about leadership when I report to two different people?"
- "My pay is good, but the no-raise policy and our benefits are lousy."
- Regarding the question about physical work surroundings, "Our work stations are attractive, but ergonomic injuries are frequent."

Similarly, many questionnaires prove difficult if not impossible to interpret because of their simplicity or brevity. For example, a single question may yield such a wide range of responses, it cannot be reasonably understood. In order to interpret and act on such responses one would have to know what influences were at work. For example, this simple question: *How satisfied are you with your pay?* What is being asked? Is pay fairly determined or is nepotism, favoritism, or discrimination involved? How closely related to performance and job service is it? Is it internally and externally equitable? Is it keeping pace with inflation? Is the pay system clearly understood? And so on. A questionnaire that fails to explore these facets is open to misinterpretation, and will surely be resented by thinking respondents. It diminishes the survey's credibility and all but eliminates any attempt to act on the results.

The foregoing is not to be taken as a general indictment of brief questionnaires. In fact, some are quite effective. Brief instruments are most effective when they deal with a limited number of topics (preferably one). In such cases, a 10-or 15-item survey can be quite reliable and very meaningful. Even the questionnaire of 15 items dealing with multiple issues that was criticized above can be effective if there is sufficient follow-up to clarify each issue. For example, employee interviews could be conducted to explore the issues that were barely touched on by the questionnaire.

Participant Interest

The degree of interest participants have in the content of a survey can be *the* overriding influence on their participation. An extreme but overwhelmingly successful example may illustrate this point. It involved the first survey ever conducted at Sears among all 18,000 managerial employees. (For many years, hourly paid employees had been surveyed, but exempt people [salaried] had, in fact, been "exempted.") The development and *accidental finalizing* of the questionnaire may demonstrate the near irrelevancy of questionnaire length in the face of high participant interest.

The process started in the usual way with a number of interviews with potential participants. From these and other sources a preliminary questionnaire of some 490 questions was created. The plan was to submit questions to the human resources staff (well known as congenital critics), with the expectation that half this number might survive and serve as a workable first draft.

In this case, however, seeing that the survey at this level was a novel idea and could touch some "sensitive organizational nerves," the officer sponsoring it decided to get the CEO's approval first. As he reported later, the CEO became intrigued with a number of items in this "unabridged" edition, and, after a brief review, said, "If this is what he (the author) wants to do, let him go ahead." Because no one knew which specific items had caught the CEO's attention, no further editing was possible. As a result, the author was faced—stuck—with a nearly 500-item questionnaire. Based on pretesting, it appeared that several hours would be needed to complete it! All survey experience predicted a disaster—a survey so long it would be ignored by participants. In fact, of 18,410 surveys, all but 331 were completed, a 98.2% return!

In addition, just over 50,000 written comments were made on separate subjects; some were only one-or two-word sentences; others were 10 typed pages. (Because the questionnaires were returned through Price Waterhouse, this very high return was taken by one Postal Service manager, who heard of it, as a compliment to her organization.)

The real catalyst for the remarkable return was easily established in later interviews among respondents. Clearly their participation grew out of their intense interest in, for the first time, letting management know their feelings about many critical issues.

SURVEY VERIDICALITY

Any survey instrument or process that somehow discourages frank and honest responses can prove fatal, and competent survey practitioners will take pains to avoid such a pitfall.

To the author's knowledge, there is no valid method for establishing the truthfulness of an *individual response* to a questionnaire. If one existed, it would probably violate the guarantee of anonymity, which is fundamental to all legitimate surveys. Although the truth of *individual responses* will probably remain an illusive construct, studying *group responses* can at least establish a ground for validating such responses. The method used is a form of triangulation. It has these three facets:

1. the actual questionnaire responses made by a group,
2. the comments group members make either in writing or in interviews,

3. the relationship responses have to actual behavior.

The triangulation argument takes the following form: When a group of respondents consistently answers survey questions in a meaningful manner, one can *reasonably assume* they are being truthful; if they provide written or interview comments that specifically exemplify or otherwise confirm their survey responses, one can feel *fairly confident* those responses were truthful; finally, if their survey responses can be shown to correlate with, or actually predict their subsequent work behavior, one can then be *relatively certain* of their truthfulness. (As some would have it: If it looks like a duck, walks like a duck, and quacks like a duck, then it is a duck.)

As already suggested there are reasons why respondents may be purposely untruthful. For example:

- Participants may distrust the sponsoring or surveying organization, especially regarding questions of anonymity or confidentiality.
- The survey may be administered in a threatening, off-hand, or inconsistent manner.
- The instructions may be unclear or confusing.
- The questionnaire may be written at an inappropriate reading level, one that threatens or alienates some respondents.
- A union or other outside agency may discourage people from responding truthfully to certain sensitive items. (For example, in a survey for a major airline, the Flight Attendant Union advised its members to be very cautious in answering pay and benefit questions in a favorable manner.)

Most of these conditions can be minimized or eliminated by (a) proper planning of the survey, (b) the careful selection of a trusted survey organization or by strict observance of professional standards in its internal administration, and (c) a strong statement of support and assurance of anonymity by top management. (In the case of unionized employees, the union should be notified of the survey and may even be invited to cosponsor it.) Each of these points bears further exploring.

- The planning of a survey should involve: some explanation of its content with prospective sponsors and recipients; proper scheduling of its administration; clear instructions on how the survey is to be completed; and a clear statement of how its results will be treated.
- If the survey is designed and constructed within an organization, it is important to follow professional guidelines. Survey work, as the say-

ing goes, is not brain surgery, but there are certain standards to be observed, and professional help can assure this (see chap. 3).

The strong assurance of anonymity from top management can take several forms. In large companies, it is done by letter, video, or in some cases, in person. However communicated, it should clearly state the reasons for the survey, encourage participation, and offer top management's *personal assurance* of respondent anonymity and the professional analysis of results.

Survey Institutionalism

A relatively obscure pitfall is sometimes encountered in postsurvey situations. After an organization carries out a survey it may then see no way to act on it, has a reluctance to reveal its results, or in some cases has no real understanding of its potential usefulness. In such cases, managers often ask, "now what do we do" and equally their answer often is, "Okay we did a survey. Now let's get back to business." The survey is, in effect, *institutionalized*, considered simply as "something we do from time to time," and treated as a separate event, unrelated to the actual workings of the organization. In the face of this attitude, even the most carefully planned and smoothly executed survey can ultimately fail. In addition, a parallel sense of indifference may be felt among respondents who sense they have been ignored or, worse, deceived. It is, therefore, a serious responsibility of management to anticipate the likely use of survey results and to plan their integration in the company's practice of management (see chap. 13 for an example of such integration).

One final point of clarification. There are literally thousands of occasions when surveys are carried out simply for the purpose of collecting information with no thought of feeding back results. When this is done, participants should be told up front that no results would be forthcoming.

It should, in closing this section, again be emphasized that most surveys proceed without great difficulty. Indeed, they often proceed well because their sponsors were prepared and knew how to avoid or to deal with the potential pitfalls covered here.

FREQUENT QUESTIONS AND CHALLENGES

Most of the questions about surveys—sometimes worded as challenges—seem to come from middle-and lower-level managers. The issues raised are usually quite reasonable and can be answered reasonably. Many others may smack of defensiveness and cynicism. Some are very minor, even frivolous—whereas others are anything but! If not addressed, however, any of these questions take on an assumed validity of their own, discouraging the very managerial cooperation needed for a survey's operational success.

Underlying most managerial concerns is the very natural apprehension that the survey results will be unfairly critical of their leadership or may be distorted by either momentary or chronic conditions, which are beyond their control. Experience suggests the concerns fall into several categories: The survey is poorly timed. The survey will create unmanageable expectations. The survey contains negative questions. The survey is irrelevant to the "bottom line."

Before exploring specific examples, it should be noted that most objections, either voiced or silently held, come from managers who are new to the survey experience. They may be members of an organization that has never used the survey approach, or are newly appointed to management and are unfamiliar with a company's ongoing survey program. In any case, and as strongly recommended in the previous section, managers and supervisors should expect to receive a complete explanation of the survey's content and assurance of its intent. Given a reasonable explanation of the survey's purpose, most managers will see it as a constructive mirror and will look to its results with a healthy curiosity.

Survey Timing

A frequent concern of managers is the timing of the survey. This is a very legitimate concern for there may, in fact, be serious reasons for not doing a survey at a certain time. In retail stores, for example, the Christmas weeks are completely out-of-bounds. Among other reasons, almost half of the employees are temporary and would not at all be representative of the regular staff. Similarly, it would be difficult to carry out a survey in a factory or plant during major renovations or partial work stoppages as stated earlier, and it would be very unwise and possibly illegal to mount a survey during a union organizing drive. Although this *would not be illegal* if the survey has been regularly scheduled as part of an ongoing program, it might still be unwise unless it had union support.

Aside from such obvious instances, the assumption that survey timing is a major or controlling constraint seems exaggerated. In Sears, for example, the huge amount of survey data collected, allowed for a detailed analysis of results from 210 units surveyed in 10 different months over a 3-year period. It showed no significant *monthly variations* in spite of wide differences among individual locations.

In a large manufacturing plant the survey was administered to small random samples of each department over a 6-month period (so as not to disrupt operations), and yielded no significant monthly variations. That is, the scores of departmental segments were consistent over time, although scores among departments varied greatly. Similarly, a safety survey in an oil refinery 1 year before and 10 months after a major accident showed no change in attitude except for the category of Physical Surroundings where one focus was Health and Safety. In this case, both the questionnaire findings and employee-written comments yielded extreme criticism of the specific physical conditions that lead to the accident, but feelings about such matters as pay, benefits, work demands, and immediate leadership were essentially constant. This kind of evidence has proven to be extremely useful in muting the concern that a survey was administered at "a bad time."

It may be helpful to managers to consider an example of how the subject of timing was addressed by one CEO in a video feedback of results from a management survey. The survey had been carried out shortly after the company had been forced, for the first time in its history, to "lay off" some of its management staff people—a bad time by all measures. In his remarks, the CEO made the point that, "While some survey results may have been unrealistic under the circumstances, had the company waited till that magical time when no problems existed, those results would also have been unrealistic."

Creation of Expectations

Managers and supervisors are sometimes concerned that simply doing a survey will create expectations that cannot be managed or fulfilled. In doing so, they fear job satisfaction may be lowered by the very process of measuring it. Again, although there is some basis for this concern, it should be recognized that it usually misses the point. When surveys generate expectations, they provide a motivational basis for constructive action. The processes by which this takes place have been covered thoroughly by Nadler (1977) and more recently, by Hinrichs (1996). Suffice it to say here that, although expectations may be created by a survey, there is little reason to fear they will be unmanageable. In fact, handling expectations is a key part of the manager's job and is not likely to be beyond his or her coping ability.

It should also be recognized that simply doing a survey is unlikely to create expectations that were not already inherent in the organization's climate. Although surveys may bring certain hopes to light, such issues do not come "out of the blue." When they do surface, a skilled manager can seize the opportunity to act on them at a time of focal interest. Rather than a reason for not doing a survey, expectations can be a springboard or, at the very least, an excuse for management action that should have been taken in any event.

There is also the real possibility that *no expectations* will be created by a survey. This is actually a very discouraging result and usually stems from a lack of action on previous surveys. When this does occur, follow-up actions are often aimed at actually stirring up expectations! In such cases, a manager may well be advised to: "surprise them—do something."

It should also be understood that a survey can sometimes be purposely designed to elicit or encourage certain expectations. It can, for example, help management anticipate employee responses to contemplated actions or decisions. This is exactly what was done by a survey of possible changes in Exempt employee compensation discussed in chapter 13. Following an explanation of several alternative plans, survey participants were asked for evaluations based on their own perspective. Not only did survey participants give management a clear idea of what was most acceptable, but their positive reaction to being asked was seen as a major reason for the plan's successful implementation.

The point here is that simply doing a survey is not an end in and of itself, and, when expectations do emerge, they should be handled in the feedback of results where systematic ways of dealing with them have been developed. It is this feedback process in which results are converted into action. This is not a negative experience. It can, in fact, bring out the best in both management and employees.

Because this is an essential ingredient of the whole survey process, it may be helpful to review three basic feedback approaches: unilateral action, no action, and cooperative action.

Unilateral Actions.   These kinds of actions usually involve management responses to important, tangible matters that require little or no discussion. In fact, discussion might seem ludicrous. For example, a poorly maintained restroom is a frequently encountered complaint in surveys and can be a source of great irritation. It is not a subject that needs wide discussion other than to announce it has been addressed. Aside from being a solution, this type of tangible action can also demonstrate management's constructive intent.

Non-action.   Taking no action is often a reasonable response to problems whose solutions are simply not possible, cannot be considered at the time, or are so prohibitively expensive as to be impractical. In such cases, a frank response is needed that clearly points out the facts. Such a communication may also give management an opportunity to explain and to educate.

In one case, employees wanted a huge warehouse to be air-conditioned. Because of the expense and physical impossibility of doing so, the manager explained the engineering and cost factors to respondents. In addition to his explanation, he did point to certain ventilation improvements that would be made and that an air-conditioned lunchroom would be installed shortly. According to his summary of the session, "No one was ecstatic, but people did understand and appreciate the explanation."

In another case, employees in an auditing firm requested that a dental plan be added to their benefit program. Because this was a matter of corporate policy, the local manager could only acknowledge the request. She added, however, that although the cost of such an improvement would be immense, such issues had come up in surveys throughout the company and are regularly reviewed. She then pointed to several other benefit improvements that had been brought about, at least in part, by surveys and hoped this request would also be considered.

In one large company, employees complained bitterly about the safety problems in their office's deteriorating neighborhood. Although the local manager was sympathetic and, in fact, shared their concern, nothing could be done at the time other than adding police at opening and closing times. Because she knew a decision had been made by top management to move the office, she asked and got permission to make an early announcement in the feedback session. Although the actual move would not be for another 6-months, people were relieved and were at least more willing to live with their present situation.

Cooperative Action.   By far the most important and enduring actions generated by the feedback process are those involving the cooperative efforts of management and employees. These combined actions are the primary focus of consultants and other professionals in the field of organizational dynamics. This is a subject in itself—actually an entire industry. On the other hand, many issues can and must be handled by line management alone and often with little or no professional background. In such cases, common sense often serves. For the do-it-yourself manager who cannot afford or who may not want outside help, a few examples of common sense actions are offered.

In a huge foam rubber manufacturing plant, one survey item revealed a complaint of "too much red tape." The plant owner, who wanted to handle the feedback in order to show his support for the process, focused on this issue and asked for examples of red tape. After a fairly lengthy silence, one first-level supervisor started the following discussion (abstracted here from tape recordings of the session):

> SUPERVISOR: Mr. Jones, I work on the night shift, and when we have an equipment failure, I have to get an Assistant Superintendent to approve a request for bringing in a repairman.
>
> MR. JONES: Well, that's not really "red tape." The cost of bringing in a repairman can be very high, so we want to make sure it is necessary before doing so.
>
> SUPERVISOR: But there is no Assistant Superintendent on the night shift any longer! That job was eliminated in the last "down-sizing." The Superintendent works the day shift so there is no one to go to.
>
> MR. JONES: I wasn't aware of this, and we will have that corrected directly, but I wonder, how have you handled this up 'til now?
>
> SUPERVISOR: Well, Joe, our senior repairman is a good friend, and usually he will come in on his own time to make serious repairs. It's the only way we can avoid losing production because of a downed machine.

This seemingly simple comment not only brought to light an easily corrected problem but also showed how serious its consequences could have been. For one, had the repairman been injured while working "off-the-clock," an indefensible lawsuit could have followed. Several wage and hour laws had also been violated for which the company was liable. The owner did not go into this problem publicly but realized its seriousness. He privately commented, "This shows how easy it is to assume things are okay because production is good and has not been interrupted." With this insight, he decided to spend several additional days exploring a host of other "red tape" problems.

The statement of a manager who had received criticism of both himself and his staff represents another common sense but very open and effective response to a common complaint. He handled part of the feedback session in the following way:

> Pardon me for reading this but I want all groups to hear the same statement. I do want to tell you that along with some very positive comments, which I want to discuss later, there was a good deal of criticism of your supervision in the report. Some of this was directed at me as well as the staff, and I want you to know I am especially concerned about it. After reviewing the findings, however, I became aware of how some of our behavior could be misunderstood and in some cases resented. Now that I understand this, I can assure you that this was not our intent, and I can assure you that a real effort will be made to correct it. I won't go into details other than to give you an example. Over the past year, I have asked

each staff person to tour the store each day after our group has lunch together. The purpose of this was to make staff people available to you and to provide help when needed. I think this is very necessary and important, but what has happened is that these visits became inspections and most of our comments during them turned out to be critical of your operations. In fact, I understand we are now called the "toothpick brigade." This was not our intent, but I realize the complaint is valid. I have fallen into the same habit myself.

I have given this considerable thought, and I want you to know that your criticism may have helped us all. I want to assure you that you can expect to see some improvement starting now. After all, whenever some member of the staff or I sit down with each of you to review your performance, we are sometimes critical of some things you have done. We do this in order to bring about improvement. Well, now, you had your chance to review our performance, and we'd be fools if we didn't try to profit from it. Hopefully, our next survey will show we have. In the meantime, I want to thank you for being candid in your comments.

Survey Use of Negative Questions

This objection is fairly common and seems to be based on the assumption that asking a negative question will elicit a negative response. There is little in the way of sound evidence to support this assumption, but it is very hard to dissuade an overly wary manager. To those of such a mind, be assured there are both technical and practical reasons for including a balance of positively and negatively worded items in a questionnaire.

Technical Reasons.   The primary reason for including a balance in item wording is to counteract the effect of *response sets*, the tendency of some subjects to ignore question content in making responses. Probably the most common of these is the "acquiescence response set." The tendency to either agree or to disagree consistently with *all* survey questions, regardless of wording. As one often-used example, some people will consistently agree with statements such as: "It's never too late to learn" and "You can't teach an old dog new tricks." Balancing item wording at least minimizes the error introduced by this habit. For this reason alone, managers should expect a strong stance on this issue from a professional practitioner, for failure to balance item wording can lead to serious difficulties. In fact, the professional literature frequently finds fault or completely rejects scales that have included items that are all worded in a positive vein.

There is one moderately successful "solution" to this objection, which the potential survey client may want to consider. It is the use of neutrally worded stems followed by both pro and con responses. For example:

My supervisor:

1. Brings out the best in me
2. Neither
3. Brings out the worst in me

Practical Reasons.   A very practical and important reason for including negatively worded statements is that they often better reflect the reality of the work place. For example, employees frequently voice complaints such as: "*Our boss bawls us out in front of others.*"

They rarely say: "*My boss always corrects us privately.*" Although the first statement might be reworded to avoid jargon ("bawls out" may prove difficult in translation), its reworded positive version may seem strained in any language. This issue seems to have been accentuated by the current tendency to have everything stated in a positive tone. Perhaps it is part of a consciously promotional world, a world where:

- "lie" becomes "misspeak"
- "used" becomes "pre-owned"
- "layoff" becomes "re-engineered"

In surveys dealing with Health and Safety matters, a similar softening is often requested:

- "accident" to "incident"
- "danger" to "correctable situations"
- "problems" to "opportunities"

In evaluating questionnaires, it is well for a survey client to remember that people still think in terms of *lie, used,* and *lay off, danger, accidents,* and so on.

Because the intent of any serious organizational survey is to provide management with a measure of workplace reality, it may occasionally include certain controversial issues. For reasons just given, this may also include the balanced use of positive and negative items. This is a frequently misunderstood issue and is often raised by managers as a challenge. One "half joking" example of this occurred within Sears when an otherwise sensible officer complained that negative questions might "unnecessarily stir up controversy" or "make things look worse than they are." This was followed by a suggestion that a "more positive slant might be considered."

The survey team decided to respond in the same half-joking manner. This was in keeping with the fun atmosphere existing in the company at the time, but like many jokes, it tried to make a point. The team created the Favorable Fortified Fathomer (see box below) as an example of how really controversial issues might be raised and "slanted" to produce the desired responses. It was also pointedly noted that not only would the instrument completely *avoid reality* but would have the added "virtue" of measuring *absolutely nothing!*

Readers may appreciate the officer's response. It was two-fold: First was a very grudging note accepting of the need for both positive and negative items—a note written in only negative terms such as: specious, inflammatory, insubordinate, career threatening, and so on. Second, he asked that the Favorable Fortified Fathomer be sent to all other officers for their endorsement!

FAVORABLE FORTIFIED FATHOMER

1. Reports of poor morale are simply caused by questions in the survey that are worded negatively.
   Strongly Agree
   Agree
   Do Not Disagree
   Strongly Do Not Disagree

2. How often do you find yourself agreeing with statements made by top management on compensation matters?
   Always Agree
   Never Disagree

3. Do you agree with top management that many of the so-called "problems" here have been exaggerated?
   Very Strongly Yes
   Strongly Yes
   No, they have actually been very exaggerated
   No, they have actually been grossly exaggerated

4. Do you continue to appreciate and understand that while the CEO and *all of his recently appointed staff* have come from the East, so did the star of Bethlehem?
   Heavens Yes
   Noel

5. In its attempt to devise a fair compensation plan, the company has succeeded in spreading dissatisfaction.

Evenly
Smoothly
Skillfully

6. Top management has definitely gotten better at making prema-
   ture judgments.
   Yes
   No, it needed no improvement

7. Do you agree with the overwhelming majority of your more
   thoughtful and competent fellow employees who say that, "Man-
   agement decision-making here is sound."
   Yes
   Yes, it is nothing if not sound
   Yes, it is nothing but sound

BOTTOM LINE CONSIDERATIONS

Why management should care about employee attitudes is a recurring question, mainly among the naïve. If, indeed, top management *does not care*, the
chances for a successful survey are greatly diminished, and a responsible professional can be expected to retire from such circumstances. In a service
economy, an argument in favor of caring about employee attitudes is not difficult to come by. Their impact of on customers (both internal and external)
seems clear and has been confirmed in a host of studies (see chap. 5). In other
types of organizations ranging from the "high tech" to "heavy industries,"
there also are negative consequences that flow from management's indifference. People may, for example, be so alienated as to quit, or what is worse,
stay on the job while withdrawing from it psychologically; seek outside help
from social governmental agencies or unions; be overly aggressive in seeking
legal redress; simply "work-the-rules" and allow delays or waste to occur
needlessly, or show a reluctance to believe or accept management directions
or communications. (Specific examples of work withdrawal behavior and its
relationship to job satisfaction are also given in chaps. 5 through 8.) There is
also management's self-interest as a bottom line consideration. Simply put, it
is *easier* to manage a high-morale ship than an indifferent or mutinous one!

SUMMARY

In an attempt to alert managers and others who may be considering a survey, this chapter first explored a few potential pitfalls that even a well de-

signed-survey might encounter. By being aware of these possible difficulties, managers can readily avoid them.

In its second part, the chapter discussed a number of commonly asked questions about the survey process. Because these are usually raised by managers whose units are about to be surveyed, this discussion attempted to provide an explanation of each issue as well as some reassuring answers.

Part II

Introduction:
Survey Research

Part II provides examples of survey studies undertaken within Sears to explore the links between employee job satisfaction and four important behavioral outcomes: customer service, absenteeism, turnover, and voluntary unionization.

It is important to note that in all four studies, the behavior studied was largely a matter of individual choice. That is, the employee decision to render customer service, to quit, to be absent, or even to join a union was more or less discretionary. In situations where such behavior is coerced or controlled by external forces (a "closed shop" is an example of the former, and assembly line is an example of the latter), employee behavior is not free to vary and attempts to study its covariation with employee attitudes are foreclosed (see e.g., Herman, 1973; Smith, 1976).

Chapters 5 and 6 focus on studies of customer service and absenteeism, respectively. Both studies were opportunistic in that they took advantage of chance occurrences. These two studies, however, provided unique evidence of the influence employee attitudes have on later work behavior.

Chapter 7 focuses on a study of managerial turnover that was part of a carefully planned longitudinal project undertaken for purely academic purposes. Its results had a very practical and significant organizational impact.

Chapter 8 describes a project that was also academically inspired. It involved a backward looking predictive study of unionization activity over a 6-year period.

Because the behaviors studied in these four examples have definite organizational implications, a modest attempt is made to show managers and students how these four studies relate to a much broader body of research aimed at identifying the conditions under which employee attitudes influence work behavior. Although this influence may seem obvious to the casual observer, any manager or student of organizations should be aware that it is anything but obvious. The influence of these conditions is, in fact, restrained by a host of moderating conditions and is enhanced by others. Because these conditions can often be controlled or productively influenced by informed management action, an awareness of their workings should be a helpful facet of managerial knowledge. The discussion of these four studies is nontechnical and references to related work are purposely limited to a few examples and parenthetical references. The hope is that it will acquaint readers with some of the research on the attitude–behavior linkage and encourage further study.

5

Employee Attitudes
and Customer Satisfaction

The study reported in this chapter was based on data collected from two separate and independent departments within Sears Canada. Aside from confirming a strong relationship between employee job satisfaction and customer satisfaction, it called attention to the opportunities for coordinated research efforts among organizational units that rarely communicate with each other.

INTRODUCTION

Everyone, it seems, instinctively knows that employee morale has an impact on customer satisfaction. What is not known is how this impact can be best managed. In a service-oriented society, this subject has become a matter of great interest to management and has generated 20 years of research aimed at discovering where, when, and under what conditions does the influence of employee job attitudes maximize customer satisfaction.

One line of the research that has extended over the entire 20-year period (Schneider, 1980; Schneider, White, & Paul, 1998) has focused on the retail banking industry. A dozen or so studies by Schneider and many others (J. Johnson, 1996; Jones, 1991; Schneider, 1990; e.g., Schneider & Bowen, 1985; Tornow & Wiley, 1996) have shown that the link between employee and customer satisfaction is strongest when management, through the use of sound human resource practices, creates a "climate for service." In banks, and by logical extension to other service oriented industries, this "climate for service" is partly a result of the emphasis placed on it by management.

The Study

The present study is, in one sense, an extension of this line of research into the retail store arena. It examines the *direct* relationship between survey results on the job attitudes of sales employees and the customer ratings of the service they received. Data were collected in 1992 from 43 Sears retail stores in Canada using two separate and independent measures.

1. Employee attitudes were measured by means of a regularly scheduled survey that incorporated 8 scales of the Index of Organizational Reactions (IOR): Leadership and Direction, Work Appeal, Work Demands, Coworkers, Physical Surroundings, Financial Rewards, Career Future, and Organizational Commitment. The survey results from the 43 stores were obtained over a 13-month period prior to the collection of customer satisfaction data.

2. Customer satisfaction data were collected by an independent research agency during a 6-month period and were based on 150 "indepth" interviews with customers in each store. In all, fourteen categories of customer satisfaction were obtained in each interview. These categories are listed in Table 5.1.

Results of the Study

Even a cursory review of the categories shown in Table 5.1 suggests that only about half were likely to be influenced by retail salespeople, whereas the others could only be influenced by the work of employees in one or more central locations totally removed from the stores served. Examples of the former are (a) allowing customers to pay for merchandise quickly, (b) short waiting times at cash registers, (c) having salespeople with good product knowledge, (d) getting problems solved quickly, (e) smiling and being friendly, (f) trying hard to satisfy customers, and (g) being clean, neat, and well-organized.

Those dimensions that are largely outside the control of local store employees include (a) having merchandise in stock, (b) standing behind its merchandise, (c) promptly crediting customer's account, (d) having a no-hassle return policy, and (e) accurate credit account statements.

To confirm these judgments, two experienced retail executives were asked to rate each dimension on a 5-point scale ranging from "completely under salesperson's control" to "completely outside salesperson's control." The results are also portrayed in Table 5.1. Only one dimension produced any disagreement, namely "having merchandise in stock." (It was noted by one executive that an experienced salesperson might make an effort to

TABLE 5.1

Customer Satisfaction Categories and Rated Employee Influence

Customer Satisfaction Category	Rated Employee Influence (5 = highest)
Allowing customers to pay for merchandise quickly	5.0
Short waiting times at cash registers	5.0
Having salespeople with good product knowledge	4.0
Getting problems solved quickly	5.0
Having good sales	4.0
Smiling and being friendly	5.0
Trying hard to satisfy customers	4.0
Being clean, neat, and well organized	3.0
Having merchandise in stock	2.5
Standing behind its merchandise	2.0
Making it easy to use a credit card	2.0
Promptly crediting customer's account	1.0
Having a no-hassle return policy	1.0
Accurate credit account statements	1.0

search a stockroom for an apparently out-of-stock item, while the other executive thought this was unlikely in that it would probably involve leaving other customers and a register unattended.)

The distinction between categories of customer satisfaction and the degree to which they are influenced by employee behavior is extremely important. It points to the need to look at individual facets of customer satisfaction that are or are not under employee control rather than on overall or global measures that may easily hide or obscure this critical distinction.

Because the study did include many separate and distinguishable measures of customer satisfaction, an attempt was made to determine how well each of these measures were predicted by the 8 scales of the IOR. This involves the use a multiple correlation technique. Briefly, this statistical technique takes into consideration the interrelationships (correlations) among all 8 IOR scales as well as their individual relationships to each of the 14 customer service measures. Each of the resulting multiple correlations is, therefore, an estimate of the relationship between the weighted combination of all 8 IOR scales and each of the 14 measures of customer satisfaction.

Table 5.2 shows the multiple correlations between the IOR scales and each measure of customer satisfaction. As can be seen, a very clear-cut differential pattern emerged. Those facets of customer satisfaction over which retail employees had control were substantially and significantly predicted by employee job satisfaction, whereas those over which employees had little or no influence showed no such relationship.

From a management point of view, these findings clearly indicate that managers may expect employee attitudes to translate into improved customer service but only in situations where employee behavior has some control over the outcome.

Discussion of Results

The present study was, as indicated, an example of opportunistic research. It depended on a chance discovery of available customer satisfaction data

TABLE 5.2

Index of Organizational Reaction Scales and Level of Customer Satisfaction
(N = 43 Stores)

Customer Satisfaction Category	Multiple R
Allowing customers to pay for merchandise quickly	.76*
Short waiting times at cash registers	.78*
Having salespeople with good product knowledge	.85*
Getting problems solved quickly	.73*
Having good sales	.78*
Smiling and being friendly	.66*
Trying hard to satisfy customers	.73*
Being clean, neat and well organized	.60*
Having merchandise in stock	.77*
Standing behind its merchandise	.47
Making it easy to use a credit card	.37
Promptly crediting customer's account	.42
Having a no-hassle return policy	.47
Accurate credit account statements	.49

*Significant < .01 Level

that were collected shortly after a survey of employee job satisfaction. Although this study was undertaken to explore the predictive validity of the IOR scales at the retail store level, its findings have apparently been extended and have become an important element in the company's strategic planning (Rucci, Kirn, & Quinn, 1998). These authors report that a "refined" attitude scale taken from the same Sears employee survey discussed here, when linked with measures of customer's satisfaction, has a quantifiable predictive relationship with company revenue growth.

The present study also lent support to a very large and continuing body of research that has repeatedly confirmed the link between facets of customer and employee satisfaction (J. Johnson, 1996; Schmit & Allschied, 1995) and other studies that have gone on to identify a causal path by which certain management practices can strengthen the link. (Rogg, et al., 2001). This line of research is likely to have considerable impact on management behavior, for it strongly suggests that certain leadership practices not only influence employee job satisfaction (well-being) but can build on it to create a "climate for service" on which customer service ultimately depends.

Although specific management practices that lead to customer service will vary from one organization to another, it seems very likely that in the growing service sector, management's emphasis on customer satisfaction will be effective to the extend that a "climate for service" has been established based on a sense of employee well-being.

6

Employee Attitudes and Attendance

Because employee absenteeism is a major cost concern of organization, liter-ally hundreds of studies of the reasons for it have been carried out over the past 40 years (Rhodes & Steers, 1991). In certain situations the cost of absen-teeism can be especially magnified by its disrupting influence on team efforts or on key projects in which unique skills, expertise, or management leader-ship is lost—even temporarily. Unfortunately, many attempts to study the reasons for absenteeism are limited by situational factors and the small num-bers of individuals who may be absent in a given time period. The present study did overcome several of these limitations. It yielded some compelling evidence of a positive relationship between job attitudes of exempt level em-ployees and their work behavior; in this case, attendance on a single day un-der very adverse conditions.

THE STUDY

The study was unique in several aspects. It focused on the attendance of exempt (salaried and managerial) employees on a single day in two geo-graphically separate locations (Chicago and New York). The day studied followed an unexpectedly heavy snowstorm in Chicago that greatly in-creased the effort involved in getting to work. In both locations a survey of work attitudes of all managerial and exempt level people had shortly preceded the snowstorm.

As will be noted, the results of the study gave considerable support to other research on absenteeism and had a modest impact on the company's human resource program.

Although the influence of employee job satisfaction on absenteeism (attendance in this study) is taken as a given by most outside observers, attempts to establish a causal connection has been forced to consider many moderating factors. As many as 209 separate influences or likely antecedents of absenteeism have been cited (Rhodes & Steers, 1991). Because the present study was completely fortuitous, it could not begin to control any of these moderating influences. Instead it looked at the attitude–behavior link as direct and uncomplicated. At the same time, the study's population, its timing, and its setting served to naturally minimize the effect of several major moderating influences. This, in turn, allowed a relatively unobstructed view of the link. For example:

1. The population studied consisted of 3,350 salaried people who, unlike those paid on an hourly bases, are not subject to any loss of pay or benefits for occasional absences. Although pay-loss is considered to be one of the constraining influences on the attitude—absenteeism link, (Rhodes & Steers, 1991) its actual measurement is usually only vaguely estimated. (Survey interviews, however, have identified it as the major influence on the decisions made by hourly paid employees to be absent.)

2. A very substantial number of people were absent on the day in question. This is an important consideration in that absenteeism rates for a short interval of time are usually small, and often force researchers to look at very limited samples or to consider long-time frames. The former created statistical problems whereas the latter introduced or allowed contaminating influences to cloud the attitude–behavior linkage.

3. The influence of "social pressure to attend" generated by supervisors or coworkers is another often powerful, influence on attendance. The constraining influence was diffused and presumably minimized here by the fact that a large percentage of coworkers and supervisors were among those who were absent.

4. The amount of effort involved in getting to work can be an important cause of absenteeism. In the present study almost all employees used public transportation and all Chicago-based people reported extreme difficulty in getting to work, in this case, to one single location (Sears Tower). This more or less canceled out any large differences in the effort involved.

5. It was possible to refine the identification of the people who were voluntarily absent only on the day studied. In studies of absenteeism, its definition has turned out to be more complicated than might be assumed (Rhodes & Steers, 1991).

6. As Herman (1973) has pointed out, many studies have failed to demonstrate relationships between employee attitudes and work behavior because the behavior studied was not under employee control. Again, in this present study, the decision to attend or not attend work was an individual matter.
7. A control group was available. It consisted of a smaller but nearly identical work population located in one building in the company's New York Headquarters. The work there was strictly related to fashion goods but was essentially the same as that carried out in Chicago.
8. It might also be noted that Ivancovich (1986) has indicated that absenteeism is better predicted by "absenteeism records" than by employee attitudes. Because "chronic absentees" would have been screened out in the exempt, managerial population studied here, this issue could not be addressed.

The Study's Procedure

Because the survey was administered anonymously, subjects were identified only in terms of large functionally related groupings. (The Men's Store for example consisted of a large group of employees working in related merchandise departments dealing with men's clothing.) A total of 27 functional groupings in Chicago and 13 in New York were used in this study. The sample sizes within each unit ranged from 59 to 228 in Chicago and from 28 to 48 in New York.

The attendance data were collected by a Human Resource Department representatives who were not aware of the study's design or intent. Because attendance data were not systematically collected for salaried people, a special effort was made to determine the exact extent of, and the specific reasons for, nonattendance. Moreover, nonattendance was carefully defined to reflect voluntary absence *on only the day studied*. Thus, subjects who were absent because of out-of-town travel, were on vacation, or were ill prior to the storm were not counted as absent on the day studied. Group attendance percentages were computed by dividing the number of people attending by those who could have reasonably been expected to attend. Thus, the measure obtained here was considerably refined.

For each departmental grouping in Chicago and New York the percentage of attendance was computed as was the average score for each department on each of six attitude scales. Correlations were then computed between these two sets of data.

The satisfaction and attendance data collected on the New York sample were for comparison purposes only. They allow for a prediction of attendance on what amounts to a random day. Because no storm had occurred in New York on the day studied, no greater effort was required in attending work than on any other day and no particular pressures to attend were in evidence.

Results of the Study

On the day after the storm, attendance ranged from 97% to 39% in Chicago (mdn = 70%). In New York attendance was much higher, ranging from 100% to 89% (mdn = 96%).

Table 6.1 presents the correlation data for both locations. As can be seen, the storm-related attendance in Chicago is significantly correlated with all six attitudes measure and, in the case of three scales, was highly significant.

Although the comparison analysis in the New York sample was limited by the small sample (13 departments) and the extreme restriction in range of the attendance rates, the small variance in attendance does represent a typical day's attendance pattern for managers in these functional units. None of the correlations was significant. (Those readers interested in the vicissitudes of research in organizational settings may find it ironic that the next significant snowstorm happened on the Friday after Thanksgiving. Because this was traditionally treated as a free day, only a handful of people came to work. By then the survey data lacked currency but probably would have qualified for a second study had there been anything to study. As a result no cross-validation of the results was possible.)

TABLE 6.1

Correlations between Job Satisfaction
and Attendance in 2 Locations

IOR Scale	Chicago Depts. (N = 27)	New York Depts. (N = 13)
Supervision	.54**	.12
Amount of Work	.36*	.01
Kind of Work	.37*	.06
Financial Rewards	.46**	.11
Career Future	.60**	.14
Company Identification	.42*	.02

Source: Smith, F. (1977). Work attitudes as predictors of attendance on a specific day. *Journal of Applied Psychology, 62*, 16–19.
* < .05 one-tailed test, ** < .01 one-tailed test

The results certainly showed a strong relationship between job satisfaction and attendance. They also suggested a casual connection in that it would be hard to argue the reverse —that attendance (or absence) somehow worked retroactively to influence attitudes.

The strength of the connection between employee attitudes and attendance shown by the correlations in Table 6.1 is higher than the reported in other studies (Hackett, 1989 reported correlations in the .15 to .20 range as typical). The much stronger relationship found here may reflect the fact that many of the factors that have been shown to moderate (lessen) the attitude–attendance link were, in fact, minimized or eliminated. In addition, the correlations obtained here were computed across organizations rather than within them (Ostroff, 1992).

The results lent support to other studies of the direct and casual link between attitudes and measures of performance (Scott & Taylor, 1985). They also encouraged the company to cooperate with other research efforts aimed at predicting absenteeism from attitude measures (Terborg, Lee, Smith, Davis, & Turbin, 1982).

The study also lent support to efforts to improve the quality of work life among employees. By demonstrating that attitudes had tangible organizational impacts, it helped convince management that efforts to improve morale that had previously been dismissed (childcare, staggered hours, flexible hours, etc.) had a definite impact on, and a place in, organizational life.

Beyond its research implication the study had one surprising impact on one company executive who had long voiced great skepticism regarding attitude surveys and their likely positive impact on his "bottom line" (his department had the highest absenteeism on the day studied and the lowest job satisfaction in the survey). When shown the results of the study and given an explanation that they related to managers in his own department, he actually seemed impressed. To his credit, he was later reported to have approached the much despised Human Resource Department for some morale building advice!

Although the present study was of a one-shot nature, it did show that a naturally occurring event could provide a unique glimpse of work behavior that is relatively unobscured by moderating factors, a situation ordinarily achieved only in laboratory settings.

7

Organizational Commitment
and Turnover

This study of turnover among management trainees was carried out within Sears in cooperation with the University of California. The study shows that even relatively small-scale, carefully planned research, undertaken for purely academic purposes can have a practical organizational impact. In the present case, the study led to a significant change in the company's management development practices, and contributed to the development of a measure of organizational commitment that has since been used in hundreds of studies.

INTRODUCTION TO THE STUDY

Voluntary turnover is a very costly organizational consideration. Even as far back as 1978 its cost to American industry was estimated to be as high as 45 billion dollars (Rhodes & Steers, 1991). In many cases, the costs are actually inestimable. They may involve an organization's very survival when special technical expertise, confidential information, or critical management skills are lost in the process. This dysfunctional turnover is itself a subject of research (Hollenbeck & Williams, 1986). Although within Sears, no exact estimate of turnover's direct costs was ever determined, its intangible costs were. In one corporate level study, turnover was shown to have an inverse relationship with customer satisfaction (Ulrich, Halbrook, Meder, Stuchlik, & Thorpe 1991). Beyond any assessment of what amounted to turnover's indefinable cost, however, was the company's growing concern over the excessive loss of young managerial candidates in its management training program. Over a 3-year period, more than half left voluntarily. This loss was especially alarming to Sears, which not only relied on, but was totally committed to, a "promotion from within" policy for future management positions.

The loss of young potential management people in their initial experience with the company was seen as a growing organizational weakness and as a threat to its future pool of executive talent. Although employee surveys had alerted management to certain weaknesses in the administration of the training program, none of these was thought to account for the high turnover being experienced. As a result, other studies were being considered. As so often happens in such situations, a research project initiated for one purpose came to serve another. In this case the author and a colleague from the University of California had prepared a proposal for a longitudinal study of turnover to be submitted for a professional award. Given the trainee turnover problem, the company readily agreed to have the study carried out among its training centers. This chapter summarizes this study and its primary results. More detailed accounts may be found elsewhere (Mowday et al., 1982; Porter et al., 1976).

Setting and Subjects

Sears had for several years established a program of hiring college graduates as candidates for future management positions. They were assigned in groups of 15 to 30 to one of 12 training centers. These were located in and were functionally integrated into large operating retail stores. The intention was to provide each trainee with a broad experience in the various operations of a store and its people over a 12-to 15-month period after which they were assigned to entry-level management positions. To insure proper exposure to all operations, each store was given a Training Director to oversee the trainees and their progression through the program.

The subjects for this particular study were 212 management candidates. All but one were college graduates and had entered Sears' program as their first full-time job. All were in their mid-20s. Out of the original group, 56 (26.5%) left to assume military responsibilities. Another 23.7% left the training program voluntarily during the first 15 months of the study. This group formed the base turnover sample, termed *leavers*, whereas those who remained with the company were the base nonturnover group termed, *stayers*.

Method of Study

To examine the relationship between attitude change and subsequent decisions to stay or leave, a 15-item et al. (1982). It was administered on the first day of training and on eight regularly scheduled dates thereafter. To insure confidentiality, all questionnaires were returned to the University of California and were identified only by a code number privately assigned to each candidate on his or her first day.

Results of the Study

In order to assess the changes in commitment scores prior to leaver's termination, three matched pairs of leavers and stayers were selected based on the number of months, which preceded the actual time leavers left the company. In addition, each set of paired trainees was from the same training center. Their average organizational commitment scores were computed at three time intervals. These results are shown in Fig. 7.1.

These results indicate that scores of stayers remained consistently high over the three intervals, while those of leavers dropped sharply the closer they came to actual termination.

This finding had important practical implications for it indicated that decisions to leave the company were likely to be preceded by a decline in commitment to the organization. This finding is also consistent with much

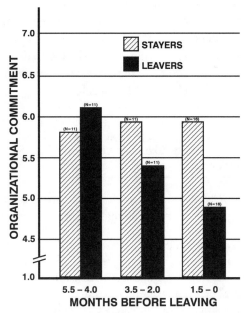

FIG. 7.1   Degree of organizational commitment of stayers and leavers: months before leavers terminate.
Source: Porter L., Smith, F., Crampton, W. (1976). *Organizational Behavior and Human Performance, 15,* 87–89.

earlier studies in which leader behavior was related to employee turnover and grievances (Fleishman & Harris, 1962).

Organizational Impact of the Study

Its findings gave management a basis for expecting early warning signs of turnover and led to further studies of how these signs might be picked up in the everyday behavior of trainees. These involved a number of interviews with Training Directors, store managers, and both current trainees and those who had left the company. From these conversations a very clear causal explanation of turnover among the majority of leavers was obtained along with some impressionistic data on its behavioral precursors. As one example, comments of the Training Directors indicated that a good deal of "bitching" had been expressed by trainees who later left. Unfortunately the significance of these comments was more or less dismissed as being "natural in most jobs." As a result, this early sign of impending turnover was essentially ignored.

More importantly the interviews revealed that although a few trainees left for entirely personal reasons that could not have been predicted, the great majority who left did so because of their openly expressed disappointment with the job's actual content when contrasted with that promised by college recruiters! It was claimed that the management responsibilities and advancement possibilities described by recruiters were in sharp contradiction to the sometimes menial tasks, the excessive hours, lack of time off, and the highly detailed nature of the work actually required. In addition, the absence of any promised interaction with management people was said to be especially galling.

Note: An interesting insight into the motivation of stayers was also obtained in interviews—a very high percentage of whom said they had understood what the job would be like by having worked for Sears as part-time employees while they were in school.

In response to the overall findings, the company made a number of changes in the training program content while maintaining its basic structure:

1. Recruiters were instructed to present a more realistic picture of the job even at the cost of obtaining fewer candidates.
2. To reinforce the hoped-for changes in recruiting tactics, a kind of "truth in advertising" program was created that included talks to groups of potential trainees by senior managers in which their own career experiences, the time demands, the detail required, and frequent moves were stressed. At the same time, they traced their own careers and rewards in an effort to "show a light at the end of the tunnel."

3. Training Directors were alerted to the signs of failing commitment—not only the "bitching" alluded to in their interviews but the behavioral and performance signs of discouragement, and so on. Rather than dismissing grumbling as "natural," Directors were instructed to use it as an excuse to counsel and discuss problems and career progress of their charges.

4. Visits to training stores by high-level executives were arranged as a means of acquainting trainees with company strategies and challenges and to have the executives get acquainted with the company's future managers. These visits turned out to have an especially significant impact on trainees.

5. Managers of the stores in which training centers were located were asked to become more involved and to hold periodic meetings with trainees to discuss store-level problems, and so on.

Note: At the time, the idea of providing realistic descriptions of the job was considered a commonsense solution to an identified problem and in this case it worked quite well. Many years later, the notion of providing realistic-job-previews (RJP) and the response to "met expectations" became subjects of professional study. (Baker & Jennings, 2001; Hom, Griffeth, Palich, & Bracker, 1999).

Attempts to provide trainees with a cold slice of reality made a significant impression. First was a large increase in rejected job offers by trainee applicants that greatly increased the costs of recruiting. Although it took 2 years to weigh these costs against the results obtained from the changes in the training program, the "final" judgment strongly endorsed the changes. It was found, for example, that (a) turnover among trainees declined (over the 2-year period, turnover was 19%) and (b) the increased costs of recruiting were more than offset by the improved trainee retention rate.

The meetings with trainees produced a reciprocal and very favorable impression on the executives involved, almost all of whom said they gained a better understanding of the "younger generation's" needs, views, and capabilities. Among the more intangible results were the increasingly favorable assessments of later trainees given by their Training Directors. It was noted, for example, that the aforementioned "bitching" had all but disappeared. The fact that turnover had been reduced was also seen as having improved the overall organization climate in that the complaints and openly expressed disappointments so often heard in the past by those intending to quit, were now said to be more or less nonexistent.

It was further stated that the recent cadre of trainees seemed "more at home" and seemed to have a greater general acceptance of, and agreement with what the company stood for. This implied sharing of personal and corporate values is perhaps one of the more significant contributing elements of organizational commitment—an issue stressed in later research (Breaugh, 1983; Finegan, 2000; Lee & Mowday, 1990; Somers & Birnbaum, 2000).

It appears that the follow-up actions generated by this one small-scale study in which job demands and rewards were frankly and honestly laid out were very effective. It may also have anticipated the attention this approach to realistic job previews would receive in later, more definite research studies. (Dugoni & Ilgen, 1981; Hom, et al., 1999).

SOME SUBSEQUENT RESEARCH

Although the practical impact of the present study was mainly limited to the Sears organization, the study was in line with subsequent research relating to the concept of *organizational commitment*, a topic that along with *job satisfaction* has been a subject of intense study for more than 35 years (Grany, Smith, & Stone, 1992). The present study's contribution to later research was primarily in the development of a useful scale for measuring organizational commitment, the Organizational Commitment Scale (OCS; Mowday, et al., 1982). Although there is some uncertainty as to whether organizational commitment and job satisfaction overlap in some predictable way (Farkas & Tetrick, 1989; Williams & Hazer, 1986) or are really separate and distinct measures (Brooke, Russel, & Price, 1988), it seems safe to conclude that both can be considered likely predictors of turnover (Eby, Freeman, Rush, & Lance, 1999).

The study reported here made the assumption that commitment was a separate concept. This is in agreement with Porter and his associates (Mowday, et al., 1982) who have maintained that organizational commitment is a more stable enduring concept than job satisfaction in that it measures the following: a more global and affective response to an organization as a whole as well as a strong belief in, and acceptance of, an organization's goals and values; a willingness to exert considerable effort on the organization's behalf; and a strong desire to remain a member of it. This definition and its measurement by the OCS has been most frequently used in studies of turnover; and has helped establish the OCS as a reliable measure of what Allen and Meyer (1990) called *affective commitment*.

SAME PRACTICAL IMPLICATIONS

Considering the costs associated with turnover, especially that involving the loss of key people or resources, those managers who are trying to control turnover in their organization may find some useful advice in academic studies of the subject. Although these studies have been carried out with ever increasing statistical sophistication, their results are often quite clear-cut and practical. For those readers who want to explore the subject further, a couple of examples are offered here.

In keeping with the view that commitment is clearly distinct from job satisfaction, one line of research has focused on the developmental of two *antecedents* of commitment within organizations. One example (Rhodes, Eisenberger, & Armeli, 2001) has shown that commitment in some situations is born of certain work experiences that create a sense of "perceived organizational support" (POS). These work experiences include: favorable opportunities for rewards; supervision that is considerate of employee needs and concerns; and a fair distribution of organizational rewards. This suggests that managers who want to foster a sense of commitment may want to encourage and build on these kinds of work experiences.

Another series of studies has looked at the *consequences* of commitment (and job satisfaction). One in particular concluded that either organizational commitment, measured by OCS or job satisfaction as measured by IOR, led to turnover by the same path (Lee 1988). Building on a theoretical model of Mobley (1977), which suggested that people rarely just up and quit, Lee identified some of the decisional steps to turnover taken by dissatisfied employees. Later, Hom & Kinicki (2001) greatly expanded these steps and identified their causal interactions. Their comprehensive model of how dissatisfaction (and presumably, low commitment) drives turnover is based on a very sophisticated analysis, but its conclusions provide a workable picture of the stepwise path by which dissatisfaction leads to turnover. In doing so, they have given managers a map of the process by which the precursors of turnover can be recognized and acted on. In over simplified terms, the path to turnover and its stepwise considerations include:

1. Dissatisfaction usually leads to "thoughts of quitting." If leaving is rejected this has negative consequences of its own, such as frequent absences and other kinds of work withdrawal behavior.
2. If the thought of leaving is entertained, this leads to a consideration of its costs—personal, career, and financial.
3. Once these considerations are resolved, the inclination to leave leads to a search for alternative employment. This is obviously influenced by the current labor market.
4. Once alternatives are identified, their comparative attractiveness is weighed.
5. Finally a turnover decision is reached.

Managers who recognize these signs of potential or impending turnover can take proactive steps to discourage or prevent it.

SUMMARY

This chapter summarized one academic study of the attitude-turnover link which had a significant impact on the host-organization and made a contribution to subsequent research on turnover. The chapter also pointed out a few of later related studies and their practical implications.

8

Work Attitudes
and Unionization Activity

The relationship between employee attitudes and union activity in a U.S. company was the primary focus of this study. Its results were then applied to a very large Canadian manufacturing organization. In both instances union activity and employee attitudes were shown to be strongly related.

INTRODUCTION

Sears had always been known as a nonunion company. Although in its very early history, it had fought against union efforts—fiercely in some cases—later labor legislation and changing cultural attitudes toward unions led to a more accepting company position. Still, at about the time of the present study only 2.7% of all its employees were union members. To the author, who came from a union background, the question naturally arose as to why so few of Sears' employees belonged to unions. Was it because enlightened human resources practices made union membership unappealing? Was it because the famous Profit Sharing plan encouraged a sense of ownership that discouraged union participation? Was it because unions were no longer aggressively attempting to organize retail employees? Was it because the company's Labor Relations Department had been successful in defeating union organizing activities? Was it because the vast majority of retail employees in Sears and elsewhere simply had what appeared to be an antipathy toward unions?

After many long discussions with employees, line managers and labor relations people, the author decided that all of the possibilities just mentioned were valid to some degree. These discussions did, however, reveal a very interesting and consistent fact that may have been crucial: In almost every case in which serious unionization activity took place, *employees had gone to the union*, not the other way around. In fact, when unions had made unsolicited attempts to organize employees in Sears, they had almost always failed. Nowhere was this observation more soundly demonstrated than in the Teamsters 1960 countrywide attempt to organize all of Sears' units. After publicly announcing its intent to do so, and after 18 months of intense efforts, the Teamsters Union experienced *a net loss of two units!* In two units, employees who had earlier joined the Teamsters Union made a decision to decertify—that is, to withdraw from union membership.

In an effort to understand the implications of the previously mentioned questions, as well as the Teamster incident, the author decided to look at the large array of survey data that existed on those units that had never experienced union activity and those that had. Due to the infrequency of union activity in Sears, the search for an adequate number of cases to study went back 6 years!

Because unionization was still a very sensitive subject within the company, the author decided to conduct the study as an independent academic research and sought the help of a Northwestern University colleague. In spite of the subject's sensitive nature, the resulting study was later published with Sears' permission (Hamner & Smith, 1978).

THE STUDY

The 6-year search for cases led to a sample of 94 units (stores, distribution centers, service centers, auto stations, etc.), that had experienced some form of union activity ranging from simply the handing out of union pamphlets and appeals to the actual loss of a union election. For purpose of statistical analysis, this range of activity was later quantified into a 7-point scale that represented the degree of union success in its effort to unionize each unit.

Method

The 94 "union" units were matched with 94 "non-union" units. Because of the huge database available, it was possible to refine this matching process in some detail. For example, units were matched by type of activity, geographic location, size, and labor market conditions. That is, stores were matched with stores of same size in the same county, salespeople with salespeople, freight handlers with freight handlers, mechanics with mechanics, and so on. For purposes of the study, survey data for all 188 units (87,740 employees) were collected. In almost all cases, the surveys had been conducted within 15 months prior to any union activity.

The Analysis

The 42 items from the Index of Organizational Reaction (IOR) obtained for each of the 188 units were correlated with the scaled union activity scores (0 = no activity, up to 7 = lost election). The correlation model used in this analysis resulted in a 13-item scale, dubbed the "Alienation Index" (AI). A weighted combination of these items resulted in a multiple correlation of .55, which was highly significant and indicated that employee attitudes accounted for 30% of the variance in union activity.

This result was then further tested by using the AI scale to "predict union" activity in another completely independent sample of 62 units for which data had either been purposely withheld from the original sample or had been collected at a later date. Half of these units (31) had experienced some union activity and the other 31 had not. Again, the units were carefully matched. The resulting correlation was .41, again highly significant. Beyond this analysis, the Alienation Index scores of the *combined* sample of 125 "union" and 125 "non-union" units were compared. This comparison again showed significant differences between the two groups on 11 of the 13 items making up AI scales. The AI scale contained the following kinds of content:

> four items referred to leadership and supervision
>
> two items referred to co-workers
>
> one item referred to career future
>
> three items referred to work demands
>
> two items referred to physical surroundings
>
> one item referred to organization commitment
>
> one item referred to work appeal

The content of the AI scale is particularly noteworthy in that the areas covered by it sharply contrast with the focus of union organizing drives. That is, none of the six pay-and benefit-questions in the IOR scales was found to be predictive of unionization activities, yet these are the very areas targeted by unions.

A FURTHER COMPARISON

Although the study just described was very carefully designed and extensive in its coverage, it was never the less only one study and in one company. In order to explore the generality of these results, AI scores were computed for several groups of union and nonunion employees in a totally different situation. The opportunity to further test the notion that employee attitudes

were related to union activity came in a survey of a large Canadian manufacturing company. Because of its very diverse activities, ranging from electric motor construction to aerospace elements, the company assigned the
activities to seven separate locations. Six of these locations had both union
and nonunion employees and a separate union represented employees in
each location. The unions ranged from national organizations to local independent groups and one formal engineering bargaining association.

From a research point of view, it is important to note that in each location the
pay of union employees was covered by a union contract. This led to a designation of every employee as either "union" or "nonunion," and in turn allowed
that designation be used as a demographic category in the same way as gender,
service, or job function. This identification of individual union membership is
not allowed in most situations and would almost always be illegal in the United
States. This probably accounts for the dearth of research on *individual motivating*
factors relating to unionization. Given this special demographic it was possible
to relate the scores of every employee to his or her union or nonunion status. It
was also possible, in follow-up interviews, to identify groups of union and nonunion people without violating confidentiality. Table 8.1 presents the overall
comparison of union and nonunion AI scores for each plant.

As can be seen, a very consistent pattern of attitudes emerged. In every
case but one, union members described their job and organization in more
negative terms than did nonunion members. In the exceptional case, no sig-

TABLE 8.1

Alienation Estimates Union & NonUnion

| Location | Alienation Centiles | |
	Union	NonUnion
Plant 1	39 (56)*	51 (36)
Plant 2	36 (33)	56 (24)
Plant 3	30 (104)	51 (38)
Plant 4	39 (250)	53 (119)
Plant 5	46 (314)	55 (134)
Plant 6	52 (41)	46 (12)
Corp. Office	—	54 (51)

* Entries in parenthesis indicate the number of employees in each group.

nificant differences were found. This fairly dramatic comparison in no way suggested a cause-and-effect relationship. However, it did suggest that union membership may not result in higher job satisfaction and may in fact have a negative or insignificant impact on it.

One explanation that seemed clear in the Sears example is that whatever facets of dissatisfaction led employees to seek unionization, these are not the same facets usually addressed by unions. That is, employees seem to have sought out union help because of their resentment toward their supervisors and working conditions, but apparently not because of pay or benefit concerns. Unions on the other hand usually concentrate on improving pay and benefits and have little to say about supervisory behavior. Ironically, when pay or benefits gains are achieved by unions, these gains are usually given to nonunion people as well, somewhat muting the original incentive, leaving union members more-or-less unaddressed. The lesson to unions may be to broaden their appeal so as to address the so-called "human side of the enterprise."

Within Sears, the AI scores were used to encourage adherence to company policies on wage administration. That is to say, in a decentralized organization local managers had been known sometimes to withhold or delay salary increases (sometimes only temporarily) to achieve a monthly or yearly profit goal. This practice was definitely "brought back in line" by the implied consequence of high alienation as measured by the AI scale. The study's results, however, were not allowed to be used as a labor relations weapon. In no case was a survey conducted to satisfy a request by a labor relations person to conduct a survey in a "problem unit." The author was strongly supported by top management in insisting that surveys be regularly scheduled with only one exception, that of the request by the local manager.

IMPLICATIONS

The main value of the study reported here was to establish the predictive validity of the survey program and to add to the very sparse professional literature on unionization behavior at the individual level. Because the study was carried out as an independent academic work, it had little immediate influence within the host company. If anything, its most informing impact may have been on unions themselves by showing how their organizing appeal might be strengthened.

> In what appeared an unusual example of union interest, a local president of a large union (who had read the published study) called the author's office to request a survey among his entire office staff. They were apparently threatening to join a union, and he wanted to "get a better handle" on the situation! The survey was conducted by a colleague.

Only later, when AI scores were routinely included in survey reports, did the study's impacts become noticeable. It was, at the very least, a "wake-up call" to local managers to recognize the importance of leadership in avoiding "labor problems." As word got around the system, a minor improvement in survey results relating to supervision was noticed as was an increased interest in leadership training programs.

Part III

Introduction: Survey Cases

The chapters in this section describe in some detail a number of actual survey cases in various organizational settings. Each chapter presents a case concerned with a particular organizational issue or set of issues where surveys had a significant role. Some are examples of "one-shot" diagnostic efforts in particular organizations, whereas others describe long-term efforts that helped design, implement, and evaluate various types of organizational interventions.

The first three cases (chaps. 9, 10, & 11) were carried out entirely by interviews. They describe three very different work settings.

The next set (chaps. 12, 13, & 14) are accounts of surveys within the Sears organization over a long time span.

Chapter 15 deals with a very long-term study of organizational well-being in two ski resorts. and chapter 16 relates to a fairly short-term study of a TV station.

Chapter 17 stands alone. It is a summary of a decade of surveys in the special field of safety and environmental issues.

The four remaining chapters deal with different kinds of survey applications: the prediction of employee reaction to organizational changes (chap. 18); the selection of a new chief executive officer (chap. 19); the design and production of a supervisory training exercise (chap. 20); and the defense of a company in a federal court (chap. 21).

It should be noted that several of the cases (chaps. 10, 11, & 12) incorporate the actual survey reports given to management. In such cases, they are presented in the *present tense* as were the reports themselves. This practice is also followed whenever excerpts from actual reports are inserted in other chapters.

9

Improving Supervisory Recruitment: A 6-Year Study of an Organizational Intervention in a Coal Mine Operation

This chapter illustrates how survey information was used to help management understand the motivational needs of employees and to facilitate interventions that improved the organization and enhanced employee job satisfaction. The organizational intervention involved here was based on a 6-year study of a large coal mine operation. This study itself started out quite conventionally but soon developed into a major problem-solving agent. Aside from its diagnostic role, it helped launch a major operational change by employing a near textbook example of employee participation, introduced in very unlikely circumstances: suspicious miners, skeptical supervisors, and resentful managers.

THE SURVEY OBJECTIVES AND PROCEDURES

This series of surveys was carried out by individual interviews with all members of mine management and a mixture of individual and group interviews among miners. In all cases a nondirective approach (explained in chap. 3) was followed. This combination of approaches allowed for a broad sampling of mine population and an indepth probing of the pertinent issues raised. The initial purpose of the study was to determine the reasons why no applicants existed for a key first-level supervisory (Face Boss) position. This position is absolutely critical in a mine operation in that a mine section (face) cannot be legally mined without the direct supervision of a Face Boss. Because a Face Boss must have either 4 years of underground mining experience or a college degree in mine engineering, the major source of applicants for this position was the miner population. Its members, therefore, become the focus of the first surveys.

During a 6-year period, issues beyond recruitment arose that extended the survey team's role from that of a passive observer to an active advisor and monitor of a major organizational intervention. In all, 12 visits were made to six mines. The first two were explanatory and dealt with the lack of Face Boss applicants. These were followed by two visits in which a major intervention was designed. Subsequent interviews were aimed at monitoring reactions of managers and miners to the organizational intervention.

THE MINE SETTING

Based on the author's experience, it is very difficult for an outside observer, or one not familiar with the mining culture, to understand the difficulty faced in bringing about change in a mine operation. This introduction, therefore, goes to some length to provide at least a working perspective on the focal job, and the hostile climate in which it operated.

The mines in this study were owned by a large oil company. All were underground operations that worked a three-shift schedule using traditional methods of mining. The management hierarchy in each mine included a Superintendent, several Mine Managers, and scores of Face Bosses on each shift. Unlike surface mines, the operations here involved the systematic removal of coal from adjoining areas (called pulling rooms) while allowing the already mined areas to collapse as a means of reducing overhead pressure created by long, hollowed-out corridors.

The work in mines is both hard and dirty and is carried out under uncomfortable conditions in far from adequate lighting. Above all, it is extremely dangerous. (Although safety had consistently improved, the ever-present danger was pointedly brought home to the survey team when three members of its morning discussion group were killed by a sudden tunnel collapse later in the day.)

In spite of these drawbacks a large number of miners find the work appealing; to some it is fascinating, "We are working alone deep in the ground and digging stuff that was laid down thousands of years ago." This is not a budding anthropologist talking but simply one of many miners who take a curious kind of pride in what they do—especially under the challenging conditions in which it occurs. What appeal the work has, however, is dampened considerably by the crude and bullying leadership miners see and experience every day. It is an atavistic style one only reads about in books—very old books. Although this leadership approach is traditional, it has become even more brutal as frustration mounted among Mine Managers and Superintendents over their inability to meet demands for coal. They relied on yelling and cursing with no thought of recognition or any sign of approval for good work. "I don't believe in coddling people. This work is too demanding for that."

This atmosphere existed in a sea of frustration, uncertain loyalties, and displaced anger. For miners, their membership in the United Mine Workers of America (UMWA) more-or-less shielded them from the constant wrath of Mine Managers. As a result, Face Bosses bore the brunt of a manager's displaced hostility. It is commonly stated that "whenever a Mine Manager sees a miner sitting down, the Face Boss gets chewed out."

Ironically, membership in the UMWA has also led to conflict and discouragement among miners themselves. Primarily interested in producing coal, they were frustrated in doing so by frequent work stoppages and wildcat strikes that they were committed to honor even when the causes seemed "silly" or were unknown to them. In a similar vein, the company is seen as ultimately responsible for the prevailing ill-will, and is viewed with much ambivalence. On one hand, the company is seen appreciatively as the chief or only source of a good living in the region; on the other hand, as the chief adversary, held in check only by the union.

There is no ambivalence, however, in attitudes expressed toward local management—Mine Superintendents and Mine Managers. Here "All unite in speaking ill." For some, this antagonism sprang from personal experience with these managers; for some resentment seemed congenital, having been passed on from father to son several times over. In general, "bitching" about management is simply the thing to do.

This atmosphere is illustrated by one group discussion that included a survey moderator, a UMWA inspector, and eight miners, one of whom was a woman: (*Because of a long established myth that women brought "bad luck" in mines, their presence underground had been forcibly forbidden until equal employment laws were introduced and enforced. Apparently no such myth applied to female influence above ground.*)

Inspector:	I am really furious about what I found out today, and the minute I get out of here I am going to write management up.
Moderator:	What was that?
Inspector:	They left a door (gate) open between sections. That is a serious violation and I'm going to "cream" them.

Female Miner: Well, I guess I better tell you. I left that gate open.
Inspector: Oh, well, honey, you should never do that. I didn't know
you did that. I thought the Mine Manager allowed it.
Moderator: Hey, wait a minute. A minute ago you were going to
"cream" someone in management. But now you are being
solicitous. How come?
Inspector: Well, she is a buddy. You can't expect me to write up my buddy.

The term buddy is not a gratuitously granted title. It is earned in part by a gross initiation rite delicately known as being "greased." The grease involved is readily available in mining machines and its application to each new miner's bare bottom is by means of group assault! The immediate effect is said to be a feeling of "frictionless mobility" but as the grease and heavy work garb became one, a miner's first day becomes a very long day. While machine grease is a lubricant, its ritual use here actually produced a remarkable cohesion. Once subjected to this socially leveling humiliation, any male or female miner is forever after known as a "buddy."

Although Mine Managers are the usual focus of miners' resentment, there is no one-on-one relationship with them. So a miner's hostility is also redirected toward Face Bosses. They are frequently the butt of miners' jokes and gibes for being "victims" rather than "supervisors." In addition, work hours for Face Bosses are usually very long and without overtime pay. In the end, the Face Boss is a nearly hopeless target of abuse from above and below. In view of this, it may surprise the reader that the original survey was commissioned to identify the reasons for the lack of Face Boss candidates—as if this were a mystery!

The Initial Survey

Although both miners and managers were, at first, somewhat guarded in participating in what to them was a new and unheard of procedure, their intense interest in the subject (and desire to see improvements) quickly led to open and candid discussions.

The interviews yielded a consistent perception of the Face Boss job, clearly explaining its lack of appeal. Both the miners and the Face Bosses agreed the position was unattractive to potential candidates and had caused many incumbents to reconsider their decision to accept it. More than 75% of the union people interviewed indicated an unwillingness to consider the job, and a good number of Face Bosses said they would return to union ranks if this were possible.

Specific examples of the drawbacks of being a Face Boss can best be seen in the following extended excerpt from the first survey report to management. It will also serve to acquaint readers with the report's form and the kind of information survey interviews can provide:

The high demand for coal production, with little prospect of easing in the near future, has intensified the situation. Consequently there is a lack of time off, the workday is extended, and the workweek often includes Sundays for cleanup or maintenance. It is also not unusual for a Face Boss to be required to fill in on the "spur of the moment" for an absent colleague. Work schedules are unpredictable, having a negative effect on home life and creating a growing dissatisfaction on and off the job.

In addition Face Bosses feel that much of the authority, status and financial significance that the job once had has eroded to the point that any sense of prestige has been replaced by feelings of relative insignificance. "Five years ago there was a sizeable difference in our pay and a union employee, but today a machine operator working some overtime makes as much or more than we do." (Both groups feel the pay is "good," but Face Bosses feel there should be a greater differential in the two positions.)

Because Face Bosses feel their job has gone from a position of reasonable authority to one of subservience, they no longer think of themselves as part of management, but rather as caught in the middle between it and the union. This situation is aggravated by the fact that union people also perceive this erosion in the job, make it the butt of jokes, ostracize those who accept it and belittle those who aspire to it.

It is stated that the union is so powerful that there is no way a Face Boss can force or even tell an employee to do something—short of "bribery."

"Bribery" is fairly common, consisting of granting overtime work for little or no purpose. "If I don't give their guys two hours overtime, they refuse to do a thing or will find a reason to 'walk off.' I'm at their mercy."

The situation is described as so extreme that a wildcat strike will be honored by the men even when its reasons are unknown or considered wrong. Management's desire to avoid work stoppages compromises the Face Boss's attempts to enforce rules and make them powerless in any attempt to take strong positions with their subordinates.

In order to get compliance and productivity, a Face Boss has to resort to an overly considerate supervisory style, using what is described as a "one of the boys" approach. Mine Managers, however, frown on this approach, preferring a hard line rather than what they see as supervisory weakness. But whenever a Face Boss takes a firm stand and is challenged, he finds that management will not stand behind him. In the end, management itself appears to be the most permissive and weak!

It is also significant that the major positive comments made about the job by Face Bosses have to do with its comparative security (mainly continued salary during strikes), the opportunity it affords for participation in the stock investment plan, the management pension plan and its platform for possible, though unlikely, advancement. Thus, it seems abundantly clear that the job's appeal is mainly a reflection of its attendant benefits rather than its intrinsic characteristics.

In spite of frustrations and dissatisfaction, it is very clear from their comments that both the miners and management share a very important, highly significant and largely latent organizational strength—*the desire to produce coal*. To most miners, producing coal is a "turn on!" However, the pressure for production is so extreme nothing else seems to matter. As a result a Mine Manager's focus becomes very narrow, measuring his whole value only by the amount of coal produced *on his shift*. Housekeeping, preventive maintenance and safety assume lower order priorities. This situation has led to a number of problems:

1. There is an unhealthy inter-shift competition between Face Bosses, bordering on open sabotage. It is stated that many Face Bosses not only seek higher production to please a Mine Manager, but go out of their way to make others "look bad" by undermining the efforts of other shifts. Comments such as 'I really screwed you today' are common. Numerous examples of inter-group sabotage are also offered:
    *   Leaving equipment in an unworkable position causing the next shift to spend time pulling it out and placing it properly before work can begin.
    *   Leaving cables in an awkward position or pattern requiring a great deal of preparatory work.
    *   Not "cutting a corner" (a maneuver which facilitates easier movement of mining machines) for the next shift, causing them to have to complete that task before being able to mine coal.
    *   Misplacing equipment so that the next shift has to waste time hunting for it.
    *   Failure to notify the next shift of broken or poorly working equipment.
2. Equipment is operated beyond endurance limits, leading to some gross inefficiencies. Numerous examples are cited in which machinery and supplies were used wastefully because of inadequate maintenance, causing breakdowns and costly work stoppage.

In view of the many drawbacks for the Face Boss position, it is not surprising that the men are aware of management's difficulty in attracting people to it. Many feel that management is so desperate it has been forced to select some poorly trained people. Some are described as inadequate, even incompetent. (It should be noted that a Face Boss's ability comes under close scrutiny by miners who are usually as knowledgeable, if not more so, and legally are as well qualified.)

In summary, a Face Boss is described as one that bears the sole responsibility for getting a job done with little or no authority to do so. The demands made on him are so numerous and conflicting there is no way he can satisfy them all successfully. It is said that he must justify the conflicting production demands of management with State, Federal, and UMW safety standards. To achieve this, he must work through men whose overwhelming allegiance is to the union and whose power to resist is far greater than his power to initiate.

The Participatory Intervention

Following the delivery of the survey report to top management, several indepth discussions led to a greater involvement of the survey team members as active agents of organizational change. From these discussions, three procedural changes were offered that were aimed at revising the negative image and reality of the Face Boss job:

1. The corporate engineering staff was asked to explore possible operating changes that might reduce the work pressures on Face Bosses and intershift conflict.
2. The impact of interview comments persuaded top management to give greater support to Face Bosses in dealings with miners—even at the risk of a strike.
3. At the survey team's strong suggestion, management agreed that any intervention would involve the full participation of Face Bosses, mine managers and, to the intent possible, miners.

Although the motivational value of employee participation in effecting organizational change is well recognized, its recommendation here was not without risk. In the very hostile climate that existed in the mines, it ran the definite danger of backfiring if expected changes were not forthcoming. For a discussion of this and related problems see Baldwin, Magjuka, and Lother, (1991). In spite of these risks, it was reasoned that in view of the strong desire to produce coal so forcefully expressed in interviews with managers and miners, any plan which served this end and was seen as reflecting their input would be accepted.

Following a review of the comments and suggestions made by both miners and their managers, the company's engineering staff modified an earlier operating plan that called for a 24-hours-a-day operation involving *only two production shifts* per mine, allowing the third shift to handle necessary "dead work" (the clean-up and positioning of equipment, maintenance and repair of machinery, and other preparatory work that would facilitate the efforts of the production shifts). In addition, and in spite of likely union objections, all routine overtime was eliminated.

The plan contained a number of features, which not only appeared to meet many needs of Face Bosses, but also held promise of increased efficiency. As one example, the intershift competition would be alleviated by moving to a total mine production measure rather than one based solely on shift production. Moreover, by having only two production shifts in each mine per day, the supervisors of each production shift would directly follow each other rather than having third production shift as an intermediary. This would reduce the likelihood of intershift sabotage because retaliation would directly follow.

Although the scheme seemed an ideal solution to many of the problems, its implementation in all three mines was dependent on having enough Face Bosses to man the production units in each mine and enough repair people to handle the down shifts as well. Thus developed a circular impasse in which the solution could be implemented only after the earlier recruitment problem had been solved. But the recruitment problem was dependent on the success of the new approach, dubbed Project X. As a result, it was decided to implement Project X in one mine and have it serve as a model. This step was not problem-free because the overall climate and Face Boss attitude was one of distrust and resentment, and there was no guarantee that they would accept a plan that did not deal with the needs of the whole group.

Several steps proved very important to the program's acceptance. The first, in keeping with the desire for full participation, was sharing the consultant's total uncensored report with all management and supervisory people. In view of its frank and extremely critical content, there was a risk that its distribution would further aggravate the situation. On the other hand, sharing the report was a clear signal that top management intended to deal with the situation honestly and was treating Face Bosses as true members of the management team. Equally important, it set the stage for the next step in the study, which was to meet with Face Bosses, Mine Managers, and Superintendents for group discussions of the report and Project X. Because many of its elements had been suggested by Face Bosses and Mine Managers, it soon became obvious to them that the plan being considered was largely based on their ideas. This may be the reason the plan was solidly approved, and a strong consensus called for its sequential implementation. Most felt there would be sufficient Face Boss candidates to insure the plan's successful extension to the other mines.

The open discussions of the plan appeared to pay real dividends. It created a sense of ownership among Face Bosses, who repeatedly stressed their appreciation for being treated as members of management and for seeing their suggestions have an impact.

First Monitoring Surveys

Project X was implemented in Mine #1 almost immediately after this meeting, and its progress was monitored by the survey team about 6 months later. The results were more than hoped for and revealed a general acceptance of the project. Somewhat surprisingly, the vast majority of union members *did not object* to the loss of overtime. (This, in turn, suggests that the miners' insistence on overtime alluded to earlier was driven more by their desire to control their Face Bosses than by financial considerations).

The tone and content of interviews in the first monitoring survey reflected a modulated elation. Supervisors in the mine most affected by Project X were extremely pleased with their new schedule but were somewhat skeptical of its probable duration. As so often happens in posttrauma situations, anxieties about the future actually mount. It was reported, for example, that rumors were being constantly circulated that the new schedule would last only to the expiration of the current labor contract. Few could believe the new schedule was "for real."

In the other mines, a kind of guarded optimism existed. The supervisors there were very happy about the elimination of overtime, but were both anxious to have Project X extended to their mines yet suspicious that this would not occur soon or at all. There were also some signs of an awakening sense of responsibility on the part of Face Bosses. There appeared to be a realization that recruitment of Face Bosses could occur only if supervisors encouraged other candidates to apply. The Project X concept, in turn, gave them a sound argument for trying to persuade qualified miners to join their ranks.

Additionally, many of the complaints regarding management's failure to support Face Boss authority, so commonly heard in the first series of interviews, were relatively absent in this series. This was, of course, most noticeable in the one mine in which Project X had been fully implemented. It appeared, therefore, that the new schedule had not only been well accepted by both Face Bosses and miners, but the spread of its effect also relieved much of the frustration, born of fatigue, confrontation, and, in some cases, wildcat strikes. In this same vein, it was reported that the intershift competition had been greatly reduced.

Another source of frustration, stemming from disruption of family life, had also been lessened by the new schedule. The Face Bosses on this schedule were high in their praise of the change, which they reported had actually improved "their whole lives." They reported feeling "healthier" and that they had begun to rediscover their families.

The most tangible result of the new schedule was the large numbers of Face Boss applications. Suddenly, from a situation in which no Face Boss candidates existed, 32 candidates applied for the first training school and 50 more applied for entry in the second round. Interviews with these trainees clearly established that a large part of their motivation was based on feelings that Project X was a reality and clearly indicated management's desire to support and upgrade the Face Boss position. Because of the new trainees, it was possible on their graduation, to extend Project X to a second and third mine.

Second Monitoring Surveys

Following several casual visits by the consultant to maintain contact with the situation, a second set of monitoring interviews were conducted about 18 months after Project X had been started.

This second round revealed a general and very positive acceptance of Project X. However, there were some noticeable cracks in its progress. It was significant that these were expressed in constructive terms by most Face Bosses. Rather than reflecting personal or self-centered complaints, the comments suggested concerns that Project X might not be satisfying the company's needs. It was recognized for example that the plan's success had been somewhat hampered by a lack of repairmen, slowing the needed maintenance. In addition, the greater support given Face Bosses in work disputes had resulted in a series of wildcat strikes.

In spite of these drawbacks, it appeared that Project X was now seen as a real benefit. A genuine feeling of responsibility for making it work had been assumed by a large number of Face Bosses who felt the plan was theirs. This feeling was strongest among those Face Bosses who had been most active in the earlier group discussions and had contributed the greatest number of ideas and suggestions. In sharp contrast, and as an example of how powerful ingrained habits can be, a few senior Mine Managers and Superintendents lamented the loss of a "hard nosed leadership." In spite of the Project X success, these managers expressed a feeling that the Face Bosses were being coddled. In their book this would eventually lead to failure. Fortunately, subsequent surveys over the next 2 years failed to support such fears.

THE ORGANIZATION'S ASSESSMENT OF THE SURVEY

Perhaps the most independent assessment of the project was given by an executive of the parent company who evaluated its impact and potential for the future:

> In reviewing the whole process, it does appear that the approach did accomplish its primary goal of diagnosing the causes of poor Face Boss recruitment and helping devise a system for correcting it. Moving from a situation in which virtually no Face Boss candidates could be recruited to one in which over 50 were successfully attracted, with every indication that the trend will continue, is certainly evidence of success. The approach taken here was behaviorally oriented, which greatly aided the development and acceptance of Project X and alleviated most of the problems discovered in the course of the study.

> In view of this, it may be instructive to consider the probable contributions, if any, of the behavioral approach to this program's success. First, by having behaviorally oriented professionals diagnose the feelings of people in the mine situation, management was able to get an objective confirmation of its own judgment and obtain additional insight into its own role in the problem.

> Second, by obtaining an assessment of the personal needs of Face Bosses in this situation, management was in a position to predetermine the appropriateness of its proposed plan and in some cases modify its content.

> Third, by constantly monitoring the behavioral implications of the study, it was possible to anticipate its eventual progress and to detect growing problems before they became serious.

> Fourth, by taking the time to discuss the problem fully with mine supervisors, a number of worthwhile suggestions were obtained. Moreover, by allowing for a good deal of resentment to be ventilated in these discussions, much of it was diminished.

> Lastly and most importantly, the nature of the organizational interventions generated a feeling of involvement in decision-making among Face Boss opinion leaders. This sense of participation, in turn, appears to have been a significant factor in the successful implementation of the program, and also in creating a much different and more constructive climate among the first level mine supervisors.

SUMMARY

Through a series of group and individual interviews, a management problem was diagnosed (the absence of Face Boss candidates) and its organizational solution suggested. Using input from Mine Managers and first-level supervisors that was gathered in interviews, along with technical help from company management, a major change was implemented in the mines that not only eliminated the recruitment problem, but greatly improved the mining opera-tion and the well-being of miners and supervisors. Each step in the interven-tion was monitored by periodic interviews. Much of its success was credited to the fact that managers, supervisors, and miners contributed to its formulation and implementation. As a result of this participation, they expressed a high sense of ownership of the intervention and its positive consequences.

Considering the long history of antimanagement feelings in the mines and the sense of management "abandonment" expressed by many Face Bosses, their constructive participation in organizational change would not normally be expected nor recommended. It was recommended here, how-ever, based on the often-mentioned desire of all employees to produce coal. That their participation not only worked but was seen as a major factor in the plan's success seems to underscore its motivational power.

The Sequel

Project X was introduced to other mines and was effective there as well, hampered mainly by lack of trained maintenance people. Only sometime later did the mines themselves fall victim to closures brought about by the growing difficulty in marketing high sulfur coal. As might be suspected, given the demise of the mines due to economic pressures, the whole experi-ence was, to all involved, bittersweet. On one hand a seemingly desperate and discouraging situation had been transformed to a livable and produc-tive one in which employers and employees (to say nothing of the survey team), felt a real sense of achievement only to have it dashed by outside events over which no one had control.

10

Identifying Disparate
Needs of Scientists
in a Research Institute

This chapter presents the report made to management based on a survey carried out during a period of prolonged and disruptive changes in a prominent research laboratory. These included a major physical expansion of facilities, a dramatic change in the nature of research, a reorganization and restructuring of the lab, and a radical change in the lab's leadership. The change in leadership became a focal issue in that the new Lab Director followed a very popular person who had recently been made a senior vice president of the parent company. His personal contact with senior scientists in the lab, however, continued.

The new leader took his challenge to be an "up-grading" of the entire lab, which he saw as having "plateaued." His efforts at "unfreezing" the current lab organization was praised by some and resented by others, and it led to a distinct polarization within the entire lab population.

The population surveyed consisted of exceptionally competent scientists in a very sophisticated work setting. Many of its problems and human interactions, however, closely parallel those found in more ordinary settings among "ordinary people."

Because the parent company had decided to carry out all follow-up action internally, the survey was a purely diagnostic effort and has no publicized sequel.

The following survey report does provide readers with an organizational portrait that can be used for discussion purposes, and has, in fact, been used as such in graduate and MBA classes. In this connection, the reader may find it interesting to speculate on the impact this report might have had if shared with all lab members.

The Survey Procedures

The study reported here was carried out by individual nondirective inter-views (discussed in chap. 3) with all 205 scientists and engineers in the insti-tute. The study's aim was to explore the overall climate of this scientific organization and to identify any problems that might exist in the aftermath of the extensive changes the lab has experienced. Because of the study's explor-atory nature the interviews were totally nonstructured and allowed partici-pants to discuss any issue of concern. This approach excluded the use of questionnaires that, it was felt, might suggest areas of interest to the company rather than those of concern to institute members. As a result, the following report does not include any quantitative data, but it does reflect the major at-titudinal themes expressed by various groups within the organization.

REPORT TO MANAGEMENT

Note: The remainder of this chapter presents a slightly edited version of the actual report presented to top management by the author. In order for it to speak for itself, it is presented without further comment.

The situation in the lab allows few generalizations. It is clear, however, that a noticeable and pervasive polarity exists in the feelings and perceptions of lab members. For most people it is *either* the best of times or the worst of times. Only a few are ambivalent, understanding and welcoming the lab's change in direction, but resenting some of its results.

Because so many of the changes are associated with the new director's ap-pointment or were brought about by him, it is not surprising that some staff members see him as the prime source of their frustrations, whereas to others he is the herald of a very exciting new era. Consequently he became the fo-cus of their interviews. He is seen as having intentionally "shaken up" the lab, for good or ill. To some he is a scapegoat for frustrations that are only co-incidentally related to his arrival. To others the problems are directly attrib-uted to his style of leadership.

This situation is further complicated by the influence of the former direc-tor, whose personal and professional ties to the lab and its people are deep-rooted. His presence as the parent company's now senior vice presi-dent is still very much felt. Because his style of leadership is in direct contrast to that of the new director, it serves as a built-in comparison. Many feel this difference not only should have been recognized by the director but should have moderated his aggressive introduction of an autocratic style. On the other hand the vice president's continuing contact and friendship with a number of senior lab members is seen by other members as an unfortunate complication to lab direction, which is occasionally turned to the advantage of these senior lab people.

Regardless of their view of his leadership style, all participants agree that the new director has a brilliant mind and a charismatic personality. He is also seen as a world class scientist who could act as a very effective spokesman and champion of the lab's efforts. Even those who are critical of his style are quick to point out his correct insistence on and advocacy of scientific excellence within the lab. To many, the "tragedy" reflected in these various views is that the hope and high expectations for a new and dynamic direction, which were universally shared, have been realized by only some members whereas seriously, perhaps irrevocably, dashed for others.

The polarity in these views is seen in both the widely rumored prediction of his leaving the lab and the contrary hope that he will continue to advance its pursuit of first rate science. In the following sections, these issues are expanded within the limits of confidentiality.

Polarity of Opinions

The division of views regarding the lab's direction and leadership is quite wide, but judging from the many interview comments, it is not apparent to a few people and is only vaguely realized by others. For example, some views expressed were held up as being generally shared by all, while in fact diametrically opposite views were expressed just as often; moreover, some people seemed to be aware of widespread dissatisfaction but did not share in it or seem to understand its causes.

It appears that people in the traditional disciplines of the lab and those who have been with the lab for some time (more than 10 years) share a rather dim view of events, whereas those who are involved in the newer "hot" areas or who have not been around long enough to react to the changes or who are removed from the "turmoil" of physical relocations, and so on, are very excited about their work, the lab's future, and their roles in it.

Physical Moves

In the main lab, the very traumatic effect of physical contractions, dislocations, and multiple moves caused by the prolonged expansion and redesign of the new facilities, as well as the anticipated growth of the lab staff, appears to have led many of most affected people to focus on change itself as a source of discontent.

The personal and work-related impact of these changes (coming one after another and complicated by shifts in directions, reallocations of resources, new administrative overlays, and rapid growth) should not be underestimated. Many people seem sincerely concerned and are under considerable strain as a result. In some cases they see their life's work being disrupted or delayed. This is not only frustrating and demeaning but could affect professional competence and development. More than anything else it has led to widespread organizational uncertainty, which in itself is seen as inimical to sustained research effort. The newer people see this instability and naturally wonder about their commitment to the lab, whereas more senior service people are dismayed at the rapid and disruptive change and wonder about the lab's commitment to them. In such a situation few are able or disposed to take a detached view. On the contrary, a kind of floating anxiety exists that finds its focus and justification in almost any object or event. As a result, seemingly trivial matters often take on exaggerated proportions and meanings.

This perhaps explains why the recent introduction of a new mail system was more frequently mentioned than any other single event. Although few actually see this, in itself, as a major organizational problem, it does serve as both a real and symbolic justification of their feelings. At the risk of exaggerating its importance, it can be used as an example of how people react to unmanaged change in a period of extreme unrest. To some the new mail system is seen as an example of management's misplaced priorities and lack of sensitivity.

In contrast some people in the lab are either untroubled by the many changes or are only tangentially concerned about them. For the most part, they applaud the direction of research and are intensely positive about the lab, their work, and the director's role. Thus, the polarized situation is real and does not appear to be fully realized by either management or the staff members. In such a situation, overall appraisal of lab morale is difficult and is heavily dependent on "who one hears." A serious mistake for management at all levels would be failing to hear all sides.

Disruptive Influences

In spite of the fact that some employees have reacted positively to many changes, more general views regard them as causes of severe disruptions in work. In addition to the general uncertainty caused by these changes, some very specific frustrations can be identified.

Change in Research Directions

The idea of a new direction in the lab's research efforts is said to have been welcomed by all, but its implementation became a source of concern. The new approach did not build on existing strengths and may have "screwed up" well-performing areas so that the lab is floundering and at the same time many promises have not materialized.

Planned Versus Chaotic Change

Another troublesome aspect of the change is that it appears unplanned. Although some of the events could not have been anticipated, others it is thought could have been better planned or at least more thoughtfully communicated. Examples are personnel growth, space needs, the administrative support organizations, and budgeting processes. Compounding these feelings is the impulsive nature of many decisions, which is said to result in crisis reactions that could have been moderated by proactive management. (Here, too, there is a balancing attitude that insists that space needs were wrong and needed change, even at the expense of delays; that budget cuts could not have been anticipated; and that support services must go through a period of learning before mature service can be achieved. These events, it is held, are only partly the fault of planning.)

To most participants there appears to be a high degree of "waffling" on promises, policies, and direction. Perhaps this is seen most clearly and painfully in recruiting plans and practices. Because so many people devoted a good deal of time to the personnel planning sessions and/or subsequent recruiting efforts, this is a widely felt "sore point." The apparent reversals in recruitment quotas caused a great deal of embarrassment to people who had approached candidates and had to back off later. Whatever the cause of this change in plans, it has been a source of resentment and doubt. To some, it has made them "gun shy" and will certainly make them more cautious in future recruiting efforts. Others feel much more strongly and suggest the required quotas were arbitrary, even "politically" inspired, and, along with other unexplained decisions, has caused them to doubt the sincerity and even the honesty of management.

Lab Reorganization and Administrative Overlay

It seems agreed by all senior people that the reorganization of the lab was too rapid and that many of the new positions should have been filled before introducing it. Probably no other organizational change was more frequently mentioned than that associated with the new Administrative Support Group. The reasons are many: The group is seen as growing more rapidly than are certain scientific groups, and this is resented. That space has been provided for them at the expense of scientific functions is a very sore point. The attitude, and to some extent the ability, of this group, as well as the results achieved so far, are objects of criticism to almost all research people.

It is claimed that administrative people are supposed to help free scientific people from routine administrative matters but in the eyes of most, it has worked in reverse. It is claimed that most (not all) administrative assistants do not have a service orientation. They are seen as "marching to a different drummer" and that their performance is not evaluated by how well they serve the lab but by how many policies are installed and procedures put in place. Instead of carrying out procedures or seeing that forms, requests, contracts, and so on, are expedited, they merely explain how this is to be done by the research people themselves. As a result, work and time is added, not reduced. "There will be a policy on that tomorrow" is the local joke in this connection. As a result such things as purchase orders and deliveries are not handled efficiently and the very important process of slide production is cumbersome.

On another line, the library is seen as one embarrassment, the stock room as too formal and understaffed, and the graphics section as too remote. Although some people feel there were good and necessary reasons for a more formal approach in these areas, most are resentful and do not understand. Most important, they do not see that it has helped at all. In this regard it is felt that the Administrative Support Group could do much more to help if it took more time to find out the real needs of lab people and sincerely tried to serve them rather than being viewed as the imposer of solutions, formal policies, and procedures that may not be needed.

LEADERSHIP STYLE

Most participants, especially those in senior positions, claim that naming of a new person who would be brought in to change the direction of research was greeted enthusiastically. Several senior people actually recommended or were involved in recruiting the replacement. In this context some very high expectations were created. In view of actual events, it appears that by striving for scientific excellence and by gaining support for the lab, some expectations were fulfilled. This cannot be overstated. Comments were supportive and complimentary in the extreme.

His style of leadership and management practices, however, have been a source of great disappointment. It is felt that he has more nearly filled the role of a research manager than that of a director of research and development. He is described as overly involved in technical details of each specialty and gives the impression of having little confidence in various lab directors. Much of his behavior smacks of a professor challenging graduate students rather than that of a top-level leader dealing with senior scientists of proven ability. (Again it is felt by some that this behavior may be misunderstood and what is inferred as a challenge or taken to imply a demeaning obligation to justify one's work is often simply his way of making intellectual inquiries. As a result, he often appeared not to understand responses.)

Personal Insensitivity

Although it is felt that the director has a unique ability to communicate ideas and can be very impressive in both group and individual settings, he nevertheless is often said to demonstrate a real lack of sensitivity in both kinds of interactions. By way of example, in one apparently memorable meeting he suggested the lab was really a Triple A organization and that his goal was to bring it into the Major Leagues. This metaphor was interpreted as an insult by a good number of scientists who felt they were already Major League.

On a personal level, his insensitivity is seen in what is described as an unfortunate habit of criticizing certain individuals in conversations with their peers. This has led to a definite distrust and makes it extremely difficult for some senior people "to level with him."

Their difficulty is aggravated by his perceived unwillingness to accept criticism or the suggestion of error. This, coupled with a tendency to lose his temper, is said to create an atmosphere in which it takes a good deal of courage to be frank with him or to offer criticisms. Although to some people who seem to know him well, this view is held to be incorrect, his image is such that people are unwilling to confront him or to be totally candid in their dealings.

Lack of Mutual Trust

The absence of subordinates' trust is apparently reciprocated in the director's dealings with them. It is said that he simply doesn't know whom to trust. Because of their long association with the former director, some still go to him with problems or complaints that they are unwilling to broach with the new director. Some see this practice as unfair and as compromising the new person's position. Others say it is natural, given the former director's deep-seated interest in the lab, his long-term association with its members, and his very sincere concern that people be treated considerately and fairly. Some feel that the new director has resented this circumvention and has openly criticized people involved. One of the unfortunate organizational results of this three-way interaction is the growing belief that a struggle is developing between the two men. There are rumors that the former director is unhappy with the way the lab is being run.

Autocratic and Secretive Climate

In contrast to his predecessors, the new director is seen as aggressively autocratic in his role. This perception is compounded by his reputation for being secretive and for "playing things close to the vest." This relates to his apparent unwillingness to delegate responsibility although surrounded by competent and experienced people. It may be that he sees no need for consultation on many issues or that because of his uncertainty of staff support he is unwilling to consult them. In any event his reputation for secrecy stands in sharp contrast to his own self-perception of being open in his dealings.

Another aspect of his perceived autocratic style is his tendency to be critical of people and to "put them down" either directly or by the appearance of superiority. To some, his ego is such that he rarely admits to not knowing a subject and often gives the impression of being obliged to know more than the other person. "I don't know" is felt to be outside his repertoire and that at times his self-oriented personality prevents his asking questions about managerial subjects he needs to learn.

Some feel this situation would not have become so serious if the new director had taken the trouble to get to know people in the lab rather than aggressively pushing his plans ahead in such a direct and independent manner. Failure to do this resulted in alienation, which may be irreversible. Unfortunately some of the most intense feelings of rejection or of strained relations are among people who work most frequently with or directly for him.

There is some feeling that he has tried to establish relationships with people "down the line" by means of his luncheon meetings. These are felt to be good, but because of their size and formality it is difficult for many people to raise issues, and because of his reputation for not inviting criticism, many people are unwilling to confront him.

In this same connection it is understood that frequent one-on-one dealings between the director and the lab personnel would not be possible but when they have occurred, their impact has been significant, "I can live on that kind of recognition for months." In fact, the expressed need for recognition of one's work and the reassurance that one's efforts are in the right direction, seem to cry out for his personal attention to lower-level people especially in the lab's traditional research areas.

Morale Commentary

Assessment of morale is difficult because of the apparent polarity within the group. It is the feeling of those who have been with the lab or see it from a distance that morale has "never been lower." Although this does seem accurate as it relates to people in traditional areas, it is a totally inaccurate assessment of attitudes of people in other areas. In fact the enthusiasm expressed by these employees is extreme.

In almost all cases there is an unfortunate air of uncertainty as to what commitments have been made, which projects will survive, and what and how resources have been allocated. Although some believe the whole situation will "settle down" once the space issue is final, the problems associated with leader–subordinate relationships will probably remain.

It is a situation that calls for communication of a high order. At least two considerations emerged from interviews and should be noted.

First, it appears that in view of the vastly changing situation, management has taken a position of not trying to communicate decisions until they are definitely decided. This often makes sense. However, in view of the devastating impact uncertainty and complex change has had on lab people and especially on their scientific efforts, it would seem that more communication rather than less is in order. The ambiguity of the present situation leads to a vacuum that is totally filled with rumors and speculation. Any move to dispel these by providing current thinking and especially the rationale behind decisions should be helpful. This includes many of the feelings expressed in this report.

Second, it is apparent from the interviews that management people at all levels probably reinforce a number of morale-depressing attitudes by overly candid comments with subordinates. In many interviews, problems were described in exactly the same words used by higher-level people. This almost always indicates a sharing phenomenon and hardly reflects independent observations by otherwise highly creative people.

There are a number of morale strengths in this organization. First, people feel well paid for what they do. Not a single complaint was made in this area. Second, people are totally dedicated to their work. Although perhaps natural in this setting, it cannot be overlooked that this is an overriding factor in the way they feel. Third, there is an immensely high regard for each other's competence and accomplishments. Although some are considered "prima donnas" (or worse), there is in almost every case, an appreciation for being associated with a top-notch scientific group.

All these strengths can be built on and should not be overlooked in any view of the group or in any actions taken as a result of this study.

A CLOSING NOTE

The survey report just presented was intended to provide management with a picture of the lab's organizational climate and an assessment of the impact of the recent changes in the lab's leadership, structure, and physical layout. By identifying the work-related needs of various groups and the barriers that frustrate them, the study identified the existence and causes of a highly polarized climate among this community of scientists. As such, the study provided the company with a platform on which follow-up action could be based. As indicated earlier, the follow-up was handled by the client company and was treated as an internal project.

11

Improving Organizational Communication in a School of Nursing

This survey was carried out entirely by interviews among all faculty members and a sampling of students in a large and long established school of nursing. The approach taken was specifically requested by the client—the school's management. It was intended to identify and surface the underlying themes of what was purported to be a "communication problem," and to make interpretations of its causes whenever possible. The school's management staff had a vague sense that "something was wrong" but none of its members could define it or its likely causes. The resulting survey report attempted to clarify the situation by presenting a portrait of the whole organization by integrating the comments and sometimes narrowly focused perspectives of its members.

SETTING AND PURPOSE

The school of nursing involved in the survey was loosely affiliated with and adjacent to a large university hospital. Its curriculum followed a 3-year course of study. Its entire administrative staff and faculty were women, each of whom possessed impressive credentials but were widely different in age and experience in their special areas.

The survey was conducted at a time of transition in the nursing field in which the traditional passive, nonconfrontational, and subservient role of nurses was giving way to one of assertiveness and involvement in hospital decisions. Even the formal dress codes of nurses was being relaxed if not abandoned.

The purpose of the survey was to explore what was termed by the school's administrator a *communication problem*. Although neither staff nor faculty had any specific insight into this problem, both were convinced that one existed. It was in this ambiguous but seemingly frozen situation that the survey was commissioned and agreed to by all 62 faculty members and the six administrative people. The author was informed that almost all major decisions were put to a vote of the entire faculty, acting as a *committee of the whole*, and that unanimity as was achieved in the survey decision, was indeed rare. The one reservation, expressed by the Psychiatric faculty, was that no questionnaires be used and that all members be personally interviewed.

In view of the undefined purpose of the survey and the insistence on the use of personal interviews, the survey was conducted by means of unstructured interviews in which each participant was free to discuss issues of her own choosing. The technique used to keep the conversations going was the same nondirective approach used throughout this book and discussed in chapter 3. It should be noted that given the interest in the process and the observational skills of faculty members, the interviews remained focused on organizational issues and required very little prompting by interviewers. It should also be noted that members of the administrative staff asked for a summary of comments that reflected on their leadership. This was agreed to on the condition that each would receive a confidential summary of only those comments made about her role and that the summary be delivered to her personally. No copies of these summaries were made and none is included in this report.

What follows, therefore, is a depersonalized but otherwise complete report presented to the school's management and all its faculty.

THE SURVEY REPORT TO MANAGEMENT

This survey involved interviews with the nursing school faculty and a sample of students undertaken for the purpose of assessing the extent and nature of a communication problem. Because such problems rarely exist in isolation, the approach actually taken examined the strengths and weaknesses of the organization as a whole and treated communication as but one of its processes.

The survey results indicate that a number of problems, including that of communication, exist as does a strong need for their improvement. However, the results also indicate that the school has a great number of strengths and that the overwhelming majority of its faculty feel it is doing a commendable job of training nurses. Indeed, even their willingness to undergo this kind of self-examination reflects a healthy motivation.

Because malice toward coworkers is frequently found in less healthy organizations with similar problems, it was noteworthy that, although a number of seemingly petty comments were made, there is a noticeable absence of destructive intent in the interviews. Therefore, it would be a mistake to exaggerate the seriousness of the problems identified or to lose sight of the fact that even the most severe criticisms offered are generally voiced constructively by people who felt the school is, at the very least, meeting its primary responsibilities in training competent nurses. In fact, a few people are actually surprised to hear that the organization has any serious problems.

With these caveats in mind, this summary outlines a number of the school's strong points but concentrates on its problems, many of which seemed solvable.

STRENGTHS IDENTIFIED

The Work Itself

Perhaps the most positive force in the school revealed by the survey is the noticeable attraction that nursing instruction held for most faculty members. The great majority seem to enjoy their work above all else. There are, at the same time, a few who are undecided on this point and who seem to be in the process of deciding whether or not they can derive more satisfaction from *teaching* nurses than *being* nurses. In addition, some have decided that teaching is not their forte, and they will probably leave. Even among these latter groups a real interest in the school is expressed, as is a willingness to help improve it.

Respect for Peers

Although a few, seemingly minor, personality clashes and conflicts exist among faculty members and between faculty and supervisory people, there is a respect for the talent and knowledge possessed by their peers that seems to outweigh the points of conflict. There was some concern and resentment that this talent is not fully utilized; that the lack of contact with other faculty members has led to misunderstandings and contributed to many problems. A strong desire is expressed for more opportunities for both work and social interactions.

Tangible Rewards

The organizational focus of the interviews may have discouraged any detailed discussion of the pay or benefits offered to the nursing faculty. However, it is obvious that very few criticisms were offered in this area—many commented favorably about the pay and related rewards.

Career Future

Comments about career prospects include both very positive views as well as some serious concerns. Although it was generally agreed that a faculty position in and of itself could be a satisfying career for many people, this whole issue is clouded by the uncertainty felt about the nursing school's future as either a diploma or baccalaureate program. In addition, those faculty members who desired to move ahead to higher or administrative levels are quite pessimistic about their chances and see little movement among people at higher levels that would allow for their own progression.

The Desire for Improvement

As indicated, almost all faculty members express the desire for improvement and a willingness to work toward this end. Although they recognize that the survey might be the catalyst for this process, they also acknowledge their responsibility to make its results work and that extra effort and pain that might be involved. Most express a willingness to try. One final aspect that seems quite positive is the feeling that the survey results should be viewed constructively and that scapegoating should be avoided—to look at *what* is wrong rather than at *who* is wrong.

AREAS REPRESENTING BOTH STRENGTHS AND WEAKNESSES

Leadership and Supervision

In general, there appears to be a good deal of uncertainty regarding the roles played by administrators and coordinators. There are also some questions about the functions the administrative staff should serve in providing leadership and about issues it should or must act on. Some leaders are seen as real barriers to progress, whereas others are viewed as helpful and concerned.

Specific criticisms of individual leaders include such mixed concerns as a perceived lack of enthusiasm, a desire to avoid controversy or conflict, and an overly controlling and unnecessary intrusive manner. Other criticisms are directed at a lack of decisiveness and the inability or unwillingness to help or guide subordinates.

There is, in short, something for everyone in this category! On the other hand, most supervisors are sincerely liked as people, and their technical nursing competence is highly respected. (In this connection, it should be noted that the phrase, "She is such a lovely person," was used so frequently in the interviews to describe individual supervisors that it was often difficult to put the criticisms that followed in proper perspective.)

WEAKNESSES FOUND

Organizational Vagueness

One of the most serious problems facing the entire school is simply that as an organization, considered as a whole, *it does not exist!*

- From the standpoint of space arrangements, the organization is too widely dispersed throughout the school and hospital facilities for effective communication.
- From a time perspective, its three academic levels (first, second, and third year) do not start, pause, nor end at the same time.
- From a psychological point of view, its members often do not perceive the total organization as the most important unit but rather tend to think in terms of their own particular groups (or levels), or even at the individual "free agent" level.
- From a motivational frame of reference, there is little evidence of overall goal direction, rather there is a feeling of separatism based on the pursuit of individual or subgroup goals.
- Last, in terms of organizational interactions, there is a lack of team effort at any but the department level, a lack of cooperation between academic levels, and a lack of mutual support between academic and nonacademic functions.

These observations, for the most part, are based on an analysis of dimensions that were thought to underlie the comments and noncomments concerning various organizational functions. Because the dimensions are latent in nature, some examples may be of help.

One of the most frequent comments made in the interviews is in effect, "that whenever 60 females get together, personality clashes occur." "You know how it is with women!" almost became an interview cliché. (A myth that seems to exist among faculty members suggests that "only women behave this way." It was the feeling of the researchers that this attitude was largely a reflection of this group's lack of experience with male-dominated groups.

If one accepts the explanation that women will always have "special" organizational problems, there is very little of a constructive nature that could be done. Although no attempt is made to dismiss the idea of "a female psychology" entirely, it was possible to view this situation somewhat differently. For example, in organizational terms, the structure and function of the school appears to have created a situation in which rewards are individually generated, rather than stemming from leaders and other organizational sources. Thus, it appears in the absence of organizational direction and recognition, that teachers, counselors, coordinators, and others have tended to seek their own sense of accomplishment by feedback and observations from their own students, counselees, peers, or subordinates. To the researchers it seemed that because these rewards are powerful and satisfying, they, in turn, encourage a protective attitude by individuals in the school toward their own separate functions. As a result, each person tends to become very possessive of her own work or function. Having been largely reduced to individual agents, they make comparisons and, as a result, jealousies and resentment at slights or criticisms develop. All this is attributed to the female personality! Although a source of high individual motivation, this kind of separatism leads to a breakdown of any organizational effort that, among other things, shows up as a communication problem.

This kind of separatism has apparently led to a duplicative overlap in content of courses taught at the three different levels and interfered with of the necessary continuity among them. As a result, the critical feedback on student performance at the three levels, which is essential to the school's overall goal, actually became a source of resentment. Because of its apparent lack of coordination among academic levels, this feedback is seen as isolated criticism rather than constructive attempts to better align course content. The resulting resentment of such criticism is sometimes heightened by being personally directed or given in a casual and informal manner.

There is also a possibility that the decision already made to redesign the school's curriculum may have led to a concentration on course content and teaching methods while overlooking the need to coordinate efforts within and among the three academic levels.

The lack of overall organizational thinking also contributes to a diminished utilization of talent within the organization. For example, the process of student admission is said to be cluttered with personal assessments of the applicant's age, appearance, family background, and so on, with little consideration of the mutual benefit or detriment these factors may have for the school or the candidate. Although some very thoughtful comments are made regarding the student selection issue, for the most part comments about such decisions reflected an intolerance of others' views and the inability or unwillingness to utilize resources within the organization. An especially cogent example is seen in the minimal use of input from the

Psychiatric or the Counseling groups on problems for which their expertise should be obvious (examples include: admissions, communication problems, committee interactions, and group evaluations).

Insecurity Regarding the Institution's Future

It is not at all surprising that, given the perceived uncertainty of the school's future, (e.g., whether it will exist at all or become a baccalaureate program), a number of faculty members feel insecure in their positions. In some cases, this uncertainty is said to have served as a positive motivation by encouraging faculty members to further their education in order to qualify for the baccalaureate status. In other cases, it has encouraged them to start "looking around" at positions outside the school in the event of its "sudden demise." All these factors continue to loosen identification with the total organization and compound the commitment problems discussed previously.

A related problem is the disappointment and frustration many faculty members feel regarding the school's relationship to the hospital. These feelings range over a number of issues including resentment at simply "being ignored." Other frustrations are expressed in being forced to cajole hospital staff people in order to obtain their cooperation; the lack of facilities provided by the hospital for clinical teaching or for discussions with students; the "haughty" attitude of medical residents and staff toward the nursing school faculty; and feelings of discrimination seen in differentials in parking fees charged to university and nursing school personnel. In brief, the survey revealed a deeply felt "poor relation" syndrome among the nursing school faculty whose members express considerable disappointment that they were not accepted as equals in what appears to them to be a "sister organization."

Organizational Climate

Partly because of the "organizational vagueness" discussed previously and for other reasons discussed here, a good deal of misunderstanding or suspicion is said to have developed among members of the nursing school faculty and administrators. Factors contributing to this organizational climate are the leadership styles of administrative and supervisory people, the age and experience differences among members of the school, and the wide variations in nursing and social orientations of faculty members.

This climate is manifested in the comments describing administrative actions and those dealing with the faculty meetings. It is reflected in the descriptions of many overly controlling supervisory actions, which have resulted in a lack of trust. It is seen in the motives attributed to a good deal of peer group behavior. Again, much of this latter distrusting attitude, which makes meaningful actions or organizational learning difficult.

An example of administrative behavior contributing to this climate is the claim that faculty members are classified as "exempt (salaried) personnel" when it is convenient for the organization, but are treated as hourly paid employees on many other occasions. This feeling is most clearly reflected in the complaints about the need to account for one's time. Administrators' phone calls, which often come at the end of the day, are often said to be for the sole purpose of checking on a faculty member. The feeling is that academic professionals "should not be treated as children" and should be allowed a reasonable amount of freedom in scheduling their time.

The Faculty Meeting: A Special Issue

Because it is the only venue in which all faculty people meet as one group, comments about faculty meetings appear to reflect the school's overall climate. It is claimed that these meetings are supposed to be open democratic forums held to decide substantive issues but because of various factors, they are felt to be dominated by trivial issues, hindered by personal animosities, and influenced by "hidden agendas." Although a number of staff pointed out that faculty meetings have shown some very noticeable recent improvement, they are still sore points for many of those interviewed.

Because no other means have been found for solving many of the organization's problems, they apparently become issues in faculty meetings. As a result some faculty members see these meetings as the actual *source* of many problems. It is felt, for example, that the Director's leadership at the meetings, in a misguided attempt at being fair and democratic has become almost nondirective, allowing discussions to become protracted and needlessly detailed. Then, in desperation as time ran short, the Director often tries to shut people off and hurry things along. Moreover, the administration's point of view on a given issue is often said to be presented just before the vote on it—a "not too subtle example" of a management's attempt to manipulate the process.

It is also felt that the faculty meetings bring out a number of antagonisms among faculty members who seem to be motivated by a desire to obstruct each other, rather than a desire to discuss issues objectively or to promote the organization's welfare. As a result, many people are "turned off" by the discussions and become apathetic about contributing or participating in them.

It is claimed that too much time is taken up with announcements and other matters that seem unnecessary and trivial. It is said that even the discussions of who is to make coffee has occasionally been put forward for prolonged discussion!

Although almost all members of the faculty seem irritated by the behavior they report, few seem willing to face the issue directly or openly. Instead, a good deal of hostility, irritation, and frustration is said to be communicated by body language and facial expressions. Rather than openly voicing criticisms, a number of members make private comments to their neighbors or group members who are considered "safe." (As a result, such comments are reinforced by implied agreement, but because they remain private, such comments serve no organizational purpose.)

Peer-group antagonisms are also brought to the fore by the meeting's climate. For example the lack of "openness" is considered a problem by most of the participants but is especially resented by younger faculty members who have been trained to be open and "up front" with problems. They not only resent the closed climate, but tend to be less tolerant of the older members who they see as either unwilling to confront anyone or as overly complacent.

In direct contrast, the older and more experienced members of the faculty, trained in a more traditional nursing climate, feel a nurse should play an accepting role and subordinate her feelings. These members are quite uncomfortable with open confrontation and express a good deal of unease at the prospect of doing so. They tend to be less tolerant of the more activist types and communication between them becomes difficult. This extends to the informal dress and hairstyles of their younger counterparts.

A particular example of this communication barrier is seen in the frequently perceived ways new ideas are rebuffed, with comments such as, "We have already tried that, and it didn't work." Aside from resentment they evoke, such comments are seen as evidence of the organization's inability to learn from its experiences—both successes and failures. For example, the question is asked, "When an idea fails why doesn't it result in some learning? Why did it fail? How can it be made to succeed?"

Because much of the behavior in faculty meetings is seen as typifying that which occurred in other forums throughout the school, the faculty meetings represent a microcosm of the larger organization. Included in such behaviors are the indirect approaches taken by administrators, occasional intra–inter groups and antagonism, attempts to advance individual goals rather than those of the school, and the tendency to avoid open discussions of problems. Although to most of the faculty, these behaviors are obvious in

faculty meetings, their general pervasiveness and influence in everyday activities was clearly recognized in the course of many interviews. In the climate created by the behaviors just described and by the climate of
uncertainty regarding the school's future, a good deal of misunderstanding
occurs. In some cases individuals are suspected of motives quite the opposite
of those actually operating. Administrators, in particular, are seen as foster-
ing problems when, in fact, it appears to others they are actually trying to
solve the problems or improve conditions.

Organizational Effectiveness

There is a good deal of frustration centered around the scheduling of classes,
the assignment of rooms, and the provision of classroom equipment and ma-
terials. The system is seen as cumbersome, poorly coordinated, and involving
too much paperwork and is viewed by the faculty as causing an unnecessary
loss of time. From the administration's point of view, the system is necessary
but made difficult by the lack of cooperation from hospital agencies and by
the misunderstanding and lack of cooperation of the faculty.

Although differences of opinion exist, it is obvious from the interviews that
this system represented a particular sore point in the school. Because much of
the work involved is of a clerical and office management nature, and considering the resentment and confusion caused by the system, it is suggested that
some consideration be given to acquiring outside office services.

CONCLUSION

In general, the overall organizational health of the nursing school is found
to be adversely influenced by a number of factors. These include insecurity
about the future, an awkward relationship with the hospital, a vagueness in
organizational structure and definition of roles, communication difficulties,
and even personality clashes among members. It is, however, functioning to
meet its goals and is seen both internally and externally as graduating very
competent nurses.

The fact that its members seem to be vaguely aware of these problems and
are willing to explore the issues with outside observers should be taken as a
sign of strength within the organization. More important, the expressed
willingness to work toward improvement is even further evidence of a potentially healthy situation. It would be a mistake therefore either to ignore
the problems outlined in this report or to be traumatized by their apparent
seriousness. The former would lose the important impetus for change,

which was both anticipated and desired, while the latter would be tanta-mount to "throwing the baby out with the bath water."

SEQUEL

The reader may see this report as a diagnosis of the school's problems. They may also have their own ideas regarding solutions. What actually resulted was a sincere effort to deal with the problems identified. For the most part this effort complimented and capitalized on the curriculum redesign work already under way that had been favorably noted in survey interviews.

In parallel with this effort and in a break with the usual committee-as-a-whole approach, a small representative task force was created to deal with the problems identified. In order to maximize the use of internal talent the Psychiatric Group was asked to form and lead this task force. It was reported later that this approach would not have been possible had the survey not brought the latent problems into the open and forced discussion without confusion or defensiveness.

It appeared therefore, that the survey had resulted in some very progres-sive steps, and the feedback received was very encouraging. As so often hap-pens however, external events overtake even the best efforts. Two years later, the school's governing board, apparently sensing the winds of change, decided to cease operations in favor of a baccalaureate program within the associated university. Although most of the faculty found positions in the new program, to the dozen or so staff people who were adversely affected, this was a disappointing end to a project that had been well received and promised effective positive change.

12

Realigning Departmental Practices With Company Polices: A Survey of a Corporate Advertising Agency

This chapter focuses on a very critical and detailed report generated by a survey conducted among a group of copywriters in what was one of the largest departments in Sears. Although part of a much broader study of the entire catalog advertising organization, the copywriter group was seen as a microcosm of the whole department. The survey became a study of what is generally referred to as organizational *empire building* as well as the effects of a dysfunctional departmental structure. The survey results dramatically called to management's attention the human costs of a failure in organizational integration. As such, it was instrumental in correcting the practices that were far out of line with those of the present company. Almost parenthetically, the survey identified the demoralizing impact of membership in an isolated "reference group." The survey itself was carried out in the 1960s and some of its findings are now of only historical interest. At the same time, the organizational issues and personal reactions of employees are still alive and well, and as can be seen in other chapters, are echoed in survey results obtained many years later.

THE SETTING

The Sears catalog advertising department (known as Department 744) was one of the oldest and largest departments in the company. Unlike merchandise (buying) or operating (support) departments whose structure, function-

116

ing, and growth had been tied to the company's spectacular retail growth, the catalog advertising department had remained a separate operation associated with the catalog—the original business of Sears. It had developed its own reporting relationships, operating practices, and to a large extent, its own personnel polices. It was in fact its own "empire" and had gained a great deal of power because of its isolation. Because of its position and history, it operated as an independent advertising agency that provided catalog services to about 56 merchandise departments but remained apart from them.

For many years, writing copy for the Sears catalog was considered to be exceptionally good training experience because of the strict standards observed in what could and could not be written. Because of the training it provided, Sears attracted two general types of applicants—those who saw it as a temporary stepping stone to a career in an advertising agency and those who saw it as a starting point in a Sears career. Although these two distinct career orientations were recognized by Department 744 management, it accepted them as a "fact of life" and made no attempt to encourage or discourage either.

Once copywriters finished a training program they were assigned to write catalog copy for one of the many merchandise departments, but their direct reporting relationship was to a single copy-chief in Department 744. In this way, all 65 copywriters reported to one copy-chief! This arrangement had traditional roots largely and was purported to be a means of controlling copy standards.

The importance of catalog copy to the company can hardly be exaggerated. It was continually demonstrated in studies comparing its effects on customers to that of personal "sales pitches" of commission salespeople in retail stores. In these studies, the percentage of customers who selected "Sears Best" merchandise (that with the highest mark-up) was higher among catalog shoppers than those in retail stores.

As the following copywriter survey report shows, this simple functional structure gave rise to a number of management practices that were out of line with company policies. These practices had the effect of turning both the work and career focus of copywriters inward toward their department rather than toward the much broader horizons offered by the company as a whole. Although the report covers only the copywriters, it depicts the situation shared by other groups within the department.

The Survey: Administration and Interpretation

The survey was carried out by questionnaire and individual interviews. The questionnaire was a modified version of one that had been used among hourly paid employees prior to the development of the Index of Organizational Reactions (IOR) described in chapter 3. The interviews were nondirective (also discussed in chap. 3) and conducted with each of the 65 copywriters.

The Questionnaire Results

A single chart of copywriter job satisfaction was created and is shown in Table 12.1.

As can be seen, the most striking feature of Table 12.1 is the consistently low levels of satisfaction copywriters expressed toward all but one category. The exception, attitudes toward coworkers suggested, a congenial and cooperative group whose members have a high regard for each other. All other facets of their work life are consistently seen as sources of dissatisfaction. This unvaryingly negative attitude leaves little room for analysis or explanation other than noting the general level of unhappiness. A deeper appreciation of the casual factors behind this general level of dissatisfaction was obtained in the interviews with copywriters.

TABLE 12.1

Job Satisfaction of Copywriter Group Based
on Company-Wide Norms
(N=64)

Category	Centile
1. Job demands	11
2. Working conditions	26
3. Pay	8
4. Employee benefits	26
5. Coworker cooperation	67
6. Supervisory relationship	12
7. Confidence in management	17
8. Competence of supervision	26
9. Effectiveness of administration	22
10. Communication	8
11. Job security	20
12. Recognition	15
13. Company identification	8
14. Advancement opportunity	11

Interview Results

As a means of demonstrating how these results were presented to management of the advertising department and to top corporate management, the actual survey report of the copywriter group is presented here in its full unedited form.

THE COPYWRITER SURVEY REPORT

Job satisfaction among the copywriters in Department 744 is quite low. A number of factors appear to contribute to the condition, which seems succinctly described by the comment, "People who have left the department generally feel that leaving 744 was the best thing that ever happened to them."

One of the most clear-cut sources of dissatisfactions among the copywriters is the universal absence of any real feeling of recognition as individuals, as professional workers, as members of Department 744, or in many cases, as employee of Sears, Roebuck and Company.

The severity of this feeling is such that it appears to have influenced attitudes toward most aspects of the work and environment. As a result, many of the extremely negative feelings concerning other job areas can be viewed as highly influenced by attitudes toward personal recognition and lack of job status. Although this lack of recognition appears to color many attitudes, other severe problems also exist. Among these are the feelings that pay is generally low and poorly administered, that opportunities for advancement are either nonexistent or very poorly defined, and that effective supervision is sorely lacking.

To a lesser extent employees are dissatisfied with job pressures, which are often excessive, and also dissatisfied with the unequal distribution of the workload. In addition, they look at Department 744 as being an entity unto itself and quite isolated from the rest of the company. In this same connection, they feel the Personnel Department is quite remote from Department 744 and that most personnel policies are completely unknown to them.

There is also a keenly felt isolation from top management of Department 744, and in most cases copywriters state they would not feel free to contact it if necessary. They describe communication as poor and are concerned with what appears to be a lack of understanding among the various work groups within Department 744.

Lacking any real basis for identification with their department or company, a majority of copywriters look to each other for much of their satisfaction. As a result, the only real strength in the overall morale picture is the generally high regard most copywriters have for each other.

Although a potential strength among members of this group is the high regard they have for Sears as a company, it appeared that many copywriters speak of Sears in an almost detached manner. Rather than expressing any real identity of feeling of belonging, they tend to describe the company "from a distance," as an observer rather than a participating member.

Although each of the factors influencing morale in this group is discussed in detail, several points should be noted that bring such a discussion into sharper focus.

Copywriters impressed the interviewers as being capable and intelligent individuals who regard themselves as professionally qualified for their work. As a result, they have a strong desire to do a competent job, to be responsible for it, and to have it recognized as such.

It should also be noted that copywriters were keenly ware of the high turnover among their group and a large percentage of those interviewed clearly indicated that unless things changed or opportunities opened up, they will leave also. In spite of this feeling, a number of copywriters expressed the desire to stay with Sears and were very hopeful that the survey would help in creating the kind of work environment that would encourage them to remain. As a result they were eager to express their feelings and were especially interested in knowing whether the survey results would be reported to them and acted on by management.

Strengths

1. *Copywriters have a high regard for their fellow workers.* Although the copywriter group is quite widespread and its members have little direct on-the-job contact, there appears to be a strong feeling of "camaraderie" among them. They look on their group as made up of semiprofessional people who share similar interests, motivations, and problems. This sharing of goals and problems has led to a strong identification on the part of many and their feelings toward coworkers appear as an important element of their job satisfaction.
    "The one thing that keeps me here is my association with other copywriters. I think our lunch hour represents the high point of the day."
    "To a large extent, copywriters are quite a bit alike. We have the same backgrounds and share the same interests. It's a darn interesting group, and a real job asset."
    Although this feeling of friendliness was obvious, there was some indication that copywriters felt some resentment over inequities that existed among the members of the group. It is interesting to note that rather than expressing resentment toward their associates, most copywriters blamed such inequities on supervision.

In addition, most copywriters state that they got along quite well with their co-workers in the merchandise departments. Although these relationships are sometimes strained by the copywriter's lack of status in those departments (this is discussed in the following sections on weaknesses) most copywriters feel that the majority of their coworkers are friendly and cooperative.

Some facets of their feelings of group solidarity are potentially negative morale factors. That is, because most members feel a close identity with the copywriter group, gripes and complaints as well as rumors are freely expressed and spontaneously spread. In addition, copywriters are quite free in discussing salary, bonus, and other personal information among themselves. The effect appears to be a constant comparing of status and salary levels that tends to accentuate any feelings of inequity that may exist.

The effectiveness of the "grapevine" has an additional negative effect. Through the grapevine, gripes and complaints are spread so extensively that many copywriters come to feel that "unless you're unhappy, you aren't a copywriter." Thus, a "negative standard" seems to exist within the group. For example, some employees feel that:

"The rumors at the lunch table are interesting, but sometimes viciously depressing. You go to lunch feeling fair, but you come away feeling that you are really low man on the Sears totem pole."

"You hear so many gripes you are convinced that things are bad, or at least could be a lot better. It's not that you ever feel things are good around here but until you hear all the sides of the problem, you don't realize how bad conditions actually are."

It appears, therefore, that the frequent airing of gripes among members of this tight-knit group act to influence attitudes of the more "satisfied" employees who neither completely identify with or personally share such negative attitudes.

Thus, the feeling of group identity seems to have both negative and positive morale elements and seems summarized by the comment of one copywriter, "Our spirit is high, but morale is pretty bad."

In essence, what appears in Exhibit 18.1 as a strength (friendliness of coworkers) can easily be read as a vehicle for reinforcing the other facets of dissatisfaction.

2 . *Copywriters feel that profit sharing and other employee benefits are generally adequate and attractive.* Although most copywriters feel that Sears oversells security in the form of profit sharing, they regard it as a good program. "If a man is going to stay with Sears, profit sharing would be a very strong point." To most copywriters, however, profit sharing represents a long-term reward, which has little appeal to them at present.

A comment, not included in the survey report, revealed a most unusual criticism of the profit sharing program. It was voiced in an interview by a man with a million dollars in the profit sharing plan.

> Int: You must feel pretty good about that.
> Emp: "Yes ... but you know, it's not all that it's cracked-up
>   to be."
> Int: How so?
> Emp: Well all my life, I wanted to have a mistress, but I
>   couldn't afford one. Now, I can afford one, but now
>   I don't want one.

3. While morale is generally low among copywriters, there is a rather clear-cut feeling that Sears, as a company, is pretty good. They feel that top company management is extremely capable and consistently above that found in similar industries. They do feel, however, that management is pretty much unaware of their particular needs and goals.

    In spite of these feelings, many copywriters do not identify with Sears but speak of it in an almost detached manner. They have no great pride nor express any real feeling of belonging to the company as a whole.

    On the other hand, many copywriters expressed a desire to remain with Sears and progress with it, but feel that other factors will have to be corrected before they will seriously consider staying.

Weaknesses

1. The universal feeling that copywriters lack any real status or recognition for their contribution underlies much of the dissatisfaction found in this group. These feelings spring from many overlapping sources that are treated individually below:

    a. Many copywriters feel that the administrative set-up of Department 744 and the nature of the administration is such that it is impossible for them or their work to be recognized. They feel that being spread out among several buildings and reporting to one man along with 60 or 70 other copywriters is an impossible situation. "The man who is really responsible for you never gets around to see you or read your copy. He may read the headlines or promotions but he never gets any further."

        As evidence of their feelings, copywriters point out that they receive no personal review of their work. They state that "rumor has it that we are reviewed, but we are never called in on it." (Interviewers were constantly asked about policy regarding such matters and it appeared evident that copywriters would welcome periodic personal review of their work.) "We never know whether we are doing a good job or not. About the only time we hear from Wilson is when an error is made…" "I guess he just can't cover enough ground, it's too much for one man…" "you always feel up in the air, never knowing whether you're lost in the shuffle or not."

A more gross form of recognition is also felt to be lacking, in that some copywriter jobs in various merchandising departments require a lot more work than others, but this is not considered by management.

"Some departments have lulls and copywriters get a chance to do extra projects. That never happens here. It takes a good man just to keep up with the routine." "Management doesn't seem aware that one department is different from another. All departments and all copywriters are pretty much the same to them."

Similarly, they feel that no distinction is made among copywriters and that such distinctions should be made. They express the feeling that some copywriters are nothing more than clerks whereas others have a quite a bit of responsibility. Some suggested that ratings should be made and a hierarchy of copywriters recognized on the basis of responsibility and contribution. Such ratings, they point out, do occur in agencies.

"I feel that I shoulder a great deal of responsibility in my department. If it were recognized by pay and other considerations, I might feel that I had a career. As it is, I feel I'm just another copywriter."

"We should have 'A' and 'B' ratings of copywriters as they do on the outside."

Thus, copywriters feel that their status is quite hazy both among the various merchandise departments and within the copywriting group itself.

As consequences of their position and felt isolation, most copywriters state that in order to get ahead or even be recognized they have to "play the right kind of politics and treat people right" or draw attention to themselves by doing a lot of special work or projects. "Wilson doesn't know what you do unless you take on a lot of extra work." Although many claim they enjoy these extra things, they aren't really sure that their efforts are appreciated. In addition, copywriters feel that extra projects are all that count, and that the copychief doesn't pay any attention to copywriting as such. "You can let the copy slip as long as you can attract attention by doing some special project for Wilson." "There should be some rewards around here for copywriting as such. After all, that's our job." This attitude is apparently a cogent source of irritation and contributes greatly to the feeling that recognition of their professional skills is nonexistent.

As indicated, the very structure of Department 744 administratively appears to contribute greatly to their feeling of nonrecognition. Most copywriters feel that they informally report to Sales Managers although they do not receive their rewards or attention from these individuals. They feel that because sales managers, copywriters, and ad reps work as a unit, it is very confusing for each to report to a different supervisor. This feeling of being supervised by people who aren't responsible for their welfare is intensified by the allied attitude that they work closely with buying organizations but don't really belong to such units. Thus, copywriters feel no basis for identification and are soon compelled to develop a number of unrealistic loyalties.

"You have to please the sales manager and the buying supervisor but they can't do anything for you in return."

Aggravating this situation further appears to be the inconsistent manner in which different sales managers "supervise" copywriters. Many state "we all know who the good sales managers are, and they are very much in demand." The individual nature of this "informal but ever-present supervision" (that of the sales manager) and their isolation from formal supervision (that of the copychief) leads most copywriters to feel that they are directed rather capriciously and exposed to inconsistent policies that grow out of each sales manager's personal point of view. As a result they have no solid basis for personal growth and development and no dependable means by which their work is recognized by their own organization.

b. Much of the dissatisfaction in this area appears to grow out of the copywriters' feeling that they lack recognition as professionals or creative workers. Copywriters describe themselves as highly trained people who are well qualified to handle the job and responsibility of presenting catalog copy in the most effective manner. They feel, however, that they are often regarded as high-grade clerks or typists whose opinions are not valued and whose skills are largely unrecognized.

In this connection, they point to the fact that any of several people can change their copy without their knowledge or permission. In addition, they feel that changes are often made that lessen the effectiveness of the copy. Such quotes as, "I can appreciate the fact that indexing is necessary, that editorial policy and standards must be observed, and that space is a controlling factor, but I don't feel that an editor or almost anyone else can tell me how to write something. That should be my job, it's what I'm trained to do best," reflect this attitude. Because people "up the line" often change copy to meet their own "personal standards," many copywriters feel that it is best to "swim with the tide" and to write to please these individuals rather than present copy in its most effective manner from a sales or promotional standpoint. Although such compromises make the job easier, it appears to lessen the copywriters' feeling of accomplishment or professional competency.

Adding to this feeling is the general consensus that "if you do stand up or ague about something you have written, you'll be pegged as uncooperative and not only will Wilson refuse to back you up, he'll criticize you for not cooperating." Thus, feeling they cannot support their own views effectively nor expect support from their own boss, many copywriters claim it is best to go along with the crowd. They state, however, "it is discouraging to read something in the catalog that is supposed to be yours, and not recognize it as your work."

c. In addition, most copywriters feel that their job has very little prestige value. "We are told that this is an important job when we start, but it doesn't take long to find out that you're low man on the totem pole." They feel left out of most department discussions and rather than being allowed to contribute ideas or suggestions, are told what to do by the various merchandise departments. In addition, if an office is needed by the merchandise department the copywriter often feels certain that his office will be the one taken. They also state that the lack of status sometimes makes it difficult to get things done and actually contributes to strained relationships between them and their associates in the merchandise departments. "No one seems to know where copywriters fit in. If you ask for something or request help even typists aren't sure they should listen to you." Copywriters claim that Advertising Representatives inadvertently "knock" a copywriter's prestige by rudely or curtly telling him what he should do or stressing the fact that a copy has to be out by a certain time. "We are responsible people and this pressure is not necessary and it is degrading to be treated like this." Most copywriters resent this lack of prestige that stands in sharp contrast to what they were led to expect when hired by

744 and to that accorded copywriters in outside agencies. "You're an office boy here, while in an agency you are pretty darn important. I'd like to make copywriting a career, but there's no sense in doing it at Sears. There is no pay or any other kind of reward for a career in copywriting here."

2. Pay is an acute and frequently mentioned problem within this group. Although attitudes toward the adequacy of pay vary, most copywriters feel that Sears does not compare with outside agencies in the area of compensation. Although the general consensus is that Sears pays starting copywriters well, progress is very slow and after several yeas a Sears copywriter is far behind the agency people. Thus, most copywriters feel that experience is not worth much to Sears and the company does not encourage good copywriters to stay. Many feel this attitude of the company is unfair and stress the fact that copywriters who have been with Sears for 5 or 10 years are worth a great deal.

"A long service copywriter is of great value to Sears. Buyers tend to respect his opinion and give him a lot more freedom and responsibility. This helps free the buyer to do his own job better and directly helps the company and the copywriter."

Similarly, this lack of progress also contributes to the feeling that inequities in compensation policy exist. For example, it is felt that increases in the cost of living have forced Sears to increase their starting rates although people on the payroll have not received such considerations. As a result, copywriters with the company for 2 years find only a slight differential between pay and that of newly hired copywriters.

Complaints were also expressed toward inequities of another sort. Some employees feel that raises are given on a highly personal and subjective basis and that often poor workers are encouraged with raises whereas more capable copywriters receive only minimal increases. This they partially attribute to the copychief's lack of knowledge of each copywriter's job contribution and partly to favoritism. Copywriters feel that it is grossly unfair that pay is determined by Wilson who is in no position to judge their performance.

The compensation policy was also generally criticized as mysterious and hazy. Many copywriters felt that if they knew how far they could go, it would help. "I can't plan a career if I don't know that the potential is." In addition, they feel that they have no idea of the standard by which their performance is judged. "Do you get paid for writing good copy, pleasing the boss, doing special projects, handling a heavy work load, or what?"

Although attitudes toward pay represent an acute problem among copywriters, it is also apparent that, in the absence of other indices, copywriters regard pay as the sole reflection of their performance. Thus, it is closely related to their feelings of recognition. "The only way you know how well you're doing is the amount they pay you ..." "Sometimes a sin-

cere pat on the back or even constructive criticism is as equally rewarding as a pay increase."

In this regard, some of the most critical comments toward pay were
aimed at the manner in which inquiries about raises were handled by
the copychief. Although this topic is discussed in the following section, it is important to note that many copywriters were intensely
critical of the "run-around you get from Wilson whenever you ask for
a raise." Feelings toward the manner in which pay is administered
both policy-wise and by the copychief personally, were as severe as
those toward the adequacy of pay.

3. *The lack of effective supervision is generally regarded as a real source of
   dissatisfaction among copywriters.* It is apparent that attitudes toward
   supervision are closely related to feelings described in the proceeding
   sections. Although most employees were critical of their relationships with Mr. Wilson, some claim the organizational set-up is chiefly
   responsible, whereas others feel that Mr. Wilson is personally at fault.

   a. Many copywriters feel that with 70 people, Wilson has an im-
      possible job. As a result, no real supervision can exist among
      copywriters.

      "Wilson probably reads our promotions, but I doubt that he
      ever reads our entire copy. It's an impossible task for one man."

      "If he had more assistants it would really help. He can't know
      what we do under the present set-up."

      "Wilson never knows what you do. He's too busy."

   b. More commonly, copywriters feel that Mr. Wilson lacks real
      leadership ability and has little personal concern for their wel-
      fare. Although many copywriters grant that Wilson is in a diffi-
      cult spot, administratively, they feel very strongly that he could
      do a much better job of fulfilling the needs and goals of his peo-
      ple. Because he fails to provide adequate attention to those areas,
      it is felt that many frustrations are only aggravated by the treat-
      ment copywriters received from Mr. Wilson. Rather than acting
      as a source of direction or satisfaction, his actions often intensify
      their concern and uneasiness.

      When expressing attitudes toward this aspect of Mr. Wilson's
      behavior, copywriters critically point to his habit of over-sell-
      ing Sears with words rather than actions.

      "He has an enthusiasm for the job which seems more
      panicky than authentic. It makes you wonder if all he wants
      to accomplish is to sell you on staying with Sears at all costs."

      His tendency to resort to highly ambiguous generalizations
      when asked about specific problems concerning the copywrit-
      ers' job, pay, or advancement also received highly critical com-
      ment. Employees feel very strongly that they get the

run-around whenever they see Mr. Wilson. The following comments toward pay reflect this feeling:

"If you ask him for a raise, he wants to know what you have been doing. Why in the hell doesn't he know?"

"When I questioned him about a raise that a 'less adequate worker' got, he told me it was intended to encourage this guy. That's kind of hard to take."

"Never get a decent answer. I've been waiting for a promised raise for months."

"If you ask about your raise, he tells you it's being held up because of the wage survey."

"You really get the run-around from Wilson."

Other comments about the nonspecific nature of his explanations reflect copywriters' doubt about his ability to lead, to teach, or to instill confidence in department management.

"One of our rules is 'always be specific.' If you ask Wilson a question, however, you get a series of generally trite remarks which give no information."

"His cliché-ridden approach is an insult to the caliber of people who work for him."

"Wilson never conducts personal evaluations with his people, and at raise or bonus time he usually kills a golden opportunity to give you an idea of your progress by offering some inane remark like 'Keep up the good work, there's more where this (your bonus) came from.'"

"He doesn't offer the kind of suggestions that copywriters, especially new copywriters, need when they're floundering around."

"If you ask for advice, you get a long talk on how he used to handle things in Milwaukee, but no real criticism or advice."

"He doesn't help or criticize his people. Either he doesn't know how or doesn't have time."

"Wilson may know his job, but he does appear to disagree with a lot of competent people in this field."

"There is absolutely no one a copywriter can go to for guidance."

"I never get any really sound critical analysis of my work."

"He fails to transfer or create any real confidence or 'esprit de corps' among copywriters."

Coupled with these attitudes is the very strong feeling that Mr. Wilson doesn't know what his people are doing. This adds to their already frustrated feelings toward lack of recognition. Some copywriters feel his assistant should handle more of the job-oriented work so he would have more time to look after his people and review their work.

"I think Wright could take a lot of the load off Wilson, but I don't really know what Wright does."

"We are never called in for ratings. It would be helpful to know how you stack up around here. The only time you know is when you are doing an extremely miserable job."

"If you are doing a good job or a bad job, it's to the company's benefit as well as the employees to tell you. We never are told one way or another."

In addition, many copywriters were extremely critical of Mr. Wilson failure to support them. They feel he will not stand up for them and will frequently take a stand in direct opposition.

"Wilson will never back you up."

"If you get in trouble, he'll never stand behind you. In his book, you are guilty till you prove yourself innocent."

"Wilson is a great hedger; he never takes a definite stand on any point."

"He just doesn't stand up to people. If one person out of 100 says you're uncooperative, Wilson accepts their word and will criticize you for it."

This lack of support from their own department, compounded by a lack of recognition bordering on indifference, is a keenly felt problem among copywriters.

In contrast to the many negative attitudes toward Mr. Wilson's supervisory behavior, a number of copywriters pointed out that he is a pleasant person and generally more cooperative than his predecessor.

" I like Wilson."

"Mr. Wilson is a very kind man, but he's too far away from his people."

"Wilson is a nice man."

"As a person, he is top notch, as a boss he leaves much to be desired."

In summary, it appears that relationship between Mr. Wilson and the copywriters group is a rather severe problem. Because of his failure to supply effective leadership, proper recognition, or personal support, copywriters feel that they lack direction and just criticism of their work. Many copywriters feel that the existence of such relationships between them and the person administratively responsible for their rewards and advancement acts only to heighten existing anxieties and frustrations.

4. *Aggravated by the lack of recognition and pay problems, the accompanying lack of career opportunity or chance for advancement is a keenly felt prob-*

lem among copywriters. They feel that opportunities either do not exist or that the avenues to such advancement are unknown to them. Among females this attitude is most strong and has led some to feel that Sears is grossly unfair in this respect. Others seem to have adjusted to the idea that copywriting is a dead-end job for females. Numerous comments such as, "chances to get ahead for men are few enough, but for women it's impossible" typify this attitude.

Generally, copywriters look for a career as a copywriter, want to advance within the field of advertising, or look for advancement in the broader field of merchandising. Within the Sears organization, each of these possibilities seems discouraging to most copywriters.

Among the copywriters who look for career opportunities, most are discouraged by the general absence of recognition "as professionals" and poor financial rewards. Although many regard Sears as a good company and would like to stay, most feel that one could do much better elsewhere.

In contrast many copywriters feel that the job could be enhanced and enlarged to attract career people. Comments such as, "if six or twelve of us could be given responsibility for preparing the format of a special book, (catalog) it would really give us a chance to show our ability and would make this job worthwhile."

Advancement within the advertising field also appears limited to most copywriters. They state that the organizational set-up of Department 744 is such that little opportunity exists for a copywriter to go to something bigger and better. Sales management appears as the only probable avenue to better jobs. Many copywriters feel that "Sales management doesn't appeal to a lot of us. It's too scientific and away from the creative end of advertising. Aside from sales management, there isn't much chance in 744." Some feel that sales management is not really a good spot to aim for, because "it, too, is pretty much of a dead-end job."

"Most of us leave the company just to get out of 744 because there's no place to go in it."

"Because there's no place to go, many of us look at Sears only as a training spot for agency work."

A large number feel that they would like to move on to the broader field of merchandising and feel that they could bring a great deal of experience to such jobs. For example, they say, "after 2 or 3 years as a copywriter, we know the merchandise as well, if not better, than many buyers do." As a result, many are looking for means of getting out of Department 744. (In this connection, there seems to be a strong feeling that people who try to get out of Department 744) are frowned on by management. Although they claim that this attitude has changed somewhat since Mr. Smith (a new personnel manager assigned to Department 744) came to 744, there is still a reluctance to approach management for a transfer.

One of the most severe frustrations in this area appears to be the lack of information concerning opportunities for advancement, both in and outside of 744. Many copywriters feel that they would like to stay in the Sears organization if they only knew where they could go eventually ... "If we only know our potential here it would help." Interviewers were bombarded with questions on this point:

"If I go to retail, do I start at the bottom?"

"What is Reserve Group Training?"

"Who do I see to find out my chances of getting ahead?"

"Nobody in 744 will give me an answer, who can I go to for a transfer?"

"I'm interested in climbing in this organization. Right now I just want to know what the ladder looks like."

As in preceding sections, it can be seen that the problem of advancement is closely intertwined with the problem of pay and recognition. It is also apparent that the lack of information about job opportunities, the haziness of explanations offered to those who inquire, and the lack of recognition of individual contributions has led many copywriters to lose confidence in, and doubt the motives of department management.

5. *Many copywriters have serious doubts about the intentions as well as the integrity of department management.* Copywriters state that management's failure to correct the high turnover makes them wonder where management's interests lie... "I should think that high turnover is extremely costly, but because they don't do anything about it, I guess they want us to leave. Maybe they feel that it's cheaper to have us leave than to pay us a proper salary."

Employees also feel that management has broken promises, especially in regard to pay increases and that the general "sales pitch" they receive when hired does not correspond to the reality of the copywriting job. Those factors have also contributed to the copywriter's doubt about management and its integrity. "When you are promised periodic raises and fail to get them, it disturbs you, and then you inquire about your pay and get the 'run-around' you wonder just what the policy is around here."

The fact that many copywriting jobs, as structured by Sears, are not as creative or "high level" as most copywriters are led to believe when hired, makes them doubt management's wisdom in insisting on such high-caliber people.

"If we are clerks, why not hire clerks. Why do they insist you be top-notch when there is no challenge here?"

In addition, the copywriters are concerned about the distance between them and management. They refer to management as the "6th floor" or the office "across the street" in an almost detached manner. Many feel that the department head has so little contact with them he doesn't even know them. They state, "management *says* its door is always open, but I don't think I would feel free to walk through it." This feeling is intensified by the attitude that 744 is an "empire" all by itself and that management is not really interested in employees' welfare, but only in keeping them within 744. "When I first came to Sears I thought I would be allowed to move around from mail order to retail to public relations, etc. and get a real background which would help me grow with the company. Instead, it appears that you're stuck in 744 once you belong to this department."

It should be noted that this attitude appears to be changing. Mr. Smith has recently fostered the idea that you can get transferred and has actually moved some copywriters into merchandise departments. At the same time, Mr. Smith, by referring to 744 as "an advertising agency all by itself" has furthered the idea that 744 is separated from the rest of Sears.

"This is a funny place (Department 744). We have our own Personnel Department, yet it never tells you anything. Smith keeps talking about it as an advertising agency, but we certainly don't resemble one pay-wise, status-wise, or even in terms of the kind of work done."

All of these factors contribute to the feeling that although copywriters belong to 744 and are expected to demonstrate loyalty to it, the department will not back them up or support them in any way. As an outgrowth of this, copywriters feel that "the best thing that can happen to you is to get out of 744."

6. Copywriters also feel that the personnel department is quite remote and has little interest in their welfare or needs. This feeling appears to grow out of the attitude that 744 is a separate organization. Copywriters think of their personnel department as a rather mysterious department and feel that personnel policies are generally unknown to them. They suspect favoritism, in some cases, because men who are selected for promotion are called for interviews, or are tested, and no one seems to know why. "It must be politics" is often the conclusion.

Copywriters feel that "personnel" should show more personal interest and should let copywriters know they count for something. Moreover, many feel that it should insist that personal reviews be conducted periodically and that employees be informed of such reviews.

To some extent, they express the desire to see the personnel department become a third party or place of appeal when they fail to get satisfaction from 744. "As it is now, I'd be quite reluctant to go to the Personnel Department. I have no idea who to see, what kind of a reception I'd get, or whether my confidence would be respected."

7. *Copywriters feel that they generally lack any knowledge of new developments or plans.* Although related to the ambiguity and mystery surrounding pay and advancement, this attitude appears to apply to the broader problem of communication, as well. They feel that they are rarely told of new plans and that merchandise departments do not bring them into their promotional planning sessions. This, they feel, makes it very difficult to really assume a creative approach toward their work. Partly as a result of this lack of knowledge of future plans, copywriters feel that they must wait till they are told what to do, at which point their work consists of carrying out a more-or-less routine assignment.

The effect of this feeling on morale can be summed up in the statement, "This place is a lot like the army. The privates don't know what the general or even the lieutenants are thinking. *Up to a point* this is as it has to be, and should be, but I think that morale is pretty much determined by *where you draw that point!*"

It is also apparent that the lack of knowledge of company or department plans is taken by some copywriters to be another index of their lack of recognition as competent, reliable, and valuable people. "If they would let us know about some of these things we might often make constructive suggestions as to how certain goals might be most effectively met. If we are worth anything at all, it is in this area."

Poor communication within Department 744, itself, also appears to have led to a lack of understanding among various work groups. Copywriters feel that if typographers and others understood the copywriter's point of view, there might be less friction created when disagreements between them occur.

8. *Although copywriters recognize a great variability in the nature and content of their work from one department to another, they seem generally agreed that much of it is routine and detailed. This they feel severely limits job satisfaction.* Copywriting at Sears is viewed as less creative and more mechanical than that carried out in agency work. Much of the routine, it is felt, results from the tight Mail Order schedule and the fact that copywriters are not regarded as creative or professional people by most of their associates. Many feel they do the work of clerks and are treated as such by most buying departments.

Because their work lacks challenge, many copywriters feel that they reach their limit after completing two general catalogs. Although many copywriters felt this condition exists, they also felt that the job could be made much more interesting and challenging.

The pressure created and the manner in which it is exerted is also a general source of irritation to most copywriters. When pressure is exerted, copywriters claim they feel it "from all directions and all at once." The erratic and inconsistent manner in which advertising representatives constantly interrupt and "ride" copywriters to get work out, is described as not only frustrating but "an awfully inefficient way of getting something done."

Most copywriters feel that the pressure, although not always present, is quite intense and that frequently they are forced to take work home. Some feel that they must take work home merely to work in a quiet spot and to "get away from the ad reps." Underlying much of the dissatisfaction toward work pressure are the feelings that the work load is quite unevenly distributed and that adequate help, such as typists, are not available to copywriters.

Additionally, copywriters feel that buyers are responsible for much of the pressure in that they "withhold" information on merchandise until the last minute. "Buyers are usually too busy or not interested enough in Mail Order to give us all the information we need to write a copy. It's only after a lot of wasted effort and red tape that we get what we need."

REPORT SUMMARY

Morale among copywriters of Department 744 is very low. Each of the many factors contributing to this situation have been discussed in the body of the report. Among the outstanding causes of discontent are the feelings that professional status and recognition, adequate compensation, and opportunities for personal growth and advancement are lacking. These feelings are aggravated by the organizational structure of Department 744 (which interferes with cooperative group effort) and the poor relationships existing between copywriters and the copychief. Cramped working conditions and excessive job demands are also seen by some in contributing elements to poor morale. The feeling of isolation from Sears as a whole, from their own department (Department 744), and the merchandise units in which they work, coupled with their lack of any real knowledge of new plans or developments, has also had a major negative effect.

Copywriters tend to see management's failure to act constructively toward improving their situation as an indication of its lack of interest in or concern for them. Thus, many copywriters feel their only course is to leave Sears. As stated by one copywriter, "we come here with high hopes and ambitions, but as we become aware that our responsibility is nil, pay is poor, progress is difficult, and our positions are unimportant, we simply drop off like ripe apples on a dying tree."

FOLLOW-UP ACTIONS

Both the report's tone and its severity regarding the identified problems had a shock effect on both company and departmental management. Because the department's size and management's vested interest in maintaining the status quo, change occurred slowly, but it did occur. Department management did, in fact, recognize the need for change and worked with policy making departments (primarily human resources) to introduce normal personnel polices and practices that were in keeping with those at the company.

It was also recognized that the traditional reporting relationships within the department were destroying its necessary link with its clients—the merchandise departments. In addition, the unmanageable span of control (65 people reporting to one person) precluded any attempt to recognize, reward, or counsel department members in any effective manner. In fact, these techniques, which normally help align separate functions in the service of clients, were actually limiting career hopes by aligning them only with prospects within Department 744. And such prospects were indeed dim.

Eventually the catalog advertising department was reorganized and copywriters were assigned to and had direct reporting relationships with their client departments, while maintaining an indirect (dotted-line) relationship to Department 744. The introduction of these changes, which in a real sense brought the entire catalog advertising function into the rest of the company, widened the career possibilities of a very talented group of people. In subsequent years, a substantial number of them went on to high levels of responsibility in other Sears departments and in advertising itself.

13

Effecting Management Change: An 11-Year Managerial Survey Project

This chapter demonstrates the role and impact of surveys in effecting substantial organizational change. Specifically, these changes involved organizational reporting arrangements, leadership practices, career paths, and compensation. A series of four surveys covering an 11-year period was the first attempt within Sears to measure attitudes of its entire managerial population, which on average involved 18,500 people.

The first survey in the series was intended to extend the company's survey coverage to its managerial level people and to explore with them a number of likely challenges the company faced or was about to face.

Because the surveys addressed issues to which only managers could respond, an in-depth level of inquiry was attained and resulted in a number of significant and long-term improvements in the organization. Included were changes in the organization's structure, and its managerial compensation and career development programs. It also helped strengthen leadership practices in key functions, improved important personnel policies and was instrumental in the redesign of one managerial assignment, which still holds to this day.

The four surveys described in this chapter were conducted over an 11-year period (1971, 1974, 1979, and 1981) covered all levels of management other than the Chairman (CEO) and President. This coverage was not only complete but was responsive to a need felt among managers. "When are you going to ask me about my opinions," was not an uncommon nor entirely facetious manager comment. Although an often quoted company joke held that "Managers get paid to have low morale, so their attitudes don't matter,"

136

it became increasingly clear to top management that these attitudes did indeed matter. As a result, a survey project was launched.

Because the population included very diverse functions and was distributed across all 50 states, Latin America, and Canada, different survey versions were created and several languages were accommodated. The first questionnaires were extremely long. However, due to the intense interest generated by the company's first attempt to survey people at this level, a phenomenal response rate (98.2%) was attained, including over 20,000 separate written comments.

The second survey and subsequent surveys were augmented by a large sampling of personal interviews. The information collected helped evaluate the follow-up actions generated by previous surveys and also provided much needed specific examples of leadership behavior, reactions to specific policies, and the perceived consequences of various corporate changes. Some of these findings were published (Smith & Porter, 1977), but most were treated as internal information.

The first two surveys received a great deal of attention. One reason, of course, was their novelty, but it was the direct involvement of top management (including the Board of Directors) in survey follow-up that carried the day. The CEO, for example, conducted a dozen meetings, each 2 or 3 hours in length, in which results were reviewed and possible actions were discussed. Similar meetings were then held by officers and other senior managers. In these meetings the results were presented fully and candidly—omitting only those that might refer to specific individuals. Follow-up actions naturally took on a longer timeline, but as each was put in place, its responsive relationship to the survey was made clear. This practice, in turn, helped facilitate acceptance of actions announced later.

THE SETTING

Throughout its long history and especially with the advent of its retail expansion, Sears had become a very highly decentralized organization with great authority delegated to its managers in the field. This freedom was in fact, a company's hallmark and attracted a very capable, enterprising, and highly paid cadre of managers in its many locations. This autonomy made for a lively and creative climate that did not yield readily to control from on high. However, with advances in data processing and national advertising, certain centralized controls became necessary and these tended to create a climate of uncertainty and concern. Top management saw this as a period of transition and held firmly to the belief that sophisticated data processing would, in fact, be the salvation of the company. It was, however, a company beginning to feel a threat to its status as number one in the industry.

It should also be made clear that the huge amount of data collected led to an impressive number of findings and specific recommendations aimed at almost all levels of the company. Although a sampling of some important issues is presented here, the account is admittedly limited, and omits dozens of findings not acted on, only half-heartedly dealt with, or simply ignored. Such are the facts of corporate life.

Survey Influence on Compensation

One result that had a positive effect on all participants concerned their compensation. For many years Sears had paid all managerial level employees a base salary and a bonus based on profit performance. For unit managers who had direct influence on profit, the bonus was a very important incentive and represented a high percentage of their total income. For others, in staff positions or in specialized functions, there was little or no measurable relationship to profit, and the bonuses became rather predictable, *pro forma*, and meaningless.

These feelings were clearly brought home by the responses to several relevant survey questions such as those shown in Table 13.1.

Table 13.1 clearly indicates that, for the overwhelming majority of exempt employees, the bonus program was poorly understood, often worked a hardship on family budgets, which led to the borrowing of funds to meet living expenses, and had, for all but very senior people, lost its incentive value. It was also seen by many as unfair and a source of dissatisfaction.

TABLE 13.1

Selected bonus and compensation items

Item	Sample	Response
How often are you forced to borrow in order to live on your salary?	Total population	82% "Occasionally or Often"
Do you view your bonuses as an incentive or as part of your salary?	Total population Senior Executive *	83% "Part of Salary" 21% "Part of Salary"
Do you understand how your bonus is determined?	Total population Senior Executive *	79% "No" 85% "Yes"
How satisfied are you with your bonus?	Total population	42% "Dissatisfied"
How fair is the present bonus system?	Total population	45% "Unfair"

*Senior Executives excluded for total population.

Results such as these shown in Table 13.1, along with several thousand written and interview comments, strongly reinforced the call for a better system of compensation. Convinced that a change was necessary, management implemented a plan that had been under study for more than a year. To do so, the consulting firm of Hay Associates, which had a long history of tailoring such plans to the needs of individual firms, was hired.

Because of their timing and relevance, the survey results were of critical assistance to the consultants in determining the new plan's structure and in recommending steps for its implementation. Once the program was designed, the survey results were used to facilitate its acceptance. Perhaps the best evidence of this facilitating role can be seen in the opening paragraphs of the Hay pamphlet that introduced the final plan to Sears managers:

> The purpose of this booklet is to acquaint you with the Sears revised Executive Compensation Program, its objectives and the methods, which will be used to achieve them. In the most recent salaried attitude surveys, people indicated a need for a better understanding of Sears' compensation practices. To this end they made a number of suggestions aimed at increasing the clarity and fairness of our system and at more closely tying rewards to performance.

Subsequent surveys indicated a wide and favorable response to the Hay plan and showed that the resentment toward the former bonus plan had been largely eliminated. This is illustrated by the responses to one item, included in the first and second surveys shown in Table 13.2.

TABLE 13.2

Comparison of Successive Survey Items Regarding
Managerial Compensation

Item		1st Survey	2nd Survey
Considering the possible effect of inflation, taxes, etc. on the one hand and increases you have received on the other, are you better or worse off than you were 2 years ago?			
	Better	29%	43%
	Same	36%	34%
	Worse	32%	21%

Survey Influence on Organizational Structure

The survey aimed a number of questions at the subject of company structure. Some were based on comments made in previous surveys, such as, "to what extent are functions seen as working at cross-purposes." Some were adopted from academic sources (e.g., "are performance measures properly aligned with corporate goals?"). And some were based on proposals that had been floating around the company's corporate headquarters (e.g., "are there activities that have become obsolete or outlived their usefulness?").

Although Sears' restructuring plans had been discussed at various times, none of these plans had assumed any sense of urgency. The survey results, especially those coming from senior people, renewed interest in the subject and led to the hiring of a large consulting firm (McKinsey & Company) to make recommendations. Because the survey had been carried out only shortly before this decision was made, its results were once again very relevant to the consultant's work.

One subject of particular interest addressed by the survey was the relationship between Headquarters and units in the Field. This age-old bone of contention had recently become a focal concern. In particular, managers in field locations felt that their input on merchandise decisions were being more and more discounted and, as a consequence, Headquarters people were assigning merchandise to stores rather than responding to store needs. The shipping of sleds to stores in Harlingen, Texas had become a topical joke.

Responses to a number of survey items that focused on these issues underscored the field concerns. Three items to which only Field managers responded:

1. Considering its growth and potential, Sears must make extensive changes in the organizational setup: 73% agreement
2. Parent (Headquarters) should take more advantage of the experience and knowledge of people in the field: 86% agreement
3. People in Parent making decisions that affect the whole company are too far removed from the real world of the field: 64% agreement

Top Management Re-organization

Another specific contribution to the re-organizational study were questions in the second survey, put only to very senior managers and administrators, asking their opinion regarding the need to reinforce Field input at top management levels. One example:

> In the last executive survey it was suggested that a senior officer be appointed to provide overall administration of field operations. What is your assessment of this idea?

The idea was overwhelmingly supported by Field executives and even by a majority in headquarters. Moreover, the consulting firm's own study apparently agreed with this endorsement and included it as a part of its major recommendations. In its cover letter to a 110-page report to the CEO, the consultant listed three factors that"stimulated its recommendation." They were:

1. Significant changes in the business environment since the last review of the organization needed to be reviewed to be certain that it was sufficiently responsive to consumer needs and competitive threats.
2. Direct comments from Sears managers who perceived that organizational problems were in some cases hindering merchandising performance.
3. Findings from recent managerial attitude surveys, which indicated increasing concern about the organization.

In effect, the consultants recommended a drastic reorganization of the company's top management based in large part on survey responses. Unfortunately, in what appeared to several management observers as a "solution du jour," the consultants recommended the creation of a three-person *Office of the Chairman* (OTC) consisting of the CEO, the President, and a Senior Officer who would speak for the field. Although this move permanently established the sought after "field voice" at the top of the organization, the implied sharing of authority contained in the *office of the chairman* concept was a major shock to an organization whose history had always been tied to one dominant chief executive. Because it failed to recognize this long embedded cultural expectation, the new structure proved ineffective and lasted only a short while.

> One rather earthy, concise, and an all-together prescient assessment of the *Office of the Chairman* concept did not stem from a survey interview but from a dinner table remark by one of three members at the *Office-of-the-Chairman*. A question posed by one table member: "Mr. Telling, how shall we address the OTC? Is it a he, she, or it?" After a pause, Mr. Telling responded with a succinct and indelicate dismissal of the OTC as masculine. In his view it lacked those male attributes so often equated with fortitude.

As can been seen, the survey results were used here to sell a major but unsuccessful change. Although the *Office-of-the-Chairman* concept did not endure, it did, at least, result in placing a field officer in headquarters. In this, the survey was something of a hand-maiden to a needed but ill-formulated change. Although the specific change did not last, one of its goals was achieved.

An account of subsequent changes, which eventually led to still another Sears structure, is given in a very detailed book about Sears entitled *The Big Store* (Katz, 1986), which in spite of serious errors, did manage an accurate account of this episode.

Merchandise Re-organization

Within headquarters another reorganization combined the 60 or so merchandise departments and their supporting functions into larger categories and were given the title of *Merchandise Groups*. It was felt that by marrying affiliated departments such as furniture, draperies, floor covering, and so on, into one Merchandising Group, decisions that had once been made at the department level (and that often worked at "cross purposes" with those in others), would be better coordinated and lead to a much stronger marketing thrust.

This combination of departments, each individually responsible for large revenues, was met with considerable initial resistance by older department managers who had long felt a keen sense of ownership in their particular organizations. Because top management sensed this resentment and was reluctant to offend some of its most respected executives, it was reconsidering the decision. Survey data were moderately persuasive in resolving the issue. By sorting the attitudes of managers, staff people, and their assistants, it became clear that the overwhelming majority actually favored the new group structure and saw it as not only wise but inevitable.

Based on this evidence, plus additional information collected, the consultants advised a continuation of the restructuring and its expansion. In this, survey results seemed to help reassure management that the changes would be accepted.

The Assistant Buyer Job Redesign

Although the survey did endorse the new Merchandising Group structure, it did not anticipate a later and troubling response among a large group of assistant buyers and other junior staff people, who came to view the new structure as a barrier rather than a boost to their careers.

This reaction was fairly subtle and went unrecognized until later revealed in a separate analysis of the interview comments of assistant buyers that seemed to reveal a pattern of "unfolding alienation." This was captured in the following profile of assistant buyers. The profile was requested by a Group Manager in order to gain a clearer picture of his subordinates' feelings and to provide a platform for action:

As Group staffs increase in numbers and decision making becomes more centralized, leadership in each Group has become more remote. As a result, many assistant buyers are beginning to sense that careers will rest on carrying out decisions rather than being a party to them. With no fixed responsibilities by which they are judged, avoiding errors is now seen as the hallmark of performance. The intermittent contact with their supervisor, who now seems to travel constantly, or with peers, who work more and more independently, leaves little opportunity to share concerns or vent feelings. With little or no reassurance from above and only fleeting interaction with peers, many assistant level people have developed a sense of being entirely isolated in their concerns. The irony, of course, is while this feeling of being alone in one's career concerns is privately held, it is, in fact, felt by almost all.

As part of his survey follow-up, the Group Manager decided to hold a special meeting for assistant buyers in his Group. It was reported later that he listened to their concerns and at one point explored the idea contained in the "composite profile" and asked for comments. Convinced that the profile did reflect their feelings, he decided to act and asked the survey team for recommendations.

In response, the team took advantage of responses to a set of independent survey items dealing specifically with job design. These items had been included in the earlier survey simply as a gesture of cooperation with a student who wanted data for a dissertation. This set of items was devised by two academic researchers (Hackman & Oldham, 1975) and was known as the *Job Diagnostic Survey* (JDS). Based on their research, the authors held that work motivation was influenced by the interaction of five job factors. Three of these are considered core characteristics:

1. Skill Variety—the extent to which a job requires the use of several skills.
2. Task Identity—the extent to which a job allows a whole process to be realized.
3. Task Significance—the perceived importance of a job by other people.

The force of these three characteristics is, in turn, multiplied by an employee's sense of responsibility for results (autonomy) and by the feedback received in doing the job (knowledge of results).

Because items dealing with all five factors had been included in the survey, they were considered a ready-made stage on which to recommend a redesign or enhancement of the assistant manager job. The Group Manager not only accepted this concept but decided to make it a basis for a major change: In addition to their regular duties almost all assistant buyers would be given responsibility for at least one line of merchandise. Because a line almost always involved well over a million dollars, this was not a small move. It was not only dramatic but was bold. It was also not *without risks*, in that most assistant buyers were young and, although carefully selected, were often inexperienced and the chance for serious error was obviously present.

This one move had very positive practical implications for assistant buyers, and seemed totally in keeping with the Hackman and Oldham theoretical model.

In the specific terms of that model, each assistant would now:

1.   be required to bargain with manufacturers and deal with Sears people in the field. From this, new knowledge would be acquired, and existing communication skills would be enhanced (skill variety),
2.   be in a position to see his or her Line from beginning to end—from its creation in factories to final sale in stores (task identity),
3.   be able to judge the Line's success or failure and effects on people in both factories and stores (task significance),
4.   have responsibility for a given Line, which automatically enhanced his or her sense of control (autonomy),
5.   receive monthly and yearly sales and inventory data, which provided ample feedback on job performance (knowledge of results).

Some Consequences of Assistant Manager Job Redesign

In what seemed a single stroke, the assistant manager's job was changed dramatically. That it was a very positive change can be seen in several ways:

First, although subsequent surveys were not able to include the JDS items, responses to similar questions dealing with "Work Appeal" showed significant gains. Second, later interviews with those who had experienced the change in job responsibility indicated they were more satisfied than those who had not. Last, the organizational appreciation of the change was demonstrated by its gradual adoption by other Group Managers.

It should be acknowledged that the Group Manager involved here might very well have made this change without any survey input or theoretical guidance. On the other hand, the survey did detect an emerging problem *before* it was sensed by management and by giving factual support for a remedy along with a sound conceptual justification of it, the survey lent a greater sense of confidence to the final decision.

Survey Influence on Leadership Behavior

The following experience is presented with some reserve. Although it happened some time ago and was unique in survey experience, the case demonstrates how surveys can help bring about significant changes that are only rarely achieved by other means.

This situation concerned a senior and very knowledgeable executive who held a key role in controlling decisions in all merchandise departments. Over a fairly short period of time, he became extremely authoritarian and very arbitrary, almost petty in his decisions. Because these in turn affected the operations of many other major executives, his style became a point of wide and bitter resentment. At the same time, the power of his office discouraged any open expression of ill will. Criticism did, however, emerge from the survey data and in a host of written and interview comments expressed anonymously.

In the version of the survey questionnaire administered only to senior people, a multipart item asked them to rate the "helpfulness" of various Headquarters functions with which they dealt. Of the 25 functions listed, the only one rated as "unhelpful or actually detrimental" was the organization headed by the executive noted previously. This executive had completed the survey questionnaire and became particularly anxious to see the results—so anxious, in fact, that he asked for an advanced presentation of them. In normal circumstances this would have been refused, but, given the startling nature of the results, and with the President's permission, the request was granted.

He sat through all the survey details and spent quite a while focusing on the ratings of his function and the pointed comments regarding it. At the end he asked only one question, "Who has seen these results?" The answer was, "The Chairman and President." He then expressed his appreciation for the courtesy and left. One week later he announced his resignation! And a not-too-subtle sigh of relief was heard.

No one will ever know what role, if any, the survey played in his decision, and it seems likely that it was only a "final straw" influence. However, as the same survey results were presented to other executives very shortly after his departure, the cause-and-effect implication, (to them at least,) appeared compelling. As a result the survey received total "credit" for his exit and, in fact, became a source of humor among the so-called inner circle.

One vice president referred to this situation sardonically in his introduction of a survey report back to his staff: "you may recall in an earlier review of the survey, some critical, almost nasty things were said about dear old Bob. As you also know, Bob left shortly thereafter—*laughter*—Now, just in case today's report is about to say anything nasty about me —*pause*—fellas, we can work it out."

To any responsible survey professional these kinds of jokes are not welcome nor encouraged. On one hand, the organization may have, in one stroke, removed a serious irritant; however, to the extent the survey was seen as a casual agent, its future acceptance by managers could be jeopardized.

Survey's Influence on Career Development

Given the number of challenges the company faced, and more important, the organizational shifts occurring within it, a growing number of managers expressed concern about their future careers. To some, the company's strong support for Affirmative Action represented a threat, whereas others complained about the seemingly rising influence of "politics—who you know," in promotions.

That career opportunities were both historically and currently the dominant concern of managers can be seen in the strong endorsement (69%) of one discerning item:

> A study of Sears managers carried out 15 years ago, concluded that managers are most concerned with setting up and monitoring long-range career expectations and will endure immediate adverse conditions of almost any sort as long as these conditions are not seen as interfering with long-range career plans and goals. How valid do you feel this conclusion is today?

Although this strong endorsement simply confirmed a culturally imbedded assumption of the company, when coupled here with the perception of narrowing opportunities, it seemed to cry out for action. It was also exacerbated by responses to another survey item that suggested the possible "hiding of talented people" by uncaring or selfish managers:

> It has been claimed that some managers go out of their way to develop young people and to push for their advancement while others show little such interest or may actually hold people back. In your opinion, how serious is this problem?

In response to these items the company looked to the Human Resource people for a "solution." As a result, a program was suggested that would first reassure managers but, more to the point, would clarify the necessary steps to their advancement and personal growth. Again much of it grew out of survey responses and a loose correspondence they had to a theoretical model of work motivation first described by Vroom (1964). In brief, Vroom's *Expectancy Theory* maintained that in work situations, motivation was largely determined rationally and depended on expectations that effort would lead to certain outcomes and that these outcomes would have certain expected and valued rewards.

Although the Vroom model was not a planned part of the survey, the very wording of many survey questions either smacked of *expectancy* concepts or explicitly captured them. In any event, the similarity was close enough to justify the model as an organizing platform on which to build the follow-up program.

For example, in addition to the two items already mentioned, several others touched on Vroom's effort–outcome expectancy:

1. "The way my future in this company looks to me now, giving extra effort seems:
   Very worthwhile … almost worthless"
   Expectations regarding the likelihood of advancement were tapped by:
2. "At the present time, do you expect to advance further in the company?"
   Yes
   No—I'm too near retirement.
   No—My job is my career assignment.
   And, the relative value (valance) of advancement was obtained by a multiple response item:
3. "To what degree are each of the following an important reason for working here?
   a. Opportunity for bonuses and merit raises.
   b. Opportunity for promotion.
   c. Opportunity for training and new experiences.
   d. Opportunity to be associated with a quality company.
   e. Opportunity to have a lifetime career.
   f. Opportunity for fringe benefits.
   g. Opportunity to work with stimulating people.

Using these and similar responses, and following the Vroom model, the expected outcomes and their values were "computed" for separate groups of mid-level managers: merchandise, operating, professionals and specialists. The results were also related to survey interview data from the same four groups. This analysis indicated that the groups had different aspirations, saw different pathways to them, and associated somewhat different rewards to them. That is, those in Merchandising, and to some extent those in Operating jobs, aspired to general administrative jobs (store management and the like). Professionals and Specialists, on the other hand, looked to growth and advancement within their fields, and attached less value to promotions per se.

From this analysis emerged an informal dual ladder approach by which opportunities were defined and the steps to them were spelled out (job rotations, field experiences, education, internal and external recognition, etc.) To this was added a new career guidance review program—"The Managerial Development Interview" (MDI) and, to monitor the effects of this program, a fairly involved item was added to later survey questionnaires.

"How accurate are the following statements regarding your MDI session with your manager?

1. Made me prepare myself so I could have a realistic conversation about what I do in my assignment.
2. Resulted in an in-depth understanding of my strengths and weaknesses.
3. Resulted in a means of thinking about what I do and how I could do it better.
4. Gave me a real chance to talk meaningfully to the manager about my present job.
5. Gave me an opportunity to have an active role in planning my career.
6. Gave me a chance to inform those people who make personnel decisions of my personal desires.

The program was further enhanced by the appointment of Human Resource Managers to various locations to oversee the career progress of current managers as well as those aspiring to such positions. Although these appointments involved a good deal of expense, they did add a personal element to a series of steps that might otherwise have easily become exercises in "paper shuffling." One final step that addressed the responsibilities of senior level people was an amendment to their contracts, which specifically rewarded them for developing people in their own units.

The reactions to this career-oriented program was decidedly favorable, although subsequent surveys did show that its main beneficiaries were not so much the members of its targeted group—midlevel managers—but rather, younger, newly appointed managers. Among both groups, however, the program was seen as providing a sense of direction to career planning, along with a degree of reassurance that the company was aware of their career aspirations and agreed with their expressed priorities.

Based on later conversations with members of top management, it appears that their reaction to the career concerns of lower-level managers was due, in part, to the compelling picture of those concerns portrayed by the survey findings. If so, this underscores importance of using a research-based model of work motivation on which to organize survey findings and follow-up action.

Survey Influence on a Specific Policy

Sears had always followed a very successful policy of "promotion from within" and developed its managers by rotating them through different assignments. In the course of a given career, this process involved a number of physical relocations. Typically, a manager in a small unit would be moved to a larger one or to a different type of assignment whenever and wherever openings occurred. The movement of hundreds of managers and their families each year was a huge expense to the company and often quite stressful to those being moved. The company considered it the necessary cost of developing executives, and the individual saw it as the price to be paid for a successful career.

Earlier spot studies had pointed out many problems created by such moves. For example, a married man (a majority of the transferees in the early years) transferred to another location usually found himself in a familiar work setting requiring only a minimal adjustment. His wife, on the other hand, had to bear the brunt of moving, establishing a new home, entering children in new schools, and finding new medical and dental care, and so on. In families with high school-age children, the separation from close friends was very traumatic and made the move all the more stressful.

Because managers rarely, if ever, openly complained about the issue—fearing a refusal to be moved would be a career kiss-of-death—this long-standing and unvoiced irritant continued to fester. By the time of the third survey in this four part series, however, a sea change in attitudes had occurred. More and more female managers had been recruited and promoted. In addition the dual-career family had become commonplace, and in turn became a major consideration for any candidate in accepting a move. Although top management was not oblivious to the trauma caused by physical moves (almost all of its members had had such experiences), its members did not sense the growing gravity of the situation and certainly did not appreciate the quandaries it created among dual-career couples.

One survey item did address this issue directly:

> "Would your spouse's career influence your decision to accept a transfer involving a move to another location?"

Once again, a survey response prompted or at least gave management an excuse to address a problem. In this case, the survey surfaced a smoldering issue and indicated its likely effect of restricting the company's future pool of management candidates. As one result, management almost immediately set about moderating its relocation practices without abandoning its promotion form within policy. It did not end the practice of moving people when truly key opportunities arose, but it did establish a policy of rotating executive candidates among units in the same geographic area—usually within a given city, which required no relocation of a home or family.

A Latent Survey Influence

As part of a presentation of survey results to top management, the responses of senior staff people to one question were pointedly compared to those of comparable executives in two other companies. The item read, *"In this company there is a considerable resistance to discussing internal conflicts."* The responses were:

Sears	63% agreed
Two comparable organizations	44% agreed

The difference seemed important and said something about the cultures of all three organizations but it received no reaction at this meting. However, some 6 months later, in a similar meeting, a vice president raised a very sensitive issue involving the allocation of funds for certain headquarters and field projects, which had become very controversial. Before anyone made a comment, the President interjected that the subject should not be discussed in an "open meeting." To this, the CEO surprisingly said, "Dean (the President), isn't this exactly the point raised in our last survey—we don't discuss internal conflicts?" The subject was indeed discussed.

The anecdote suggests that not all management reactions to a survey are immediate or direct.

SUMMARY

The results of four surveys over an 11-year period helped strengthen the commitment of all management levels during some of the company's most trying times. The company's structure, managerial compensation, and career development programs were improved, as were some leadership practices. In addition, a key junior level position in which future executives were developed was permanently redesigned to expand its responsibility and intrinsic appeal.

The chapter was intended to demonstrate the impact of survey information on management's efforts to bring about successful organizational change. In some cases, survey results directly influenced these efforts whereas in others, the results proved of value to outside consultants hired to design the changes.

14

Influence of Surveys in Initiating Top Management Action

This is an account of a survey's influence on decisions made by a company's top executive. The survey results were first used to call his attention to a serious morale situation and later to initiate a timely motivational program. This process is an example of a survey's unique role in speaking for a whole population of employees who would otherwise lack a unified or undistorted channel to top management. It also demonstrated the organizational advantage of having a continuous means of gauging employee opinions, allowing changes in attitudes to be interpreted within their past and current contexts.

THE SETTING

Throughout the later half of the 1970s, the annually scheduled surveys conducted throughout Sears indicated a growing concern about the future among employees. This trend was compounded by the results of a series of managerial oriented surveys that pointed to an increasing sense of despair among middle-level managers. These trends occurred during some difficult economic and political times and were not limited to Sears. The economy was depressed, inflation was increasing, the Iranian "hostage incident" came to dominate foreign relations and the media. Although the trends from both survey sources certainly reflected these conditions, they also pointed to problems that were peculiar to the company—problems that were especially foreign to the company's culture and its general sense of itself. In the face of these issues, the traditional proactive and enthusiastic approach usually taken by the company seemed to be giving way to a fatalistic attitude.

After repeated meetings with various officers regarding the trends shown in both surveys, it became clear that many of them simply did not want to hear or deal with this kind of information. Most chose to rationalize the situation, seeing it as a reflection of the times and beyond one company's control. This internalization by top managers of what seemed to be a general countrywide malaise had a stultifying effect. Rather than marshaling their resources, as had always been done is past crises, they seemed resigned to simply waiting out the depressed state of the economy, an attitude they thought was shared by management everywhere.

At the same time, the survey data were actually indicating that Sears *was not* in the same situation as others, but had problems peculiar to itself. As the "wait-and-see" attitude persisted among many senior managers and was adopted by those down the line, the situation cried out for action. This became a point of serious discussion among the Human Resources staff, who agreed that a challenge to this "wait-and-see" attitude was needed and that it could only come from the CEO.

The staff recommended that a memo be sent to the CEO that would make him fully aware of the situation. To underscore the notion that the information contained in the memo came from the "horse's mouth" (that is, directly from survey data) the author was asked to prepare the memo along with a summary of the surveys' findings.

> Note: At the time this struck the author as a shrewd and typically heartless suggestion. Should the memo backfire, it was apparently reasoned, it would better to lose one horse than the whole herd. It was perhaps fortunate that the current CEO expected and encouraged frankness and honest opinion in communication and had an ability to see humor in even darkest days.
>
> As an example of the Chairman's more sardonic side, when introduced to the husband of an attorney recently engaged to deal with a major legal proceeding (with possible liabilities of nearly a billion dollars,) he asked casually,
>
> "What do you do?"
>
> "I'm also a lawyer.
>
> "'I am counsel for the Democratic National Committee."
>
> "Oh, I didn't know your firm practiced criminal law."

Recognizing both his humorous side and his respect for candor, it was also recognized that memos from subordinates suggesting a CEO personally do something were more than a bit unusual and did seem to reverse the natural order of things. The following memo, therefore was introduced gingerly and fortified by only as much detail as thought tolerable.

May 1, 1978

Mr. E. R. Tall

In view of the Company's manner of dealing with many current problems, it seems appropriate to summarize some of the effects these efforts have had on employees at all levels. This is especially appropriate in view of the announced plans for the future which will certainly depend on the attitudes and behavior of the people involved.

The attached summary may not be totally surprising, but its implications certainly call for top management attention if we are to continue to succeed while maintaining our proven traditional reliance on people. I am convinced that many of the problems alluded to in the summary can be corrected if a renewed sense of dedication to employee well-being is more directly voiced by top management.

If the summary seems critical, I assure you its intent is totally constructive. If a defense for this is necessary, I offer Ecclesiastics Chapter 7: Verse 5.

(For the uninitiated: "It is better for a king to hear the rebuke of the wise than to hear the song of fools.")

The following five-page summary of managerial job satisfaction was forwarded to the CEO. Although it is now mostly of historical interest, at the time, it proved very influential in generating top management action. Because it may be of interest to the reader as an effective use of survey information, the entire summary is given here with only minor editing. It was entitled "Some Thoughts on Morale Here and Elsewhere."

In the last few years, a series of articles and reports from widely different sources have pointed to a steady decline in the work-related attitudes of American workers. While there are many contributing factors to such a trend, the prominent influence seems to be the change in values and expectations of newer employees in the work force. Because they are better educated than previous generations and have generally been reared under favorable economic conditions, this emerging wave of people seems to have higher expectations of what work and organizations should offer. For the most part, organizations have failed to understand these changes or have simply been unable to take definite steps to respond to them. As a result, dissatisfaction has occurred on an increasingly widespread basis, and a kind of malaise has developed among many people in the workforce.

Because Sears has seen a similar downturn in job satisfaction, there is a widespread belief among management that we simply reflect the kind of world in which we live. This view, however, is largely contradicted by the comparison of our own survey data with the findings of large scale outside studies, which monitored the attitudes of American workers over several decades. They not only confirmed the *general* decline in worker satisfaction, but pointed to an increasing gap between the attitudes of managerial people and those of white and blue collar workers. They concluded that while the satisfaction of managerial people has remained more or less constant, that of non-managerial employees has declined dramatically.

This particular finding contrasts sharply with our own survey data and clearly contradicts the view that we are simply "like everyone else." In fact our survey results indicate that not only has no such management–employee gap emerged but that, in fact, *with the possible exception of our top administrative people, the morale of managerial and supervisory employees has declined to even lower levels than that of hourly paid employees.*

The number of organizational and operational changes the Company has undergone during the past few years has certainly served to frustrate many people. This, coupled with a centralization of authority, has created a situation in which many managers feel they no longer have control of their operations. Indeed, it appears that some executives and managers have all but given up trying to deal with morale, and some have even expressed disapproval of attempts to measure it.

In addition, many managers in all areas of the Company feel their status has been severely reduced by the restructuring of the organization and their career opportunities have been narrowed by the relatively slower rate of expansion and by the influence of equal opportunity guidelines.

In spite of all these adverse conditions there remains a general hope and expectation that many of the changes introduced by the company will eventually correct or at least improve some of these conditions. Moreover, it is generally recognized that many improvements in the current situation are dependent upon factors outside the control of the company: the general economy, the success of the government's anti-inflation programs, as well as the resolution of international problems.

Most employees also realize that the extent to which job opportunities and tangible financial rewards can be increased is dependent upon the success of the economy and the success of the Company within that economy.

On the other hand, there is a general view that some significant internal improvements could be made which are under the direct control of management. In this regard, a very prominent concern is the sense growing of indifference among many of our managers toward our traditional concern for people. This, coupled with a noticeable and growing sense of impersonality throughout the company, contributes to a general negative corporate climate. Whatever its cause, there is a prevalent feeling that "nobody cares" and that nobody understands the impact that many recent changes have had on employees and their work. These conditions are, in part, a result of our size, our increased use of automated programs, and certainly our increasing dependency on centralized control of the business. In the resulting climate, the concern for people, always our hallmark in the past, is seen as having deteriorated. This is not only foreign to our tradition but is a source of real concern to our employees. It has, in fact, created some doubt as to the kind of company we are, or are becoming.

While to some extent this climate is perceived as almost an accidental or natural result of the changes in the company's operations and structures, it is more often perceived as reflecting a diminishing commitment to an employee-oriented organization. As a result, many feel the current management philosophy subscribes to the adage that the end justifies the means; that short-term gains are to be pursued even at the cost of mutual respect and confidence which have been the cornerstones on which our survival and success have traditionally rested.

Closely related to this trend are the findings from a number of our studies at the hourly and salaried levels which clearly show that both morale and productivity are directly influenced by personal recognition of employee efforts. In this context, the growing sense of impersonality in the Company makes any plea for recognition almost meaningless.

While the importance of recognition has been stressed in training younger managers, the lessons learned are frequently discarded on the job in the absence of encouragement or reinforcement from higher levels. Also contributing to this climate are the extreme pressures associated with frequent organizational changes. These allow little time for even well-intentioned managers to attend to people-related problems. Unfortunately, that does not change the effects of such perceived neglect.

Considering the difficult times the company and the nation are experiencing, it is understandable that the traditional concern for employees may have suffered but should not be a reason for allowing it to continue. In fact, such a concern is more important now than ever. Supervisors at all levels should feel a sense of accountability for emphasizing this tradition of our company. To achieve it, all managers should be reminded that employee welfare is not a fair weather concern but is an everyday commitment. Unless all employees can see that their efforts are recognized, a great many will feel they are struggling for nothing.

The CEO's response to this fairly long summary was quick, direct, and amazing. He directed that the entire memo and summary be formally printed as a booklet and distributed with his own very strongly worded cover letter to all executives and senior managers.

The Chairman's letter which accompanied the booklet is given here in full.

Chairman of the Board

All Officers

Attached is a concise and, I believe, thoroughly reliable evaluation of overall morale in Sears. It does not make for pleasant reading, but it is the sort of thing we and our managers should understand ... and understanding, accept the responsibility for the improvement of morale.

Sufficient numbers of copies of this report are being mailed to your Personnel Director for distribution to each of your managers. In your letter of transmittal, I believe you should emphasize that this is privileged management information and that we hold managers accountable for the morale of the employees reporting to them. Sears has always taken great pride in the high level of employee morale, and we must not permit this erosion to continue.

All of us understand the great expense control pressures we have placed on management, but we cannot allow managers to use these pressures as excuses for abdicating their prime responsibility to their people. Our employees are to be treated with dignity, respect, fairness, and with personal interest. Doing so will ensure improved morale and will at the same time encourage similar treatment of our customers by our employees. Recently conducted independent surveys indicate a serious need for improved customer service. Thus, acceptance of the need for action, the recognition that the responsibility for morale belongs to unit management, and immediate and intelligent constructive steps to improve morale will serve two very serious and current problems.

Reactions to the Booklet

The reaction to this booklet among senior people was surprisingly positive. The feeling expressed was that "what it said had to be said." One territorial vice president did express a reluctance to distribute the booklet to his managers, feeling it would only add to the pressure they were already under. The CEO, however, saw this as an indication of how deep the state of depression really was. The booklet was distributed.

For the most part the booklet became a subject of broad conversation among managers. Although it did not lift the sense of malaise, the booklet did have an impact. It and the CEO's cover letter clearly reminded managers that high morale was still a fixed corporate value. Rather than representing an added managerial burden, the development of high morale by managers was held up as an asset; an important value by which Sears carried on its business.

On a more tangible level, the CEO's cover letter and later remarks gave tacit approval for expenditures aimed at improving the lot of middle managers. For one, it gave the "green light" to the Human Resources department to implement an already prepared management development program. This move led to some improvement in career expectations as mid-level managers could see the company was taking direct action to develop promotable people. However, it's immediate reach could touch only a sample of managers and limited its immediate impact. A more generally positive effect was generated by the acceleration of efforts to improve compensation (discussed in chap. 13).

A Suggested Intervention

In spite of these efforts, later interviews indicated a continuing concern about the future. These feelings became even more specific when the first steps were taken in carrying out the next regularly scheduled survey of managerial level employees. Its preparation proceeded as usual, including interviews with a small but fairly representative sample. In these interviews a curious mixture of hope and despair became obvious. The hope was that top management would take even more vigorous and tangible steps to invigorate the business, while the despair focused on the continued concern about limited career opportunities. There was also a concern that many higher level managers were retreating to the earlier "wait-and-see" attitude. On the basis of this limited information, it was decided to make one more attempt to engage upper management's interest and response.

Reporting preliminary survey results can be dangerous because the data may later be contradicted or greatly moderated by the results of the more conventional survey approach. And the release of preliminary results may lead management to act prematurely on the wrong problem at the wrong time. However, in this situation, the risks seemed outweighed by the intensity of some of the early comments and by their close parallel to those obtained in the earlier studies.

Another factor influenced the decision to again encourage management to act. At the time, Sears stock, which was widely held by employees both individually and through the profit-sharing plan, had hit what almost all believed was an all-time low. It was reasoned that a stock option offered at this low level would not only offer an attractive potential, it would further convince managers that top management was listening to them and was taking tangible action—this time aimed at everyone. This reasoning led the author to forward the following memo:

Mr. Charles Bacon, Vice President Human Resources
March 11, 1980
Re: Stock Options

In preparation for the next exempt level survey, we have and are conducting a number of interviews. While I would normally wait until the formal survey is completed before making any recommendations, the fact is the survey will not occur until later this year, and in the meantime, even our preliminary interviews suggest one positive step (a stock option) whose impact is largely dependent on timing.

By way of background, I am sure it is no surprise to you that exempt employees are deeply concerned about economic matters and are very depressed about such things as inflation and Sears stock prices. On the other hand, there is still a reservoir of hope and a degree of optimism among many that the company is getting back on track and will not only "pull through" but will prevail.

Given these attitudes, it would seem that a meaningful stock option now would be very resonant with their needs and responsive to their concerns. There is also a fairly common feeling that "the stock is so low," and given its return, "it can't go much lower." Perhaps more importantly from a psychological viewpoint, a significant and general option would give concrete evidence of top management's confidence in its corporate plans and would both reinforce and capitalize on the latent optimism we sense.

While there may be economic or even political reasons for not taking this action, which I am not competent to comment on, I do feel that this kind of top management action in these difficult times would have a very salutary effect and would further increase respect for management.

As so often happens in large organizations, the memo was acknowledged by Mr. Bacon with no hint of its probable disposition. This uncertainty was somewhat lessened a very short time later when a stock option was announced to *all exempt employees*. A short time later the memo's influence was more clearly acknowledged. It happened in a way that students of organizational communication and its vagaries will appreciate.

As the author entered the Drake Hotel in Chicago, the chief financial officer (CFO) of Sears was just leaving a fund raising dinner for candidate Ronald Regan. The dinner had apparently gone well, the champagne had flowed freely, and the CFO's own stock option had been sizable. Not surprisingly, even given his accounting background, he was quite buoyant. After literally bumping into one another, he even more unnaturally blurted out, "Boy, do you know when to write a memo," this was followed by a brief account of how the memo had actually triggered the stock option decision!

From numerous later conversations with management people, who were involved in the stock option decision, it became clear that the impact the memo and booklet had alerted the CEO to the need for action and apparently created the necessary receptive climate for the stock option idea. If so, it suggests that the line from survey results to follow-up action is not always a straight one.

15

Contrasting Use of Surveys in Organizational Development: A 19-Year Project in Two Ski Resorts

This chapter is an account of a longitudinal study of two successively owned ski resorts. The sharp contrast in their use of survey information paralleled an equally sharp contrast in organizational performance. This account therefore can be read as a practical lesson on how survey' should and should not be used by management. In both resorts attempted interventions were of necessity based almost entirely on "common sense" interpretations of survey data. In the first location, corrective steps either failed or were avoided altogether, whereas in the second location, they not only succeeded but were remarkably enduring.

Based on his past use of survey information, the resort's owner had adapted the survey process in all of his enterprises. Its inclusion here was simply a continuation of a managerial philosophy based on listening to what his people had to say about an organization—its leadership, its operation and its climate.

The survey projects are reported here in two parts, covered a 19-year span, and involved approximately 13 survey visits to two resorts that the owner owned successively. Because of the study's long duration and the number of surveys involved, its progress is summarized first through tabulated responses to questionnaires that were periodically administered. These are accompanied by commentaries on a series of excepts from actual survey reports to management that summarized employee interviews. These commentaries are purposely limited to those observations and insights that are thought to be of most interest to managers and students of organizations. To this end, the present summary emphasizes the role of leadership, which in both resorts was of crucial importance and was observed under the following reasonably controlled conditions:

- Both resorts were new ventures and were studied from their start-up stages onward.
- Both were located in the same community.
- Both were intended to offer essentially the same product and services.
- Both were successively owned by the same person.
- Both began with the same organizational vision.

These circumstances allowed variations in leadership behavior and its covering effects on organizational results to be gauged (over a considerable length of time), under conditions rarely encountered in field studies.

As is shown later, the implementation of survey results in the first resort was not only ineffective but came perilously close to accompanying a disaster! In contrast, the acceptance and constructive use of survey findings in the successor resort contributed to the development of what is now one of the premiere ski resorts in the United States.

> Note: Because the focus of this chapter is the survey's influence on management, this influence can be easily exaggerated when considered in isolation of other factors. It should be recognized, therefore, that although survey findings did have a definite influence on both resorts, they were only one of a host of considerations which required management attention.

SURVEY OF RESORT I

Surveys in Resort I started with exploratory, unstructured interviews with its management staff and key assistants regarding the resort's progress and departmental needs and problems. This coverage was continually expanded in subsequent visits and on three occasions full-scale surveys were conducted in which questionnaires were administered to all employees. The questionnaire findings provided viable longitudinal "hard data," which helped alert staff members to problems in their areas, whereas interviews provided a more in-depth portrayal of each resort's appeal and perceived promise as well as its organizational drawbacks.

The Early Survey Interviews

During the early stages of its development, the resort was operational but was also adding new ski lifts and the construction of new condo units was proceeding rapidly. Members of the management staff were all specialists and each operated his or her department more-or-less independently. (The Ski School, as but one example, interacted with other departments only as the need arose, although the Ski Patrol, Lift Maintenance, and Marketing were obviously dependent on the school, as they were on each other). This led to a number of "turf" conflicts that involved competition for various resources. At the same time, both management and nonmanagement people expressed an unqualified enthusiasm for the resort's future and its "idea" as envisioned by the owner.

A glimpse of the perceived strengths and potential weaknesses of the organization can be seen in brief excerpts from an early survey report.

The strengths revealed in interviews included some very important assets that all managers agreed on. These are noted here:

1. The easy geographic accessibility of the area in comparison to other resort complexes,
2. The vast, private ownership of land and its control by the parent corporation,
3. The financial support of the owner,
4. The "unique and historic" attraction of the area,
5. The ideal snow conditions during the ski season and the very attractive summer climate,
6. Career interests of management and personnel are closely tied to the successful operation of the corporation.

The weaknesses revealed some serious challenges, to the resort's future. Some were seen as "growing pains," whereas others seemed more intractable. Some of the major drawbacks are seen in excerpts from the survey report:

> The personnel function is reported as practically non-existent. As examples: overtime pay is a question mark in certain areas, the policy on skiing privileges is also not well understood. (People in the Design Group not only have free skiing but also are said to get passes for family members, while other employees do not.) The compensation and training programs are apparently not receiving needed attention from management and even the vacation policy is not spelled out nor consistently administered.

There were also a number of comments about other personnel and financial matters such as the questionable quality of employees being selected, problems with individual supervisors and other key people, which go unnoticed or are ignored. On occasion unionization was suggested as a remedy. Again a brief excerpt:

> It is felt that control over financial matters has been extremely loose. It is reported that decisions have been made to spend large sums by individual department mangers, with little regard to overall budget considerations or control. Personal expense accounts are filed without proper documentation, and bills are submitted long after being received with no advance notice to the accounting department. At higher levels, deals are negotiated without being properly communicated to those who need to know.

Some managers viewed these problems (occurring as they did in the early stages of the Resort's existence), as part of a developmental process. At the same time, their seemingly unnoticed entrenchment might have sounded an alarm. It did not! In fact, the lack of attention to these problems was already having serious repercussions. Thus, the survey report stated:

> A number of other incidents suggest a general lack of discipline and overall managerial control and coordination of the complex array of corporate activities. It is said the organization is fragmented, and each department tends to operate on its own, setting its own goals often at cross purposes with those of other departments. For example, the contrasting and often conflicting approaches taken by the design department frequently results in re-work or wasted time for construction people.

> One problem that seems to be growing as a result of departmental fragmentation is the development of more or less defensive posture by each. Fault finding and "finger pointing" occur in place of constructive problem solving. As a by-product, employees tended to identify only with their department or with some outside group rather than the resort as a whole. Instead of being an asset to the resort, they became its chief critics. For example, negative comments about construction of condominiums is said to be very common on the ski slopes, which hardly helps in the sale of the units on which the resort's success depended. Another example could be found in the tendency of many employees to voice or share the negative attitudes of old-time community residents toward the resort. Rather than trying to persuade their fellow citizens of the organization's virtues, employees reinforced the expressed resentment. In a sense a "shame society" had developed in which criticism was rampant, silenced only when overheard by a supervisor.

Lack of management control and organizational discipline was also seen in the absence of attention to costs—such things as waste, loss of large quantities of construction material, and accumulation of miscellaneous charges were said to be rarely questioned. It was claimed that department heads are simply not asked to account for their functions. An excerpt from the survey report provides some examples:

> While numerous mistakes are seen as natural in a rapidly growing corporation, there is a feeling that many are unnecessarily repeated. One of the more glaring examples of a repeated error is the placement of unprotected water pipes in an outside wall of the condominiums. This, it is said, occurred in one set of units because the out-of-state architects were either unfamiliar with Utah weather or refused to consider its effects. As a result, the pipes froze and tenants and owners were inconvenienced. The same kind of mistake was repeated in the succeeding group of buildings.
>
> The importance of priorities for internal services is also confused. As a result, friction seems to be developing between lower level employee groups, making cooperation and the once strongly expressed pride in the overall organization almost impossible. As an example, it is said that the ski school is very demanding of services and seems to insist on them regardless of the needs of the rest of the organization. This has caused members of the ski patrol, normally a closely related function to the ski school, to say they are treated like "poor relatives" and have come to feel their function is not respected nor supported by its own departmental management or that of the resort as a whole. Its members are particularly resentful of what they see as a "put down" of their professional status, their skills, and their efforts. As a result a real antagonism has developed between the patrol and the ski school as well as between the patrol and top management.

The General Manager's Leadership

Interviews with staff and supervisory people gave detailed descriptions of the general manager. He was generally seen as a very likeable person whose gruff approach to subordinates, although not exactly appreciated, was at least tolerated. Sometimes, jokingly, he was seen as that "lovable bastard." His background was thought to be in the construction industry, and to most staff people he seemed to have little experience in ski operations. As a result many of his judgments were said to be intuitively based on his personal observations while skiing or "driving around."

The interviews also revealed some important facets of his management style. Above all, he was said to have a remarkably short span of attention—"22 seconds" was the common estimate. This was coupled with, and seemed to reinforce, his disdain for discussing management decisions with people below him in the organization. Although he recognized the abilities of individual department heads, it was claimed he rarely delegated any responsibility to them that went beyond their individual functions. This in part resulted in the development of several "dominant" departments, which continued to "do their own thing" with little thought given to the effects on the overall resort.

It later became clear from staff comments that the general manager also resented the whole idea of employee surveys, seeing them as intrusive and ill timed. In fact, he constantly questioned their timing although they were regularly scheduled over a 5-year period! Under the circumstances his initial resentment was understandable, but its persistence proved very unfortunate as survey results unfolded. Rather than being ill timed, they actually proved to be very opportune.

> Note: Because the surveys had been requested by the resort owner, it was assumed they had the agreement of the general manager. This turned out to be a serious error in judgment by the survey administrator. The agreement should have been confirmed and any resentment regarding the survey resolved before the process began.

Communications barriers added to the organization problems. Given the general manager's staff relationships, and his reluctance to treat survey results seriously, communication problems multiplied and soon became threats to the organization's well being. An excerpt from the report:

Some people report that top management simply does not communicate decisions, and an aura of secrecy surrounds most activities. Whether this is due to a reluctance to communicate or to an uncertainty regarding corporate directions seems to be unknown, but it makes the immediate communication of specific decisions difficult, if not dysfunctional. In the end it not only creates feelings of uncertainty but of non-involvement as managers and supervisors retreat from decision making. Sudden arbitrary changes in decisions add to this problem, and are compounded by the absence of problem-oriented discussions. While the recent scheduling of regular staff meetings is seen as a move toward correcting this, there is still a strong feeling that too often only unimportant things are discussed while major matters are ignored.

Probably the most telling example of communication failure was seen in an excerpt regarding the general manager's behavior in staff meetings:

The general manager's reactions are said to largely control communication in the meeting. It is generally recognized that by raising of an eyebrow, a chance remark, or the wave of a hand, he can shut off most subjects rather quickly. His ability to intimidate others is apparently much greater than he is aware. As a result, many subjects are neither raised nor explored. This, in turn, results in the non-utilization of lower level input, knowledge, and experience in most decisions. Perhaps more importantly, it creates the false impression that all top decisions have been accepted without objection. The failure of subordinates to speak up or confront either each other or the general manager has, it is thought, led him to believe that all is well and that his decisions are totally supported. While this avoidance of constructive confrontation is seen as a serious obstacle to healthy organizational growth, it is a problem most members are *unwilling* to face openly. In short, rather than being a vehicle of communication that helps to pull the organization together, the staff meeting all too often illustrates the problems that tear it apart.

As might be expected, the communication barriers created at the top level led to other difficulties down the line. This was also described in another excerpt:

A major problem appears to be the lack of information regarding just what the corporate goals are as well as the avenues by which the goals will be reached. It is reported that the company is seemingly changing its direction, but no one seems to know what impact this will have on specific functions. If additional condominiums are to be built, will the engineering and design department have a hand in it or will outsiders be utilized? How many will be built, and how will they be maintained or serviced? What about sales plans and advertising plans? Obviously, the lack of knowledge leads to speculation and doubt about the management's intentions.

In part, the manager's preoccupation with "other resort matters" was a cause of communication problems, but much more central was his almost automatic defensive reaction to even implied criticism. (For example, the description of his staff meeting behavior produced no insight nor any attempt to moderate his intimidating style.) As problems mounted, his ability and willingness to share information with his staff and explore solutions actually declined. This trend is clearly seen in Table 15.1, which shows the drop in staff and supervisory responses relating to his leadership in three surveys spaced over a 5-year span.

As can be seen from Table 15.1, existing problems found in the earliest survey tended to persist while potential problems only worsened.

Sensing that any general change was unlikely, the survey team shifted its focus to just two critical problems: staffing and customer safety. The hope was that any recommended improvement in either might have a "spread of effect" influence on other areas and might, in any event, reassure employees of a responsive intent on the part of management. The recommended staffing action worked very well, but recommendations concerning safety failed miserably and dangerously!

TABLE 15.1

Resort I: Trend in Staff and Supervisory Perceptions
of the General Manager Leadership

	Percent Positive Response		
Our General Manager:	Survey 1	Survey 2	Survey 3
1. Consistently gives clear goals, instructions	40	35	30
2. Seems to lack job knowledge	61	60	55
3. Gives all issues an open hearing	60	47	26
4. Knows me well enough to judge my work	40	48	55
5. Shows an interest in our ideas and suggestions	37	37	26
6. Is in touch with problems at my level	60	46	37

The staffing suggestion was to have the owner create a "buffer" between the general manager and lower levels and to help solve the multiplying number of "people problems" by appointing a personnel manager. It was hoped that should a strong person be selected he or she might play a "chief of staff" role. This suggestion was apparently seen by the general manager as a way of divorcing himself from many of the issues found in surveys and was agreed to almost immediately. Perhaps as a result, the appointed manager was given a free hand and over a relatively short time made a great deal of progress—as noted in a subsequent survey excerpt:

> One of the more recognizable improvements made in the organization has been the emergence of the personnel department. While almost all the individuals interviewed agreed that its manager still has a number of problems, there is a rather widespread agreement that this department has already made significant changes. He now coordinates all recruitment and hiring, taking a considerable load off other executives. Similarly, his attempt to oversee all salary adjustments is applauded, though people are quick to point out that he is still not in full control of this function and can often be circumvented.

The safety suggestions were based on growing concerns about the likelihood of serious accidents. These fears increased with each survey. In the first survey, the chair lift operators pointed out that maintenance had become rather lax and that attention was being placed largely on construction of new lifts. This concern was reported to the general manager as part of the survey feedback and was summarily dismissed. In the second set of surveys, this issue became more critical, as the following excerpt reveals:

> Because of the extremely poor morale existing in the lift department, there are frequent comments about leaving before the season is over. The problem is generally attributed to a combination of factors, but centers on the lift manager. His behavior strongly suggests incompetence, which contributes to an extremely disorganized, unsafe, and poorly equipped department. *The existence of unsafe lifts is emphasized.*

Again, this issue was included in the survey report and was again dismissed in a way that revealed an almost unshakeable refusal to hear disturbing news. The general manager simply denied the lifts were unsafe saying: "I use them myself almost every week!" Obviously, on any of these occasions he could have asked operators about the lifts or checked them personally. He apparently did neither. In the third survey an even more strongly worded excerpt stressed the danger:

> The lack of attention to maintenance, which has been complained about for almost four years, has led to what operators claim is a critically dangerous condition. Many lifts and chairs are said to be in very bad shape and are now seen as definite safety hazards. The Gondola and Bunny Hill lifts, in particular, need work. It is claimed the Bunny Hill has not been properly inspected in two years, is rusting, and has been ignored by the lift manager. The men further claim that they are not allowed to work on these jobs until an actual crisis exists. They all feel that the resort has been extremely fortunate in having a good safety record to date but are fearful that some major accident will occur soon, possibly involving loss of lives, for which they will be held responsible.

It appeared that all the general complaints made in earlier surveys had coalesced and now described a palpably dangerous situation. Although only 6 weeks remained in the season, the concerns seemed so critical they were again taken directly to the general manager and again went unheeded.

Sequel

The sequel to this chronicle is chilling! Its sequence was later confided to the author by the resort owner. Two weeks before the close of the season, the lift operators carried out a routine test of the Bunny Hill lift using 50 pound bags on each chair. As the loaded chairs came around the lower turn, 3 fell! The lift was closed and in an immediate inspection 14 other chairs were found to be in danger of falling. In addition, one emergency brake was found to be inoperable!

The reader can imagine the likely consequences of a sudden failure of the operator's brakes—the only ones working properly. Picture 50 or more skiers sitting in nonsecure chairs when suddenly the entire lift started to move in reverse with no way to stop it. The owner had no difficulty visualizing such a scene and later commented, "If I ever doubt the results of a survey, please remind me of this one."

SUMMARY—RESORT I

By way of a quantified summary of events, Table 15.2 based on questionnaire results over a 5-year span clearly shows unfortunate and seemingly inexorable decline in the resort from its heady expectations and promise to its near disintegration!

For a number of reasons, including those reported here, the resort was closed. In retrospect, the lesson learned was not that survey findings are always correct or even realistic, but that ignoring them or refusing to consider them is wasteful of time and money and can be dangerous. In this case, the findings did predict a disaster that came very close to happening. That this message never got across is a fault of the survey administrator (in this case, the author). The intransigence of the resort executive did not help.

These and other lessons were not only learned but sincerely applied in the successor organization.

TABLE 15.2

Resort I: Trend of Overall Resort Survey Results

	Centile Scores		
IOR Category	Survey 1	Survey 2	Survey 3
Leadership and Direction	56	35	21
Work Involvement	65	63	58
Work Demands	54	53	50
Teamwork	82	66	54
Physical Surroundings	81	61	25
Career Planning/Security	50	54	36
Financial Rewards	50	52	41
Organizational Commitment	86	60	25

SURVEY OF RESORT II

In contrast to the surveys conducted in Resort I, the survey experiences in Resort II reflected a solid success. That success was mainly in the survey's role in aiding and monitoring the development of what became the Deer Valley Resort.

THE SETTING

Following the demise of Resort I, its owner began development of a second resort, literally a few miles away in the same small community. Like its predecessor, it "started from scratch," on an adjoining mountain that had an unusual promise for skiing. From inception, it was to be a first-class operation oriented toward family skiing and would offer superior facilities, service, and accommodations.

To fulfill his dream of a world-class resort, the owner brought in as its president the current manager and principle developer of what was at the time, one of only a handful of Five Star hotels in the United States. To handle construction of the ski slopes and support facilities, he hired a young general manager with fairly broad construction experience. Thus, the resort began under the leadership of a managerial "odd couple."

The president was a sophisticated executive, a highly respected member of the San Francisco business community and something of a dreamer. The new general manager was bright, narrowly focused on work, and a no-nonsense, down-to-earth realist. The former, as the saying goes "did not tolerate fools gladly," whereas the latter tolerated hardly anyone!

Both were faced with enormous construction challenges and both worked very hard to achieve the envisioned result. Because of the president's hotel background, he concentrated on the development of restaurants, food and beverage, and many off-slope accommodations. The general manager focused on the "mountain"—that is, the ski slopes and lifts along with the ski lodges. Although the president had overall responsibility, his leadership and that of the general manager were felt separately because of this agreed-on division of labor.

Early Stage Surveys

During the early stages of resort development, a series of preliminary interviews were conducted among both the management staff and employees in various functions. These were summarized in informal discussions with the owner and president. Aside from essentially personnel related complaints (pay inequities, benefit questions, work rules), a couple of potentially critical issues were identified: Communication was said to be confused and poorly timed, resulting in uncertain construction priorities, delayed arrival of equipment, and wrong work schedules. Added to this was a seemingly growing resentment of leadership "on the mountain." Both of these issues were confirmed by a full-scale survey, which used questionnaires and interviews. Its overall results are given in Table 15.3.

Interviews with both staff members and employees attributed much of the leadership problems to the general manager. He was said to have consistently bypassed supervisors and managers in dealing with work teams in a manner that was charitably described as harsh and overly emotional. Although the owner and president were aware of the situation, they attributed much of the problem to the pressures on the general manager and his almost 24-hour-a-day work schedule. This rationalization seemed reasonable under the circumstances and was, in a sense, buttressed by widely expressed enthusiasm for and commitment to the resort and its future, which in turn seemed to balance the resentment toward the general manager.

> Note: This enthusiasm for the resort future and its unique concept continued to be expressed throughout future surveys. It seemed to be a kind of "organizational glue" holding the resort and its people together in both very trying and very agreeable times.

TABLE 15.3

Resort II: Overall Resort Survey Results

IOR Category	Centile Scores
Leadership and Direction	44
Work Involvement	35
Work Demands	35
Teamwork	55
Physical Surroundings	53
Career Planning/Security	41
Financial Rewards	97
Organizational Commitment	88

The resort became operational in 1981. Although construction-related problems became manageable, many new challenges emerged as the resort continued to grow and expand.

During the first 4 years of the resorts operation, a number of spot inter-views were conducted that were aimed at diagnosing the extent and inten-sity of any new or emerging problems. Although communication issues were again reported as serious concerns, most of the other problems were more-or-less routine—the kinds of issues often encountered in any rapidly growing operation (perceived favoritism, interpersonal conflicts, crowded facilities). These were turned over to the personnel manager, who, with help of other supervisors, corrected all but one or two chronic issues.

Of greater significance, however, was the discovery that efforts by the personnel manager and her associates went well beyond routine personnel matters. They in fact had an impact on the whole resort, which for reasons to be explained, were almost completely unrecognized by management or even by her. (Because this kind of subliminal influence is frequently found in organizations, the process by which it was brought to light here may be of particular interest to managers and students of organizational dynamics).

Hints of her influence were given in scores of off-hand interview com-ments in which individual employees alluded to the assistance each had received from the personnel manager and some of her like-minded super-visors. It appeared that by advising, coaching, cajoling, and even con-fronting they had instilled a benign sense of discipline centered on service to customers. All of these incidents, however, were separately ex-perienced—known only to the individual recipients. As such, they re-mained isolated events in the flow of organizational life. Not until these fragmented comments were integrated by the survey analysis did their organizational impact surface. When their cumulative effect on the en-tire resort was pointed out, it was realized that the work of this small group was one of the key instruments by which resort values were rei-fied—translating its lofty vision into observable employee behavior. (Having emerged early in the resort's development, this finding was par-ticularly important for it identified a process by which an organizational vision was being made operational.)

Note: As noted in chapter 1, the surfacing of influences and incidents that often lie beneath the organization's purview goes to the heart of survey prac-tice. It is one of a few unobtrusive vehicles by which management can learn of significant but latent organizational strengths or weaknesses—in the present case, the unseen but significant impact of a manager and her associates.

The Initial Full Scale Survey and Follow-up

Other issues that arose in interviews had wide organizational implications and were presented to the resort's president in a detailed report. Some of the issues included were:

1. People were becoming alarmed at cost over-rides, which they felt might lead to downsizing or resort failure.
2. Working hours were excessive and seemed to be increasing.
3. Many female ski instructors felt their male counterparts treated them as second-class people.
4. A number of people felt the resort was too restrictive in its ski privileges and resented the "no mingling" policy and the references to them as "servants."
5. One manager had become an obstructionist to efforts of other departments and was widely reviled.
6. Bottlenecks in the communication chain were creating problems on the job.

The response of the president was initially in the form of a long letter to the author in which he commented on each point raised in the survey report. Because his comprehensive response set the stage for the follow-up steps taken in future surveys of the resort, it is reproduced here in full. It is also a model of constructive use of survey information by an executive.

Dear Frank:

I'm in possession of the meaningful survey, which you conducted a few weeks ago. Your observations certainly bring forth some warning signs towards which we must exercise vigilance and alertness. It never ceases to amaze me as to the subtlety with which these signs exist on the surface, while in reality seething emotions could possibly be raging far beneath.

As I summarize your report, I find six issues emerging that will require our thinking in terms of problem solving. After listing these issues as follows, I would like to comment on each according to my own viewpoint:

Alarm over Escalating Costs and Overruns

There is no question we've had some rather dramatic surprises in this specific area of concern. Mostly, it is happening with the two buildings. While such circumstances are never very pleasant, they are not out of the ordinary in these unpredictable times. While we are aware of these cost problems, we are not alarmed or fearful that they will prevent us from opening and getting into business. We are not fearful that we will have to face doing anything that might be termed a "short cut," nor do we see having to pare our staff compliment or wage and salary commitments.

<u>Female Reaction to Male Chauvinism</u>

Times have really changed on this question, and I am at the top of the list of those who believe that equal rights to women is way overdue. On my own hotel staff many of our women have advanced to positions of significant responsibility. They are dealt with equally in every way. Each has become a very effective leader and, as we all know, the hotel's business has been sensationally successful. We must all, just as quickly as possible, erase any doubts we might have about the potential of our women. I can't stress this point enough.

<u>Unnecessarily Long Working Hours</u>

This is serious. Very serious. Putting in very long hours should be done so only against identified reasons and objectives. Leadership (department heads and division heads) should have the choice in terms of exercising their own judgment as to the hours needed to accomplish the necessary tasks at hand. Measuring one's performance by using numbers of hours contributed to the job is a fallacy. There are those who are sufficiently capable of achieving their tasks within normal time constraints, and there are those who face longer periods of time. It is important that top management recognize that the quicker and faster a standard week becomes reality, the better the morale and the resulting spirit of loyalty. Also, it has been my experience that top management can much quicker determine the effectiveness of a given supervisor's capacity to lead and direct when not under the pressure of an hours-worked measure of performance.

<u>Negative Reaction to the Issue of Ski Privileges and Facilities Access</u>

In no way has this policy been designed to make lives miserable or to cause a kind of deprivation of the less privileged.

It is, more than anything else, a continuation of the common thread we want to see laced throughout this whole venture ... a structured disciplined environment within which to exercise and function. In my surveys and analyses of other ski areas, I find that the ski privilege aspect is virtually without any policy whatsoever, other than to say, "ski all you want, on the house, as long as you are not required to be on duty!" If anything, we're saying nearly the same thing, but we want to be in control. I really see this as no different than in the hotel business ... It can be said that ski slopes are like sleeping rooms and like chairs and tables in the restaurants. We have to be in control of who eats and sleeps where and when. This now will have the impact of making the staff realize what the product is and that it has value.

As for the "servant" bit, I'm probably more to blame for this specific reaction and/or sensitivity than anyone else. I clearly remember a couple of months ago we staged a full department head staff meeting addressing this issue. Here is what I said: "It is a hard fast statistic as confirmed by a recent Louis Harris poll, that the United States is a post-industrial civilization, where a majority of our people are no longer employed turning out physical goods. Instead, 63% of the employable sector now work at service trades." Then I said, "I am a servant, a lawyer, a banker, a cab driver, a department store clerk ... we're all servants." Then I made a big point of how unhappy most of working America must be because they're seemingly so miserable at giving service.

Consequently, we want to make a big thing about this and just to prove to everybody that we're not kidding ... everything about this resort has been designed primarily for the visitor's convenience and pleasure. This has got to come across loud and clear, that the guest is of TOP priority! This is precisely what I feel will bring us to the level of success and prosperity, which we are seeking to achieve.

Managerial Obstruction

Frankly, I've never been comfortable with this individual as one who possesses the innate leadership skills with which to exercise at the level of management in which he has been cast. Also, I believe his style of operating technique, or lack of, has cost our firm an enormous amount of money. His style is one of embarking on small missions and tasks and making them appear monumentally complex. There is a kind of pseudo-intellect, which he brings to bear on the most fundamental issues, thus complicating them unnecessarily. This is one situation we should discuss privately.

Communicating to Lower Staff

The solution to this problem is obvious. Regular top management staff meetings should be conducted, which I believe are now being done on a regular schedule. Well-documented minutes should be recorded on a timely basis. Each department head should receive a copy and in turn should conduct his or her department head meeting, thus giving insight to the issues, which prevail.

In your message of September 14, you indicate you will be in touch with me before visiting again. Please do this, as I would really like to become more involved in this aspect of organizational exercise. I think I can be of help, having had so much of this kind of experience previously.

Regards,

James Nassikas

This letter from the president of the resort illustrated an exceptionally open acceptance of survey information and was coupled with a clear statement of the organization's dedication to customer service. *It also indicated a commitment to act on the survey results.* The sincerity of his intent was seen in the actual fol-low-up steps he initiated. Some were carried out immediately, some took time and all but one were addressed, and all were reported back to employees:

1. The expense concern was addressed by reading and discussing the president's response given in his letter—to the staff and supervisors who were asked to "pass it on." It not only surprised them but seemed completely satisfying. Although costs rightfully remained a concern of managers, their expressed alarm over the resort's survival disap-peared in further survey interviews.

2. The issue of excessive work hours was addressed directly and effec-tively and soon seemed to solve itself. Again, his written response was read to the staff who were, in turn, strongly encouraged to make sure their own work behavior was not seen by subordinates as a model to be emulated, or more important, rewarded. These moves were very help-ful, but as so often happens in organizations, the issue slowly disap-peared as the organization became better "organized," and the need for extra hours lessened naturally.

3. The male chauvinism issue was primarily the ski school issue, but given the resort's emphasis on gender equality, it had more general and serious implications. These were made clear to all managers and supervisory people and any incidents smacking of discrimination were to be recognized and firmly "extinguished." Another step was indirect but certainly helpful. Intra-and interdepartment ski contests were set up in which females acquitted themselves very well. Finally, as subsequent interviews suggested, the growing professionalism within the resort seemed in-and-of-itself, to eliminate any vestiges of chauvinism or even implied discrimination.

4. Employee ski privileges and the "no mingling policy" were handled differently and probably require some explanation. The existing priv-ileges were actually seen as quite liberal but for some people use of them was made difficult by conflicting work schedules and the afore-mentioned extra-hours problem.
    The policy remained, but definite steps were taken by managers and supervisors to insure work schedules did not discriminate or unfairly limit ski time. Although the problem became a chronic one, its fre-quency and intensity did diminish greatly.
    The "no mingling" problem had been a problematic result of the president's otherwise successful attempt to transfer the five-star-hotel culture to the ski resort. It affected all employees but was most keenly felt among ski instructors who, under this rule, were not al-lowed to accept an invitation to lunch or an after-lesson drink by

their clients. This, in turn, became a source of resentment to employees and clients alike. It took over a year to persuade the president that this rule, which seemed appropriate in a hotel, made little
sense in a ski resort. It was rescinded.

5. The obstructionist manager problem was "solved" even before the
report of survey results. He was asked to leave! Under normal circumstances such action is discouraged when a problem is surfaced in
a survey but in this case, the resentment toward him by other staff
people was so intense and the president's own views were equally
strong, so the action seemed appropriate. Certainly, no mention of
this was made in reporting back survey results but its consequences
were obvious to all and all seemed quite relieved.

6. The communication issue was not solved as easily as the president
had suggested. The leadership problem that discouraged any upward
critical discussion continued. Moreover, selective perception and
personal biases of both listeners and leaders are not eliminated by
schedules or by taking minutes of meetings. Although communication remained an issue throughout much of the resort's history, for
reasons discussed shortly, it vastly improved and became, if anything,
a very minor concern.

Management Turnover Issue

In spite of their expressed commitment to the resort and its likely career opportunities, several managers resigned, citing work demands and what was
termed the unyielding demands of the general manager. Fortunately for the
resort, the void created was readily filled by promoting people from within
the organization whose managerial promise had been recognized by top
management and whose people skills had been emphasized in surveys.

At the same time, the turnover of key people did again signal the seriousness of the leadership situation "on the mountain." Although earlier survey
results had been used in a series of coaching exercises with the general manager, any improvement was fleeting. Even the urgings of the president to
take a more open approach and to make better use of the proven abilities of
the staff were to no avail. Even as construction problems lessened and the
mountain took shape, the original manager's emotional outbursts continued—even to non-problems.

Probably the general manager's most damaging outburst (which unfortunately became widely known throughout the resort) was reported to have occurred on his birthday! As a gesture, the large clerical staff and management
team decided to surprise him with a birthday cake. Upon seeing the cake,

> however, he exploded saying, "Don't you realize if you do this for me, it will have to be done for everyone?" At this point he pushed the cake across the table and onto the floor. In that one push, social equality in the workplace was acknowledged and ruled out of order.

Although normally a detailed account of a manager's idiosyncrasies would be irrelevant to this discussion, readers may have an interest in seeing some of the ways emotional volatility can all but destroy real and demonstrable leadership accomplishments. Although the general manager's achievements in building a series of first-class structures, extremely safe ski lifts, and appealing ski slopes were clear, these were slowly overshadowed by an irrational leadership style. His apparent intolerance of organizational uncertainties coupled with a tendency toward stereotypical thinking finally countered an otherwise very credible performance. It gradually became obvious to him that his leadership style was increasingly at war with that expected in a world-class organization whose unique sense of service depended on a demonstrated commitment to it and to its employees. He left to take on another assignment in his chosen field of construction.

> One seemingly humorous but eventually destructive example of stereotypical thinking was the general manager's openly voiced distrust of employees who were skiers—this is a ski resort!
>
> His rationale was they would shirk their work in order to ski. Because 90% of the employees were avid skiers, his perspective here was rather broad and was broadly resented.

Selection of a New General Manager

The search for a new general manager was surprisingly short-lived. Although both the owner and president had considered a replacement from outside the organization, survey interviews conducted at the time with the management staff and supervisory people clearly pointed to one of their own as an ideal candidate. In fact, their judgment on this was unanimous, which in itself usually indicates that a topic has been discussed beforehand. In this case, any such "constructive collusion" made their recommendations seem all the more impressive.

An informal presentation of the staff's recommendation to the owner and president was warmly received. It apparently agreed with their own assessment of the candidate and led to his official appointment almost immediately. The staff recommendation was later documented in the written survey report, and was used in the feed-back survey results to employees. This, in turn, had the effect of adding an even wider endorsement of the new "boss"—being seen as one of their own. Subsequent developments over many years have only served to confirm the staff's wisdom.

The new general manager's considerable experience within the resort and his solid acceptance by coworkers allowed him to "hit the ground running." Most important, his promotion brought a synergy to resort management in which his management style and philosophy now merged with and was reinforced by that of the owner and president. As one manager put it, "Now we are all reading from the same page."

His management style was characterized by his staff as open and considerate. Although he had his own view of resort operations, he was said not only to listen but to solicit advice and opinions of others. This extended even to the lowest level of the resort through a practice he established of holding biweekly group discussions among randomly chosen employees. In these meetings, it was later reported, problems were openly discussed and dealt with. In a sense, this routine represented an internalization of the survey process—a very difficult step for any top executive. It takes a great deal of time, requires a keen ability to listen, and succeeds only when a high degree of employee trust in a manager's fairness exists. Because these conditions often are not present, the general manager's success in "pulling it off" here certainly attested to his acceptance throughout the resort.

Emergence of a Considerate Management Style

As the operation matured and dramatically improved, the survey retreated from a *diagnostic* role to one of *monitoring* employee reactions to a host of issues arising from the organization's amazing growth. In that role, the surveys gradually noted an evolving style of management that seemed to emerge naturally rather than being intentional. It involved elements of strategic thinking in which decisions were seen in an organizational context and their likely consequences were given careful thought. Complimenting this was a continued and dedicated concern for employee welfare. Both facets of this emerging style showed up in many management actions—both contemplated and achieved. Two examples of the employee welfare concerned solutions to employee housing and the initiation of drug testing.

Seasonal employee housing in most ski communities was usually reserved and made available to visiting skiers; almost always at rates well beyond what seasonal employees can afford. This not only led to a number of employee hardships but was a major cause of turnover during the season and often discouraged employees from returning.

Management had been greatly concerned about employee hardships and had tried a number of possible solutions—providing busing to a nearby major city, where housing was available, was one example. Management also saw the long-term, and in some ways unique, implication of this situation for the resort as a whole. It realized that the exceptional level of service it held out to customers could not be assured without some seasonal continuity in trained people. The level of training required to continue a culture of service would indeed falter if it had to be introduced each year to a whole new employee population. It was decided, therefore, to take steps to retain at least a core group of returning seasonal employees.

Because employee housing had been shown in surveys and exit interviews to be a major factor in seasonal turnover (and the resulting discontinuities in training), a solution to it was necessary. It was also likely to be very expensive! The steps taken were indeed expensive, but were justified by being both satisfying to employees and beneficial to the resort. Through its real estate department the resort located an available motel and adjacent private housing and acquired them for the use of selected seasonal employees. It resulted in a win–win solution in which both employee welfare and the resort's dedications to service were assured.

Drug testing of employees demonstrated and tested the commitment to strategic thinking among managers. In order to provide for customer safety and minimize resort liability, management felt it necessary to initiate a drug-testing program for its employees. The resistance to this was loudly and widely expressed. Even among department managers the policy was objected to as an intrusion on personal freedom and as being professionally demeaning.

Although management listened and showed an understanding of the complaints, it held to its decision. Again, the general manager openly faced and discussed all sides of the issue, and through persuasion and rational explanation of the immediate and long-term consequences of the program (the liability of the resort and the threat to its customer's pledge), a firm and unanimous agreement was reached to publicly endorse the program although private objections and resentment might remain. This was no small achievement in a ski culture where drug use is probably tolerated to even a greater extent than in the general society. Without the unanimous endorsement for drug testing, skier safety and the resort's promise to its customers would surely have been compromised.

Spread of Strategic Leadership

The open management style, which came with the new general manager along with his awareness of employee needs, was welcomed by department managers and the spread of its effect was reflected in surveys of their peers and subordinates. As one example, a simple survey exercise demonstrated an unusual sensitivity of managers to the feelings of their people. In it, they were asked to estimate the average scores likely to be obtained in an upcoming survey of their departments. With one exception, their estimates were within 13 centiles of the scores actually obtained!

At peer levels, the evidence was more observational, but no less significant. Whereas the staff members had mastered the demands of their individual functions (some, in fact, were nationally recognized), they also reported that interactions across departments became less parochial as they learned, for example, that sharing resources and people was far from being a threat to departmental performance and actually enhanced it. Moreover, exchanges of people led to the surfacing of latent talents and a broadening of aspirations among those "loaned out." These developments were said to almost force closer attention to the likely consequences of their actions, not only within their own operations but those of the whole resort. In this very real sense, they became resort executives.

Much of the change in behavior was attributed to the general manager and it was his style that was actively emulated. This can be seen in quantitative terms in Table 15.4, which compares employee perceptions of his leadership and that of his staff obtained in successive surveys.

As can be seen, perceptions of the general manager were initially quite positive and remained so while employee attitudes toward his staff gradually improved over time, as his style was copied.

TABLE 15.4

Resort II: Comparison of Successive Perceptions of Staff
and General Manager Leadership

Management Level	Percent Positive Response		
	Survey 1	Survey 2	Survey 3
General Manager Leadership	70	69	71
Management Staff Leadership	56	61	68

Note: Organizational theorists have recently referred to some of the elements outlined here as disciplines, (personal mastery, team learning, shared vision), which combine in a "systems thinking" approach to management (Senge, 1990). It is perhaps ironic that they emerged here as simply a natural way to manage people and an organization.

Assessment of Organizational Climate

As intimated, the improvement in, and maintenance of, a positive organizational climate was almost universally attributed to a climate established by a new general manager and the earlier efforts of the resort's president. This can be seen in graphic terms in Table 15.5, which shows the trend in overall employee survey responses before his appointment and in the years following his appointment. (The last survey conducted by the author was in 1997.) The program has since been internalized.

TABLE 15.5

Resort II: Trend of Overall Survey Results 1984 to 1997

IOR Category	Centiles			
	1984	1990	1994	1997
Leadership and Direction	44	75	63	70
Work Appeal	35	58	49	62
Work Demands	35	79	64	61
Teamwork	55	58	50	62
Physical Surroundings	53	68	63	60
Financial Rewards	97	56	45	54
Career Future	41	67	61	66
Organizational Commitment	88	79	76	82

The general manager's influence can also be seen an excerpt from the final survey summary of interview comments:

Much of the reactive and self-serving protective behaviors seen under the previous administration have been replaced with a cooperative spirit. This kind of teamwork is largely attributed to Bob Wheaton, who is said to be universally respected as both a knowledgeable and sensitive general manager. He is seen as knowing "what's going on" in the resort and is able to mobilize his people to achieve its goals and visions. The fact that these goals and visions are solidly shared by the management team has historical roots but is reinforced by Bob's approach (even the new and very controversial drug policy is publicly supported by his staff even though some members personally object to it).

Such glowing endorsements of a manager are usually expressed early in a leader's term and often result from a kind of "relative deprivation" effect by which comparisons are made to a disliked predecessor. But these comments were made some 9 *years* after his appointment!

Summary

This chapter traced the parallel relationship between survey use and organizational effectiveness in two successively owned ski resorts over a 19-year period. In the first resort, attempts to use survey results to guide or influence management actions generally failed, as did the resort itself. In the second location, survey data were used as a normal adjunct to management and assisted in the development of a now world-class resort.

The chapter laid particular emphasis on the critical role played by leadership in both the effective and dysfunctional use of surveys. It also demonstrated the functional use of surveys in identifying the ways organizational strengths were brought to the surface as were the underlying processes by which the resort's values were implemented.

In sociological terms, Resort I came to represent what has been referred to as a "shame" society in which discouragement of employees led them to publicly complain about the company and its leadership—held in check only by supervisory disapproval. In Resort II, a "guilt" society developed in which employees internalized the resort's values and took personal pride in expressing them.

16

Diagnosing Organizational Unrest: A Study in a Television and Radio Station

This survey was the first of several carried out in a major TV and radio station in a large southern metropolitan city. It is as an example of how surveys can prevent, or at least minimize, a very common error of managers, especially top managers, of taking the loudest voice to be the representative voice. The survey also made management aware of a wide spectrum of emotional reactions existing in one organizational setting. In one group, it found an outstanding example of intrinsic motivation stemming solely from work appeal. In contrast, in another small department, the survey surfaced the devastating effects of inadequate supervision exercised in organizational isolation.

THE SETTING

The survey occurred in the early years of color television. In that era stations had very large technical staffs as well as a great variety of on-camera personalities and supporting personnel. In this particular station, the owner had taken a very personal interest in the station's editorial stand on human rights and had firmly supported the editors in the face of great pressure from advertisers and the resistance of large segments of the public. He was also very involved in the early development and workings of the station and would even accompany field technicians during on-site coverage of hurricanes or other major news events.

Because the station had grown rapidly, the owner had recently pulled back from these activities and delegated responsibility to a new professional manager. At the same time he continued to find opportunities to meet with employees and to feel a sense of camaraderie with them. It therefore came as a major shock when the new station manager reported that the technicians were threatening to strike because they feared new automated equipment would cost jobs. The owner was quite taken back by the news, which he took quite personally, feeling he had been deceived by people he thought were not only loyal but friends. This "hurt" reaction led to an unnatural expression of anger and to a decision to hire a well-known antilabor attorney to "prepare for a fight." At this point a mutual friend suggested he talk to an industrial psychologist before taking any action. It was this chance recommendation that led to an exploratory survey.

After a briefing on the events leading up to the present conflict, as well as the owner's present state of mind, a decision was made to survey the entire station rather than single out the technicians. This turned out to be a wise decision in that other problem situations were developing that went beyond the problems thought to exist in the technician group.

RESULTS

The job satisfaction levels among the major departments in the station are shown in Table 16.1.

The data presented in Table 16.1 indicated that, to a large extent, employees were quite satisfied with almost all aspects of their work. Some interesting and surprising variations did exist, however. For example, the level of satisfac-

TABLE 16.1

Job Satisfaction Centile Scores of Major Departments in a TV Station
(N=161)

Category	Total Station	Technicians	News and Editorials	Production Staff	Marketing Department	Radio Section
Top Leadership	80	65	96	81	81	61
1st Level Leadership	69	71	92	82	72	31
Work Appeal	75	80	99	76	61	70
Work Demands	52	55	70	45	48	60
Physical Conditions	51	45	76	50	47	31
Co-workers	70	83	89	56	66	43
Financial Rewards	63	68	85	61	71	61
Career Future	61	58	81	56	72	42
Organizational Commitment	73	66	99	71	70	40

tion with work appeal and leadership expressed by the news and editorial people was among the highest ever obtained (centile scores of 99 and 96 respectively). These scores were in sharp contrast to those obtained toward local leadership in the radio group (its members scored at the 30th centile). Some variation was also seen across departments in attitudes toward physical surroundings and coworkers. The most surprising results of all, however, were found among the technicians. Considering the imminent labor conflict that was purported to exist among its members, their scores were astoundingly high. In order to explain these unusual results and to explain the likely causes of the identified strengths and weaknesses in the organization, reliance was placed on the findings of the interviews conducted among all employees. What follow are summaries of these findings in three key departments.

News and Editorial Staffs

Some of the most thoughtful comments regarding the intrinsic nature of work and commitment to the organization came from this group. Although its members were generally pleased with their pay, physical surroundings, and career opportunities, they uniformly pointed out that they were probably no better or no worse than competition would offer. At the same time, they were extremely proud to be working at this particular station and, in this regard, saw their situation as unique in the industry. They were particularly appreciative of their freedom to cover what they thought were important public issues, which were either avoided or "toned down" by other stations. Above all was their pride in the editorial stances taken on equal rights and other social issues. This pride certainly magnified their positive endorsement of other facets of their job and surroundings, and the feeling of organizational identification expressed was so pervasive and sincerely expressed it bordered on a kind of zeal found among committed members of a religious cult. In a profit-making organization, this seemed unique.

The Radio Station Group

In stark contrast to the TV news and editorial people, the relatively small radio staff expressed very mixed but generally negative feelings about the company, their supervisor, and each other. From the comments about coworkers it appeared that some "red necks" (as some were described) among them actually resented the station's human rights stance and were unhappy with those who disagreed with them. This internal conflict was aggravated by a supervisor who would not confront this discord but contributed to the problem by showing blatant favoritism and a decided indifference to subordinates' feelings. Because this department numbered only 13, was not highly profitable, and was physically isolated, it was treated as a sort of "distant relative" by the more glamorous TV operation. As a result the new general manager was *as yet* unaware of its situation. All he seemed to know about the radio group was what its manager told him in staff meetings. What actually went on, however, bordered on mistreatment of people.

The very positive sense of camaraderie that existed throughout the TV station was almost absent within the radio group, and considerable resentment was expressed toward a company that allowed these conditions to exist. The combination of fear for one's job and the belief that their manager enjoyed upper management's favor apparently kept the radio staff people from voicing their concerns. In fact, before the staff would agree to cooperate, the interviewers had to convince them that their comments would be treated confidentiality. In cooperating, they presumably saw the survey as the only safe way to make their feelings known.

The Technicians

The Index of Organizational Reactions (IOR) scores for technicians were at first baffling. How could a group of resentful people on the verge of a strike produce such positive survey results? Although there was always the chance that they had misunderstood the questions or had given false responses, neither explanation seemed likely given the high intelligence required by the job and the intense concern they were said to have already expressed quite openly. After interviews with 12 of the 35 technicians, no hint of resentment or intent to strike was heard! Instead a stream of comments were made about how good the company was as an employer! At this point, the interviewers felt it necessary to inquire directly about the new automated equipment that was supposedly viewed as a threat.

It soon became clear that the threat had been voiced by only three group members who were technically unskilled and were convinced that their jobs would be eliminated once the equipment was installed. These three men apparently were vocal in expressing their concerns and resentment. Because they met no argument from other technicians, they assumed they spoke for all. In fact, they spoke only for themselves but did so very loudly. As so often happens, their complaints were magnified as they were reported up the line. Actually, it was discovered that the technicians (almost all of whom had electronic background) were eagerly anticipating the challenge of working on the new equipment. In spite of this enthusiasm, their sense of solidarity kept them from contradicting the views expressed by the three unskilled coworkers. In the final analysis, the positive questionnaire results were confirmed by the interviews. The survey had revealed a classic example of a small vocal minority being mistaken as representing the view of a much larger group who in no way shared it.

The new station manager might not have misjudged the situation so badly had he been around longer and had been able to develop closer ties with the technician group. In any event, the insight into the group's real attitude was gratefully accepted by him, especially when supported by the "hard survey data."

This case demonstrated the ease with which communications are distorted and magnified in the face of ambiguity. Although little professional skill was needed to discover the simple dynamics of this situation, given the uncertain circumstances in which it occurred, the new manager had simply responded to rumors that were rapidly taken up as a major corporate concern and as a personal affront to the owner.

FOLLOW-UP ACTION

Before leaving the station the survey consultant assured the owner and station manager that the "technician problem" was apparently a pseudo problem. He added that, should a vote be taken, the issue surrounding this misunderstanding would become "crystal clear." The owner, in fact, did just that. As he reported later, he called the technicians together, explained his purpose in bringing in the equipment, and reassured them it would cost no jobs and even might make life more interesting. Their response was unanimously in favor of the change and expressed some surprise that their views had been thought otherwise.

The radio department was a different matter. Although its manager had certainly "crossed a line" in his unfair treatment of people, he was not fired. Instead, it was suggested that a documented corrective interview be conducted by the station manager and that the tenure of the radio department manager be made conditional on improvement.

> Note: This recommendation is in keeping with widely shared opinions of professionals in the field that survey results alone should not be used to fire people. Instead, survey results should be learning devices—even if painful devices—and should allow problem situations to be corrected internally and fairly.

This recommendation was followed and, somewhat painfully, it did work. A survey done 18 months later verified that the manager had made a sincere effort, which was reflected in subsequent comments of his subordinates. A comparison of the earlier and later survey's questionnaire results are shown in Table 16.2.

TABLE 16.2

Comparison of Survey Responses of Radio Department
over an 18 Month Period
(N=13)

	Centiles	
Category	1st Survey	2nd Survey
Leadership Top Management	61	70
Leadership 1st Line Management	31	65
Kind of Work	70	68
Amount of Work	60	61
Physical Surroundings	31	39
Co-workers	43	51
Financial Rewards	61	64
Career Future	42	51
Organizational Commitment	40	54

SUMMARY

This chapter described a fairly typical survey function in which management was given a more accurate and *representative picture* of the human side of its organization. Armed with these quantitative and behaviorally based data, management was able to act responsibly rather than responding impulsively on limited or exaggerated rumors.

> This situation should not be left without reporting one incident that could only occur in a TV station. The survey had taken place shortly after a major hurricane. To say the least, the viewing public was still upset and paid particular attention to weather reports. Because the professional meteorologist did much of his reporting from field locations where damage had occurred, his program was anchored from the station.
>
> On one afternoon during the survey, it was necessary to present breaking news about an altogether different subject than weather, but a weather update was to be included. Because the regular anchor person was off duty, the job fell to the man who played a character on the afternoon children's show. This character had spent the week literally "breaking up" the survey team with one joke after another, and it was with great interest that its members gathered to watch him "play it straight."

He carried out the whole newsbreak in a remarkably professional manner, and at the end reassured the audience that no further signs of bad weather, let alone a hurricane, were in sight. Then he did it—not being able to resist the opportunity to revert to character, he added that "rumors of World War III were also false!" This was at a time when people were still considering bomb shelters! The station switchboard lit up for hours. The character friend was not fired but his short career as anchor ended as abruptly as it had begun.

17

Employee Attitudes Toward Health, Safety, and Environmental Issues: A Decade of Surveys

Between 1988 and 1998 a series of surveys designed to measure employee attitudes toward health, safety, and environmental (HS&E) issues were carried out among 51 locations of several large petro-chemical companies. This Chapter is a synopsis of results obtained in 22 representative production sites that were surveyed twice. The following summary is based, in part, on a survey report prepared for discussion purposes with company management.

THE SURVEY COVERAGE

The series of surveys reported here were part of a much larger effort carried out by the author aimed at surveying Health, Safety, and Environmental (HS&E) issues that involved hundreds of locations in the United States, Latin America, Europe, Indonesia, Philippines, and Canada. Although the present report deals with a selected sample of units from companies based in the United States, the conclusions reached from this sample were fairly consistent with experiences in the broader effort. The sample was selected on the basis of similarity of work carried out, (administrative and distribution facilities were excluded in the study). Most of these locations had been surveyed between 1985 and 1988 and all shared the similar HS&E standards. The time frame of the surveys carried out after 1988 is especially significant in that a good deal of evidence collected over this period pointed to definite and positive changes in attitudes among employees in these production sites. However, as will be shown, a number of serious problems remained and a growing sense of safety professionalism seemed apparent from both the questionnaire and interview responses.

The survey was conduced by means of questionnaires administered to all employees and by a sampling of employee interviews in each site. An HS&E questionnaire was developed that consisted of approximately 65 to 70 items, depending on the version used. These items were divided into five separate scales that measured attitudes toward the following five categories:

1. Priority—the extent to which employees see safety and environment as a top priority in this location as shown by the emphasis and support given by management.
2. Climate—the extent to which safety and environmental matters are a focal issue in the day-to-day activities of supervisors and work groups.
3. Assurance—the perceived danger or potential for accidents and environmental damage among the various jobs and areas in this location or site.
4. Action—the perceived likelihood that management will take preventive or corrective action regarding environmental and safety-related incidents.
5. Ownership—the influence of company training programs both on-the-job and at home. It reflects the degree to which employees have internalized or taken ownership of positive safety attitudes.

In the resulting HS&E report, scores on each scale were plotted against industry norms, and responses to selected items were shown in terms of the percentage of agreement or disagreement obtained.

SURVEY RESULTS

The overall comparison for the 22 selected surveys after 1988 and those obtained earlier is shown in Table 17.1.

As can be seen readily, the more recent results pointed to very significant improvement in employee assessments of HS&E issues in their locations. It was also apparent that attitudes in the "Action" category showed only a modest gain and more-or-less remained at the industry's average level. This suggested a continuing area of concern, which was discussed throughout the report.

Development of Professionalism

Scores obtained in the other four categories were generally at the high end of industrial norms and suggested a significant and positive change in atti-

TABLE 17.1

Comparison of HS&E Survey Results From Two Time Periods

	Centiles	
HSE Scale	*1985–89* *(N=3,116)*	*1989–92* *(N=4,076)*
Priority	54	63
Climate	57	66
Assurance	63	69
Action	39	51
Ownership	65	69

tude toward HS&E issues. When examined further, these results indicated a change in attitude that could be maintained and reinforced by appropriate management actions. This impressive change in attitude was undoubtedly a reflection of a number of internal and external pressures on the industry but also pointed to a personal acceptance of responsibility for safely and environmental protection by individuals at various job levels. This was seen in both questionnaire responses and interview comments—some examples are to follow:

> "If this company was anymore committed to safety and environment, we'd probably have to close our doors."
> "Bosses who used to only think about production now zero in on safety and spills."
> "Violating a safety rule around here is a good way to get fired."
> "Its almost funny to listen to the old guys who used to laugh at spills. Now you would think they are Sierra Club boosters."
> "I even get the message at home. My kid is picking up the environmental stuff in school and every once in a while I get grilled on what we are doing to keep the water clean."

Table 17.2 shows the specific quantitative evidence of this growth in positive attitudes toward HS&E issues.

As can be seen in the survey, there was a growing tendency for employees to point to internal influences: (e.g., "carelessness" and "acting without thinking") as the main causes of accidents whereas external influences ("heavy work pressures, unsafe conditions, and untrained people,") were increasingly down-played as major causes.

TABLE 17.2

Changes in Perceived Causes of Accidents

Perceived Cause	Percent Indicating a "major" Cause of Accidents	
	1985–1988	1989–1992
Carelessness	39	55
Acting before thinking	40	56
Heavy work pressure	46	21
Unsafe condition other plant	36	20
Poorly trained people	21	16
Poor communication between workers	24	17
Bad luck	5	6
Drug/alcohol abuse	1	3

The acceptance of responsibility for one's own safety also extended to co-workers. As a result, a work group "climate" was said to exist in which people looked after themselves but also look out for the safety of others. It is in a very real sense a form of group discipline. To follow are some relevant employee comments:

"I get the feeling that people here look after each other and help each other out."
"It used to be the boss who yelled at safety violations—now any guy on the team will let you know when you are making a mistake."
"I almost got hurt yesterday. Two of the men stopped a new guy from turning the wrong valve while I was tying to clean a pipe."

These comments, hallmarks of a professional outlook, strongly suggested that the development of such an approach to work and environmental safety was equated with job competence and pride.

Effects of Training

Changes in behavior and attitudes are often attributed to training. In this particular industry, training had two faces. A good deal of it occurred in formal classroom exercises, and perhaps even more critical were the efforts occurring on the job. Because of the importance of both kinds of training, a group of items were included in the survey that were intended as "inferred measures of training." They gauged the attitude changes that should result from both types of training. These are shown in Table 17.3.

Table 17.3

Changes in Perceivd Influence of Training

	Percent 'YES' Responses	
Survey Item	1985–1988	1989–1992
Know the procedure for evacuating this facility	85	94
Could show HSE procedures to a new employee	79	96
Training and "real" world job experience agree	65	78
Been taught safe procedures	51	72
Know how to handle Hazardous Materials	41	51
Regularly asked for ideas and opinions	40	42

It is worth noting that even among those positive attitudes that seemed already well entrenched, some additional improvement was made. For example, in the earlier survey, a very large majority (85%) indicated that their training had enabled them "to explain safety procedures to new employees." In the more recent survey, that response rose to 93%. A significant gain (72% vs. 90%) was also seen in the number of people who felt, "classroom training made sense in the real world of work." Only one item suggested a need for improved on-the-job training: only 60% said they were "regularly asked for their ideas and suggestions." Overall, these findings clearly indicated a greater acceptance of training than once was the case. Comments that in the past often belittled training as unreal and theoretical now seemed to smack of appreciation. Nowhere was this more clearly seen than in comments about training's influence on safety off the job. Some examples of these comments are as follows:

"I never wore a seat belt cause I couldn't reach the cigarette lighter. Now I wear one even to go to the grocery store."
"Our training guy has shown me a dozen things done at home that are terribly unsafe—they never occurred to me."
"I never thought about how dangerous mowing the lawn was—now I wear safety shoes."

Perception of Management Action and Nonaction

As is shown in Table 17.1, employees were far less positive in their assessment of the actions taken by management regarding unsafe conditions and environmental threats. Although this suggested an indifferent attitude on the part of local managers, interviews with site managers and their staff people painted a very different picture. In these discussions, it was stressed that all managers were concerned about safety and that no sane manager would be unwilling to act on unsafe conditions. In the eyes of many workers, however, the idea persists that management is often "indifferent to safety."

Both sides of this issue surfaced in a discussion of survey results in one of the company's offshore facilities. Although only an anecdote, it seemed to capture the perceptual differences in a "nutshell" and may be generally instructive. In this discussion a fairly serious employee complaint centered on the rusted and deteriorated condition of metal stairs on an offshore platform. As the discussion proceeded one of the operations managers interrupted saying, "Look, I don't deny this can be a serious problem, but am I supposed to authorize a boat and crew to go out and fix something that will normally be taken care of in the next scheduled maintenance visit?"

Although this seemed to be a reasonable question, it did provoke other points of view. For example, it was noted that, should an injury occur, its cost to the company would surely be higher than that of a boat and a repair crew. It was also asked, 'why weren't the stairs (fixed) in the last maintenance visit' Thus, it appeared that management was clearly *not unwilling* to act but saw little reason to disrupt normal and scheduled procedures. Workers on the other hand, seeing their complaints go unanswered, interpreted this as management's indifference.

Because dozens of similar incidents were raised in this discussion, it seemed to have a wider relevance and undoubtedly reflected everyday occurrences throughout the company. The conclusion reached in the discussions may also be of interest: In most cases, what is seen as management indifference should be recognized as a valid concern. It also should be recognized that responses should reflect judgment and be coupled with reasonable explanations. That is, if the incident is judged to be serious or of immediate concern, it should be addressed—even with added cost. If it is decided the problem can be corrected using routine procedures, that decision should be fully explained and made as a commitment to employees.

The general applicability of this conclusion was further seen in a rather dramatic comparison of survey results from two of the company's refineries. The comparison is especially pertinent in that both locations were of the same age and size. This comparison is shown in Table 17.4.

In Refinery #1, management was seen as placing a high priority on HS&E matters and as being reasonably responsive to potential incidents. Employee comments generally supported this assessment:

> "Our manager is pretty friendly and approachable. You can show him a problem and not get yelled at."

Table 17.4

Comparison of HSE Survey Results Refineries 1 & 2

	Centiles	
HSE Scale	Refinery I (N=24)	Refinery II (N=136)
Priority	67	49
Climate	68	63
Assurance	60	55
Action	61	39
Ownership	67	68

> "He walks the talk and seems interested in our opinions."
> "The big boss relates well to our supervisor—that helps."
> "When I broke my arm, he called me at home to see how I was."
> "He knows this place from A to Z."

In contrast, management of Refinery #2 was seen as unresponsive and uncaring. Employee comments here bordered on open resentment:

> "That guy (plant manager) doesn't give a damn about us."
> "Rather than seeing for himself, he sent a flunky to check out a serious incident."
> "All he cares about is production."
> "The only time you see him is when a 'Cat' breaks down."
> "He must know that our safety reports are juggled just to get him off our supervisor's back."

Although these results and comments certainly pointed to management's indifference as the source of concern in Refinery #2, interviews with its management staff again revealed a much different view. Staff people claimed the manager actually was very concerned about safety and environmental threats, but that he had a "short fuse" when he thought a complaint was unjustified or if he felt the union was "pushing him around." As a result he often refused to get involved or to act unless he was sure. Although this point of view seemed to suggest a management style and judgment issue rather than a lack of concern, to employees it was seen as management indifference.

It should also be noted that, in spite of their concerns about management's willingness to act, employees in Refinery #2 evidenced the same kind of personal concern for their own safety and that of coworkers mentioned earlier. In this case, however, it was a means of self-protection. Rather than depending on management to respond they took the problematic course of "working around" unsafe conditions! In such situations, an uneasy sense of professionalism may still be generated, but it is one in which workers observe safety and environmental standards in order to protect themselves, rather than from a sense of personal pride or confidence in management.

The irony is that both sides of the issue have a point and both views might be moderated greatly by mutually constructive communication and leader behavior that openly recognizes the other's position.

One final example of perceived management indifference to HS&E issues can be placed directly at top management's doorstep. It concerned the apparent practice of treating certain sites as rotational training grounds for potential executives. In two locations, which were so identified, management indifference was strongly pointed to as a major concern of employees. Here the attitudes had a very genuine ring and complaints were supported by examples—sometimes scary examples.

The problem seemed to be that managers in these locations usually saw their assignments as temporary and their goals as quick gains in production. Unfortunately these goals were said to be achieved at the expense of other considerations—including safety and environmental standards. It appeared to be an example of a common management tactic, making one's mark at all costs and "leaving the mess for the next guy." It is not a practice unique to this industry and, in fact, it is seen in retail stores as well as in high-tech manufacturing plants. It is, however, an especially critical problem in the petro-chemical industry because of its safety and environmental implications.

SUMMARY

A series of repeat surveys in 22 production units pointed out some attitude trends that have a wider relevance to the petro-chemical industry. Foremost in these trends was the growing acceptance of personal responsibility for one's own health and safety, and to a great extent, that of one's fellow workers. This trend was made even more apparent by employee downplaying of other factors such as, "heavy work pressures" or "unsafe conditions" that in an earlier survey, had been voiced as the major causes of accidents. In many units this growing sense of professionalism was seen, in part, as a reflection of employee pride and, in part, a consequence of management's support of formal and on-the-job training.

At the same time, in a number of the units surveyed, employees held management responsible for various environmental infractions and unsafe conditions. In these cases, management was perceived as either refusing to act on employee complaints or as indifferent to them. Even in these units, there also appeared to be a developing attitude of personal responsibility. In these situations, however, it seemed to derive from a sense of self-preservation rather than from personal pride in work or from confidence that management was concerned about safety.

18

Survey Prediction of Worker Reactions to Organizational Changes

This is an account of a post-survey prediction of the likely reaction of a group of construction workers to an intended organizational change. The prediction was based solely on responses to a questionnaire administered several months earlier. The mustering of data for this predication is an example of the so-called "cause-and-effect" analysis of survey results alluded to in chapter 3.

THE SETTING AND PROCEDURE

A large construction firm located in the Appalachian region was the client in this project. It had been taken over by a large conglomerate and was under considerable pressure from its new owner to improve profit performance. It had, in fact, received a rather direct "suggestion" to introduce two major organizational changes toward that goal. One involved a change in work rules that would allow for more efficient use of equipment. The other called for the cross-training of workers in the various skilled trades, and would require workers to learn each other's skills and to perform them when and where needed. This would in turn create great flexibility in the use of labor and probably lead to cost savings. Although cross-training is a red-flag issue with union workers, there was no indication of how this large non-union group would react to either change.

The construction employees, approximately 400 in number, were divided into five closely located "regional" divisions within which more-or-less permanent teams operated. These were usually lead by two or three supervisors. Almost all traditional trades were represented: carpenters, electricians, plumbers, roofers, and heavy equipment handlers. A group of relatively unskilled laborers helped out where needed.

Within a team, the work of each skilled trade was scrupulously observed and guarded. This was partly traditional, but also allowed for the ready identification of, and responsibility for, errors or any need for rework. Supervisors were almost all "graduates" of one or more of the skilled trades and had held their positions for at least several years. Their median age was 49. All supervisors had attended a supervisory training program at the start of their assignment but had been left to develop their own leadership styles in the field.

Management had traditionally maintained a fairly distant relationship with both supervisors and construction crews and interacted with them through a small group of roving superintendents who visited work sties fairly often but irregularly. As a result, management was seen as quite remote and largely unknown. This remoteness gave management very little basis for judging employee acceptance of new work rules and cross-training. Management was concerned, however, and because a survey had been conducted only a few months earlier, it naturally turned to the survey idea again for a prediction of the probable employee reaction.

The Survey and Post Survey Analysis

The survey had been carried out by means of a questionnaire that included the Index of Organizational Reactions (IOR). It used seven of its eight scales (The "physical surroundings scale had been omitted because each team worked in ever changing locations and surroundings.) Although a few interviews had been conducted as part of the survey's "groundwork," no interviews were part of the survey itself. All employees were given a brief report on the general survey findings from company management and later participated in informal discussions with the company's personnel manager, that were held in various field locations.

Survey Results

The overall results for the supervisory and nonsupervisory groups are shown in Table 18.1.

The supervisory results shown in Table 18.1 indicates an only modest level of job satisfaction with very little variation across all seven categories. This is a rather surprising result for a supervisory group and, in itself, suggested a potential problem.

TABLE 18.1

Comparison of Supervisor's and Nonsupervisor's Survey Results

| IOR Category | Centile | |
	Supervisors (N=29)	Nonsupervisors (N=376)
Leadership & Directions	54	35
Work Appeal	51	66
Work Demands	57	44
Coworkers	59	65
Financial Rewards	44	54
Career Future	49	51
Organizational Commitment	49	52

Results for the nonsupervisors, in contrast, indicated a good deal of variation in attitudes toward different aspects of work situation. Taken as a whole, it could not be thought of as a "happy group" but there were several facets of the work that were well regarded. That is, whereas attitudes toward their supervisors and work pressures were fairly low, the attitudes directed toward the kind of work done, coworkers, pay and benefits were quite positive.

Although the overall survey results did offer a clue to the likely employee reaction to the intended change, a search for an even more refined predictive base seemed advisable. To this end the category results were broken-out further in search of the likely causes of employee dissatisfaction. This analysis had a two-fold aim—one obvious, the other not. It would first of all provide a basis for making the requested prediction. It was also hoped that by giving management a clear picture of the causes of workers discontent, it would encourage further constructive action. By this means, the level of job satisfaction might be raised and any suspicions workers had regarding the intended organizational changes might be lessened.

Supervisory Analysis

In the introduction of any significant change in an organization, first-line supervisors usually play a very influential role. Their support is often *the* critical influence. Likewise, their resistance can be fatal, whether voiced or seen only in gestures and the like. The level of dissatisfaction with pay that was expressed by the present group of supervisors and their only luke-warm commitment to the company suggested their support of organizational change would be at best a passive one. In view of this supposition, a search was made for the causes of their dissatisfaction in all survey categories. Two of these, which seemed most significant, "financial rewards" and "organizational commitment," are reported here.

As noted in chapter 3, the IOR survey questionnaire contained two sets of items. One set was crafted to measure job satisfaction, whereas the other set simply asked employees whether or not certain conditions existed in their work settings. In order to determine which of these conditions had the greatest impact on job satisfaction, an analysis was made of the extent to which each was said to exist.

The analysis of financial rewards is shown in Table 18.2. In it, the workplace conditions thought to influence satisfaction with pay are listed. Next to each, are the percentages of supervisors, in above and below average job satisfaction groups who indicated the condition existed.

As seen in Table 18.2, pay dissatisfaction is almost solely accounted for by the condition of internal pay inequities. Almost all of other conditions were dismissed or were said to be "unknown."

TABLE 18.2

Percentage of Supervisors in Above-and-Below Average Job Satisfaction Groups Indicating the Existence–Nonexistence of Conditions Influencing Satisfaction With Financial Rewards
($N = 29$)

	Job Satisfaction Level				
	Above Average		Below Average		Don't Know
	Exist	Nonexist	Exist	Nonexist	
	Percent		Percent		
Equal Opportunity					
Age	88	12	88	12	10
Gender	–	–	–	–	100
Equity					
Internal pay	66	34	80	20	10
External pay	–	–	–	–	85
Promotions	–	–	–	–	70
Benefit Coverage	88	12	76	24	10
C.O.L.A.	10	20	70	30	10

In this particular case, the only internal group to which supervisory pay might be compared was the nonsupervisory group. Thus, the source of their feelings of pay dissatisfaction seemed clear as was the strength of its influence. For these reasons management was strongly urged to act on the perceived gap in pay levels of these two groups.

Organization commitment scores were analyzed in the same way. This is shown in Table 18.3.

Again the pattern of responses is quite revealing and, for a supervisory group, somewhat alarming. Those expressing below average satisfaction with the company generally gave more critical descriptions of management's communication efforts and its awareness of problems, and both groups saw the company as viewed more positively by the outside community than by employees. This suggests a serious absence of management involvement with supervisors and, by implication, with all employees. Because supervisors also saw the organization as unconcerned about supervisory problems or employee welfare, the likelihood of their support for a major organizational change would be doubtful. In addition, perceived absence of management communication would seem to make their support even more unlikely.

Nonsupervisory Analyses

The previous analyses were extended to nonsupervision people. Because they constituted a much larger population, an even more reliable estimate of casual factors could be obtained. As shown in Table 18.1, nonsupervisors

TABLE 18.3

Comparison of Responses to "Organizational Commitment"
by Supervisors in High and Low Job Satisfaction Categories
(N = 29)

Descriptive Items	Job Satisfaction Level			
	Above Average%		Below Average%	
(Paraphrased)	YES	NO	YES	NO
Corporate good citizen	80	20	70	30
Community trust	80	20	65	35
Aware of problems at my level	40	60	30	70
Effective communication of corporate plans	45	55	38	65
Considers employee welfare in decisions	49	51	49	59

expressed the greatest dissatisfaction with their supervisors and work pressures. As a result, an analysis of these two categories was carried out.

Attitudes toward leadership and direction were examined in some detail because of the number of questionnaire items devoted to the category. In examining the conditions that influence satisfaction with leadership, the major focus was on the specific elements of supervisory behavior. A sample of those that were included in the survey are shown in Table 18.4.

As seen in Table 18.4 a fairly distinct pattern of supervisory behavior emerged. That is, almost all of employees said their supervisors were knowledgeable, were available, gave clear instructions, and knew good work when they saw it. At the same time, supervisors were said to be indifferent to employee feelings, unaware of their problems, uninterested in their ideas, and unappreciative of good work.

This pattern is an approximation of a well-known style of leadership: *high initiation of structure and low consideration.* As can also be seen, this description of supervisory behavior was most critically expressed by workers in the "below average" satisfaction group. Those in the "above average" group tended to see their supervisors as somewhat more considerate. It appeared, therefore, that even among a group of supervisors who shared an amazingly similar leadership style, the relatively small differences in their behavior pro-

TABLE 18.4

Comparison of Responses to "leadership and Direction"
by Nonsupervisors in High and Low Job Satisfaction Categories
(N = 376)

| | Job Satisfaction Level | | | |
| Descriptive Items | Above Average (N = 199) % | | Below Average (N = 177) % | |
(Paraphrased)	YES	NO	YES	NO
My Supervisor:				
is available when needed	81	19	75	25
gives clear instruction	76	24	80	20
is knowledgeable	71	29	62	38
is aware of problems	51	49	39	61
is helpful with problems	45	55	41	59
considerate of workers feelings	39	61	35	65
recognizes good work	42	58	39	61

duced different levels of satisfaction among subordinates—a finding that had definite implications for future training efforts.

Work demands were examined by means of a series of responses to a single question: "To what extent would each of the following factors lead to improved output in your work?" The responses are shown in Table 18.5.

Given the overall low level of satisfaction among this group with the "work demands" category (as shown earlier in Table 18.2), it is not surprising that both the above-and-below average satisfaction groups largely agreed on their responses to this issue. Members of both groups stressed "less pressure from supervisors" and the receipt of "more recognition for good work" as the most influential factors. The significance of these findings is particularly heightened by the fact that they are seen as outweighing the importance of such bread-and-butter issues as "more money" and "more opportunities for promotion."

In addition, some direct hint of employee reaction to the intended organizational change were noted. For example: "More interesting work" and "increased training" were among the factors employees saw as least in need of improvement.

TABLE 18.5

Comparison of Responses to "work Demands"
by Nonsupervisors in High and Low Job Satisfaction Categories
(N = 376)

To what extent would each of the following factors lead to improved output in your work:	Percent Endorsing Each Factor	
	Above Average Satisfaction	Below Average Satisfaction
1. Better working conditions	37	43
2. Less supervisory pressure	56	69
3. Less "red tape"	41	40
4. More coworker cooperation	10	6
5. More money	26	35
6. Improved training	10	8
7. More communication from management	35	39
8. More recognition	52	63
9. More interesting work	5	6
10. More promotional opportunity	36	46

Alienation estimates for employees in the five regions was also computed. Although the preceding analysis seemed to present a fairly clear indication of how employees would respond to an intended change in work rules, and so forth, one further analysis of the data was taken. It involved the rescoring of 13 items that previous research had shown to predict employee withdrawal behavior (Hamner & Smith, 1977). These thirteen items, when properly weighted, formed an "alienation scale." The results are shown in Table 18.6.

Although these results indicated that definite regional differences existed, they also showed that all five groups displayed fairly high levels of "alienation." (It should also be noted that the least alienation was expressed by the smallest group.) It was decided therefore, to ignore regional differences and to consider all employees as one group for purposes of prediction. This decision seemed well justified because the change itself would also apply to all employees regardless of region. These estimates of "alienation" among all five regions were consistent with the previous analysis, and seemed to support a rather strong recommendation *against* the introduction of a drastic organizational change.

Predictions

Based on the survey responses, the "alienation" estimates, as well as considerable experience with similar employee groups, the following comments were presented to management:

1. If both the cross-training and work-rule changes are unilaterally announced, the likely reaction of nonsupervisory employees will be ex-

TABLE 18.6

Alienation Estimates of Nonsupervisors in Five Categories
(N = 376)

Region	N	Centiles
1	90	31
2	41	38
3	60	28
4	120	32
5	65	34
Total	376	32

tremely negative. In addition, given its current attitude, the supervisory group will probably be of little supportive help.

2. If the intended changes must be introduced, they should be presold to employees. These changes actually contain some very appealing elements that, if properly explained, could result in considerable enrichment of jobs and could make workers more valuable both within and outside the company. As matters stand now, however, employees are likely to see these changes simply as a means of reducing the workforce and increasing their job pressures.

3. If the intended changes are an economic "must do" step for the company, this should be clearly and dramatically explained. *This step can hardly be exaggerated.* Unless people are convinced the change is inevitable, necessary, and legitimate, they are likely to reject it—especially if announced without warning or explanation.

4. If the changes must be made, some consideration should be given to a sequential introduction. If, for example, only the work-rule change was introduced and people could be reassured of its intent and its positive features, the later introduction of cross-training might be better accepted.

5. If the changes are introduced, supervisory people should be enlisted to support them. But to achieve this, the company will have to increase its efforts to include supervisors in management discussions and to consider them as legitimate members of the management team. In addition supervisory pay inequities noted in the survey analysis should be seriously addressed. At present, the supervisors may actually encourage resistance to the intended change.

The Sequel

Management of the construction company accepted all of the comments and recommendations and announced its intention to present them, along with other concerns, to the parent company. Management also admitted that it had asked for an opinion of a third party (in this case, the survey) in the hope that it would advise against the introduction of the intended changes. Such a finding, it was reasoned, might help convince the parent company that the planned change would boomerang. Unfortunately, management's entire argument was rejected by the parent company and the work rules were announced, as were the plans to introduce them, almost immediately.

What happened next was reported to the author by a parent-company staff person some 13 months later. First, the employee reaction was even more resistant than predicted. Having little faith in the company's intention and shocked by the abrupt introduction of the changes, the nonsupervisory people contacted a local union and, by a 4 to 1 vote, elected to unionize. Although in-and-of-itself, such a move might have helped resolve the dispute had both sides tried to do so, it apparently only served to strengthen resistance on both sides, and a costly strike resulted.

Although the purpose of this chapter is to demonstrate a method of analyzing survey data, it also attempts to show how data can be mustered to form a prediction. In this case, the response of workers predicted by survey results actually occurred, but the question remains whether a more successful solution might have been achieved had management acted more cautiously, or had not totally ignored the survey's best estimate of employee reaction to the organizational changes.

Proving "what might have been" is of course a logical impossibility. In practice, it is even more difficult.

Technical note: The so-called "cause-and-effect" analysis demonstrated in this and other chapters is essentially a comparison of responses to different items in the same questionnaire. In this case, responses to *descriptive items* that describe work place conditions that have been shown to influence job satisfaction are compared to responses to sets of other items that actually measure satisfaction.

Because similar methods are used in obtaining both types of responses, any comparisons between them is likely to be influenced by the similarity of their methods. That is, attitudes measured by the same methods yield results that are often different than those obtained by measures that are clearly different from one another.

Although the present analysis is open to this method-variance influence, it is argued here that this influence is minimized by the following elements:

1. The actual measures of job satisfaction are obtained from carefully crafted multi-item scales that have met sound psychometric standards. Descriptive items on the other hand, are single, neutrally phrased questions, which ask only whether certain work place conditions do or do not exist. Although the methods are similar, the responses called for are quite different.
2. The "causes" of job satisfaction identified by this type of analysis have been fairly consistently supported by interview results—which, of course, represent an entirely different method of measuring attitudes.

19

Use of a Survey in Determining CEO Succession

This is a brief account of a very unusual use of survey information—the selection of a new CEO of a subsidiary corporation. This application shifts the survey from a purely passive, largely diagnostic role, to that of an active change agent. In doing so, it also draws pointed attention to the important requirement that observers should not interfere with what is being observed. Although this requirement is an axiom of any objective or scientific approach, it can be an insidious influence in survey work, often going unnoticed by managers. The care taken in avoiding this pitfall is noted here as a means of alerting managers to its potential effects.

Although none of those directly impacted by this study is still active in the company, their names have been purposely disguised or omitted.

THE SETTING AND SURVEY OBJECTIVES

The role of human–resource tools in facilitating management decisions or in anticipating postdecision reactions is fairly common. The growing use of these tools in the selection of a top management candidate has been emphasized in popular management publications (e.g., Leonard, 2001). In the present case, the employee survey greatly extended the role played by a human resource vehicle to the point of all but making a final personnel decision: the selection of the first Mexican national as the CEO of the Sears Mexican subsidiary corporation.

The situation described involved the Sears International Department, which, at the time, had an extensive chain of subsidiaries throughout Latin America. It also had a long-standing policy of placing U.S. citizens in CEO positions in all of its Latin American locations. Increasingly, this policy had been questioned for many reasons, not the least of which was the presence of several very experienced and qualified nationals on the staffs of most of the company's subsidiaries.

The opportunity to change the policy came rather suddenly when the president of the Mexican Corporation became seriously ill and asked for medical retirement. As it turned out, three senior members of the current Mexican staff had been considered as eventual candidates for the presidency and, although their strengths varied, they were essentially considered equally qualified. However, an important consideration was their likely acceptance by the large Mexican managerial staff, as well as other employees. Because staff acceptance had been stressed in the earlier discussions of the succession policy, it became *the* major concern. To assess it, a survey of the entire large Mexican staff was requested.

In what appeared to be a classic instance of "all things being equal," a survey was mounted that had a "hidden agenda," that of determining who, among the three candidates, would be most acceptable to Mexican employees. Given its likely historic significance, as well as its practical importance to the Mexican Corporation's future, the survey was announced and carried out with particular care.

Although the probable early retirement of the current president was sensed among his senior staff, the severity of his illness and his actual imminent retirement had not been announced. The survey process, therefore, had to respect both his feelings and his present condition. It also had to avoid any speculation regarding the survey's role in the selection process. Such speculation might have led to all sorts of political jockeying, and would have committed the aforementioned cardinal sin of allowing observations to influence what is being measured!

Survey Procedure

The survey was simply announced and carried out as part of a regular standard procedure. It included a questionnaire written in Spanish that was administered to all corporate office employees, coupled with nondirective interviews with all corporate staff members as well as a random sample of field managers. The Index of Organizational Reactions (IOR) was used in this study. Its development and that of its Spanish version is discussed in chapter 3. It measures eight aspects of job satisfaction: leadership and direction, work appeal, work demands, coworkers, physical surroundings, career developments, financial rewards, and organization commitments.

A major procedural problem concerned the use of a nondirective interview approach, which is, after all, *nondirective*. Because topics are almost totally determined by the interviewed person, it was possible that all sorts of issues might be discussed without ever getting to the subject of primary interest—the acceptability of the various candidates for the presidency. At the same time this approach had the important advantage of being passive and unobtrusive.

In keeping with sound survey tactics, a contingency step consisting of a structured interview protocol was prepared should the nondirective approach falter. As the program proceeded, however, it soon became obvious that such a contingency was unnecessary. Among senior staff people, the retirement of the president and his likely successor was practically the sole subject of their conversation. At the junior staff level, there was far less awareness of the impending change, and the subjects discussed were more varied but typical of those found in other morale-oriented conversations. They did, however, express an unusual number of comments about their present department managers—the current senior staff—and these comments, in turn, proved very valuable in supporting and elaborating the comments from the senior staff themselves.

The questionnaire responses pointed to several organizational strengths and weaknesses that were generally known and acknowledged by the management of the parent company. Other findings, however, came as a surprise and played a major role in the final selection of a new CEO.

> Note: As might be expected, the resulting summary of departmental morale issues had to be held back until a new CEO was named, but a report was prepared and given to the parent company for later feedback and action. That feedback became one of the first actions taken by the newly appointed CEO.

SURVEY RESULTS

The overall survey results did bring to light a noticeably strong point that seemed especially relevant to the selection process—it was the extreme sense of pride the employees took in their company. This was underscored by such comments as, "This company was the first in Mexico to share its profits with employees," "Our president is not afraid to talk to us on his visits," " We are 'numero uno' in Mexico," "I am the second generation of my family to work for Sears. My son will, too."

> The expressed identification with the company by Sears employees, especially those in Latin America, is by no means an empty use of words. It is real and palpable. Nowhere was it better seen than in one of the more serious riots

in Panama during which the Sears store was left untouched. The reason: the stores' Big-Ticket salesmen took guns from the sporting goods department and stood guard outside to protect their store! Obviously they also protected their jobs, but because employees of other stores also had guns and did not do this, the action of Sears people did indeed demonstrate an identification with their company. A similar incident occurred in the Los Angeles Watts riots in which a *lone* security guard voluntarily stayed inside the main door with only a shotgun to protect "his" store.

It also became apparent in interviews that an additional component of employee feelings of identification was the high regard they had for the current president, Mr. Scarborough. These feelings were clearly reflected in the following summary of interview comments about him.

Some of the most positive comments gathered in this survey were those concerning Mr. Scarborough, President of the Mexican Corporation. He was said to be "the great white father" (a reference to his snow-white hair), and was greatly respected and sincerely liked. Although most employees below the level of his immediate staff said they saw him only infrequently, they responded very positively to his warmth and sincere interest in them whenever they did interact with him. Among his extended staff, he was described as a man who delegates well and allows people to carry out assignments without "looking over their shoulders." He apparently enjoyed healthy competition and not only allowed constructive conflict, but actually stirred up a good deal of it among his staff.

What was described as a minor criticism of Scarborough was his "detachment" from the day-to-day operation. (Because many employees were not aware of how seriously ill he had been, that criticism has to be put in perspective.) As a result, information coming to him is said to be filtered and often "softened." More important, because it was recognized that he was a busy man who had to deal with many political, social, and financial problems that obviously extended beyond the internal affairs of the company, there was a reluctance to bring problems to him. On the other hand, he was said to be open and willing to see people when problems occurred and was consistently fair in dealing with them. Both in interviews and questionnaire responses he was seen as a top-flight executive and a very warm human being. The almost glowing attitudes expressed toward Mr. Scarborough actually served to magnify the importance of the survey. Certainly any recommendation it made was bound to strike a sensitive nerve and, in order to preserve the staff's very positive attitude, would have to resonate with their feelings.

As indicated, Sears had three Mexican managers in mind as potential CEO candidates. In order to unobtrusively explore their likely acceptance by the Mexican corporate staff and field employees, two analyses were carried out. The first required comparative analyses of the questionnaire responses made by each candidate's subordinates. This was followed by a summary of relevant interview comments made about each candidate.

Questionnaire Responses

The job satisfaction levels of the employee groups reporting to each of the three candidates are shown in Table 19.1.

The results shown in Table 19.1 indicated rather clearly that employees reporting to Mr. Lopez or to Mr. Weider had roughly equal or above-average levels of satisfaction on all 8 categories included in the questionnaire. The results also showed that the people reporting to a third candidate (identified here only as Mr. X) were less satisfied and had a negative view of the leadership they received from him. Although these results alone suggested an unlikely acceptance of Mr. X among Mexican employees, the accompanying written comments of his direct reports raised even further doubts about his candidacy. In them, he was described as a dictatorial and uncaring manager who led primarily by threats.

In subsequent interviews with his peers an even more disparaging assessment of his executive abilities was offered. The totality of criticisms

TABLE 19.1

Job Satisfaction Levels of Subordinates Reporting
to Each of Three Candidates

| | | Candidates / Centiles | |
Job Satisfaction Scales	Lopez	Weider	Mr. X
Leadership	67	65	30
Work Appeal	70	69	54
Work Demands	51	54	48
Coworkers	70	65	55
Physical Conditions	60	58	62
Career Future	52	54	43
Financial Rewards	61	61	51
Organizational Commitment	90	87	81

leveled at Mr. X not only eliminated any chance that he would be recommended, but raised the obvious question of how he could have been considered as a CEO candidate in the first place. When this same question was in fact raised by the officer who had commissioned the survey, it led to some additional interviews with the international management staff. An approximation to an answer was offered in the following very brief memo that was later sent to the same officer. It may be of interest to students of management:

> Both peers and subordinates pointed to Mr. X's destructive influence on morale and his non-constructive opposition to any suggestions other than his own. While these comments have been covered elsewhere, it is significant that the negative reaction to him by employees came as a surprise to U.S. management. In later discussions, the reasons for this seems clear. His English is impeccable, he dresses very well, makes a very impressive appearance, and in social interactions with U.S. managers, has exhibited a degree of charm. Apparently, most U.S. executives, who spoke little or no Spanish, assumed he made the same impression in Mexico. Ironically, the only reservation Mexican people had in criticizing him was their fear he might actually be promoted to the CEO position some day.

Comment Summaries

The following profiles of the two remaining candidates, based on interview comments about them, were included in the final report to management.

Jorge Lopez

> Mr. Lopez is "Mr. Mexican Executive" to a vast majority of the Mexican Exempt employees. While he was criticized by a few for being egotistical and occasionally harsh, the overwhelming reaction to him is very favorable. Much of this positive reaction seems to be a reflection of the almost symbolic role he plays in the minds of most Mexican employees. Because he came up through the ranks, is very well known to all, and has achieved high stature in the Corporation, he is the one person with whom all Mexican Exempt people seem to identify. On a more concrete level, Lopez is considered to be a very effective executive. He is said to be particularly impressive in his dealings with political and business leaders and thought to be highly regarded in such circles. Within the company he is equally respected, well received and admired. The only serious criticism of Lopez was focused on his tendency to assume too much authority and to exercise it in a rather arbitrary manner. (Again Scarborough's illness has forced Lopez to assume this larger role and may inadvertently account for the perception of this taking

on authority.) As a result, some viewed him as a rather ego-centered person, and some of his direct subordinates and a few field managers react to this occasional aspect of his personality. By far, however, his strengths were seen as outweighing his weaknesses, even among those who criticize him. There is little doubt that he was the most admired, well-liked, and respected member of the Mexican Corporate staff.

Guillermo Weider

Although generally unknown below the staff level in the Corporation, Mr. Weider is considered by those who do know him to be extremely competent and knowledgeable. To these he is looked on as a financial genius. While his main strength is said to be in the financial area, he is considered well versed in the business. As one manager commented, "He is the only Controller I've ever met who thinks like a merchant." At the same time, he is regarded as something of a "poker face" whose appearance and actions create a rather imposing facade, which seems to threaten people.

Paradoxically this facade, which everyone recognizes, is variously interpreted. To some, it is a reflection of his real personality, in that, he is said to consider most people as his inferiors and is rather quick to dismiss or ignore their opinions. He is also said to make decisions with very little concern for the reactions of people affected. To others, Weider's facade is described as misleading. While admitting it is formidable, it is nevertheless only a facade. To these people, he is viewed as a very fine and thoughtful person, possessing a keen sense of humor "once one gets to know him." While it appears Weider is something of an enigma, even to close associates, he is simply unknown to the majority of the Exempt people in Sears Mexico.

Recommendations

Based on all the survey information collected, the following memo was presented to top management:

Comments Regarding Future Leadership of the Mexican Corporation

The subject of a Mexican National succeeding to the presidency is a topic of everyday discussion and frequently raised by senior Mexican staff members in interviews. A large majority expressed great enthusiasm and hope for the idea. It is felt that a Mexican president would be a giant step forward, and its effects on Mexicans at all levels would be extremely positive. It would remove the career ceiling, which most have seen as being below the president's job. It is also seen as a real asset to the company in the political arena, especially in view of the nationalistic spirit, which currently is being supported (sincerely or not) by the new Mexican government. Lastly, as a public relations move, it also has great merit with no apparent drawbacks.

To almost all, however, it was stressed that no Mexican should be made president just because he is Mexican. Only a capable and qualified national should be considered. In this regard, only two names are mentioned: Bill Weider and Jorge Lopez. *None of the other executives is even thought of as a possibility* although several were said to be likely potential candidates in time. Ironically, in spite of the idea's great appeal, the expectation is that Scarborough will not be succeeded by a Mexican.

It should also be noted that among a handful of American managers and a surprising number of Mexican nationals, there is actually some opposition to promoting a Mexican to the presidency "at this time." Among American managers, two objections are raised: it is argued that the Mexican Company is not ready for such a move and that a Mexican would lack the experience and especially the discipline necessary to run the operation. While it is hard to believe that men with the background of Lopez and Weider would not have enough experience, the reservations are expressed rather pointedly. (I have the definite sense that these criticisms were based on very subjective, even biased, views of Mexicans since none of the interviewees could give a concrete example of the weaknesses they say exist.)

The other objections stem mainly from nationals who feel a Mexican president would be much less understanding or sympathetic in his leadership than would a "North American." This may be solely a reflection of their feelings about Scarborough, who is seen as both understanding and "sympatico." His predecessors, on the other hand, were apparently not chosen nor necessarily known for being either.

In spite of their hopes to the contrary, most Mexican executives feel a U.S. national will again be named president and, if so, the hope is *it will not be one who is nearing retirement.* They feel a man should be of such an age that his tour in Mexico would not be his last, but rather, a part of an extended career which would be determined by his performance in Mexico.

This feeling seems to stem from their impression that Scarborough has not been as involved as he might have been at a younger age. As a result, they say a number of recent problems have not reached him, and his previous strong sense of direction has been lacking. While they truly love him, they are aware of this drawback.

My strong recommendation at this time is that Jorge Lopez be appointed to the presidency. He is not without faults, but he is a solid executive who will be warmly received by the staff and employees alike. While Weider is probably more intelligent than any staff person I encountered in all of Latin America, my reservations about him are that he is unknown and would not be the kind of person with whom the Mexican nationals identify (quite the contrary, he seems to "turn them off"). Lastly, while he is a Mexican national, his name is not Mexican, and I am not sure he is even perceived as one. He is relatively young, and should Lopez be appointed to the presidency, he could probably be moved to where his considerable talents could be put to use.

CLOSING NOTE

About a month later, the memo's recommendation was implemented. Lopez's appointment and subsequent performance was such that the parent company established a policy of appointing nationals to the presidency of all of its Latin American subsidiaries.

It is hoped that the reader will agree that the corporate-level decision made here based largely on the survey information was a correct one. It should also be noted that the same information served to prevent what, in all probability, would have been a disastrous selection.

20

A Survey-Driven Supervisory Training Exercise

Information obtained from surveys is frequently incorporated into company training programs. In the present case, the survey staff itself created and conducted a supervisory training program based entirely on information obtained from survey participants. It is presented here as an example of how survey data can be effectively used by managers to tailor training to the needs of their specific departments or organizations.

INTRODUCTION

A frequent function served by surveys is the assessment of training needs. The most cogent of these needs is often found when new programs or major procedural changes are introduced. Initial training in these situations is often quite intense, but tends to drop off as the programs become established and trainers move on to other areas. As new, largely inexperienced people are added, new training needs emerge, and it is often the role of an employee survey to bring these needs to management's attention. Quite a different situation is encountered when training is needed to bring about behavioral changes among long-experienced people who having done the same thing day in and day out and have failed to adjust to new conditions. This is a far more difficult training challenge.

This latter situation was clearly identified by a series of surveys carried out in 1963–1964 within 12 large catalog distribution plants. One of its consistent findings, which became a major management concern, was the growing and open resentment directed toward first-line supervisors and managers. The following are a few examples of this behavior:

- Criticizing employees in front of others,
- Making sarcastic or personal (even ethnic or racially biased) criticisms,
- Playing favorites,
- Picking on and exploiting subordinates' weaknesses,
- Failing to acknowledge good work,
- Acting arbitrarily and discourteously,
- Showing little interest in employee ideas, suggestions, or feelings.

Most supervisors had held their supervisory positions for some time and had been trained and conditioned to a rather harsh style of leadership by "old-school managers." (In one infamous example, a plant manager reprimanded a subordinate manager for having *above average morale* in his department, claiming it was a sign of weak leadership!) The situation became especially frustrating to a new generation of management who had gradually taken over the plants. Their efforts in dealing with a seemingly frozen supervisory style led to a request for "some kind of training." Because the survey program had consistently pointed out the problem, the task of developing a training exercise was assigned to the survey group.

THE SETTING

The 12 plants ranged in size but generally had 50 to 80 mid-level managers and supervisors, almost all of whom had worked in the same plant their entire careers. Although each plant had several college-educated management trainees, the remaining supervisors had relatively limited education. Having risen through the ranks, they felt a special sense of gratitude to the company. They were, in fact, considered by management to be one of the most dedicated groups in the company—dedicated but increasingly difficult.

The work they supervised was hard, tightly scheduled, and largely carried out by younger people who possessed a *somewhat* higher level of education and definitely different attitudes and values. Put simply, the problem was the increasing dissatisfaction of younger employees with their supervisors—a situation they no longer felt obliged to endure.

Because the level of dissatisfaction was increasing and past efforts to improve human relations skills had failed, any thought of traditional lectures or other passive learning techniques was clearly dismissed as inappropriate and certainly unlikely to produce positive change. It was decided, therefore, to create an exercise in which the actual effects of the supervisors' own leadership could be directly experienced by them. This task of designing "some kind of training" of course, runs into the classic problem first raised by

Fleishman (1953) and noted ever since by those involved in human relations training (discussed in chap. 3). Essentially, Fleishman pointed out that training of this kind was likely to be effective only when it was personally acceptable to participants, could be incorporated into their behavior, and supported by the leadership climate they experienced "back on the job." In the present case, the "leadership climate" requirement seemed assured by the commitment made by the newly appointed plant managers. Because they had made the request for a more considerate style of leadership training, their support of it "back on the job" seemed very likely. On the other hand, the personal acceptance of this "new" approach among a group of long service people—thoroughly indoctrinated with a belief in direct, blunt, and uncaring leadership was very doubtful. It was decided, therefore, to meet the challenge head on by including an element of shock! This was accomplished by designing an exercise in which the participants would be abruptly placed in a situation in which they would experience examples of their own negative leadership behavior. Through follow-up discussion they would also be able to see the benefits of a more considerate style.

Aside from its hoped-for shock value, the exercise was in keeping with common behavioral training approaches.

Training Exercise Procedure

The procedure followed in this training exercise was carefully orchestrated in terms of the stages involved, the physical layouts used, and the leadership roles played.

The Stages of the Exercise

The exercise in each plant followed the following plan:

1. Plant management invited all supervisors to a meeting of an undefined purpose.
2. The leader of the exercise was introduced as a headquarters manager who wanted to carry out a working discussion of some company problems.
3. The meeting room was then judged to be too large for discussion purposes (providing an excuse to divide the group into two subgroups). To minimize the presence of a disproportionate number of males or females, or close associates in either subgroup, the division was done randomly by the traditional counting-off procedure. The even numbers were sent to one room and the remainder to another.

4. A leader (again from headquarters) was assigned to each group. In Group One, the leader played a very considerate role in which he avoided any of the objectionable behavior noted in the survey results. In sharp contrast, the leader of Group Two adopted the style of the autocrat and portrayed as many of the identified objectionable behaviors as possible.

5. Each leader had the same task to accomplish in approximately 45 minutes.

6. Each leader distributed a series of business-related questions that were to be discussed and answered by the two groups. To create a realistic situation, the questions involved such things as returned merchandise, its cost, causes, and reduction, as well as some problems dealing with arithmetic calculations, which were said to be a frequent source of error. One calculation was purposely designed as a trick in the hope of eliciting different reactions from each group.

7. To avoid ethical problems, as well as any embarrassment to unsuspecting participants, a shill was employed in Group Two. This was usually a management trainee who volunteered to be the butt of most criticisms and was also directed to play the role in secret and to purposely answer certain questions incorrectly.

The Physical Layout

Each room was approximately the same, and each contained an adequate number of desk chairs. In one room, however the chairs were prepositioned in a classroom arrangement, whereas the other room had an informal semicircular pattern, usually of two or three rows. Each desk had a small ashtray (smoking in such rooms was then a common practice).

The Leader Roles

The leaders were selected for their acting ability. In all meetings, the same two actors were used. For simplicity, the two roles are referred to here as "the good guy" and "the bad guy," the titles later conferred on them by the subjects.

The good guy always entered the room, which had a classroom arrangement. After introducing himself and suggesting that people call him by his first name, he asked that the chairs be rearranged in a more informal manner. He also noted that although ashtrays were on each desk, people were asked not to smoke. The reason given for this was purposely somewhat strained, but plausible: It was explained that the plant had invited visitors from the American Cancer Society who, later in the day, were to conduct a test that required a smoke free room.

The leader then passed around copies of the problems to be reviewed and discussed. Throughout the discussion, a decided attempt was made to do the following:

1. Make sure the obvious resources in the group were utilized by asking women to discuss female-oriented issues such as dresses, and men to answer male-oriented questions concerning hunting goods, and so on.
2. Ask people to offer suggestions.
3. Encourage everyone to participate.
4. Insist that answers or appropriate solutions be reached and seriously presented issues in an attempt to solve problems the company was currently experiencing. This included a series of calculations said to be a source of repeated errors. As indicated, one such calculation was purposely planted as a trick; it simply asked $20 + 10 \times 10 = ?$ The convention is, of course, to multiply before adding so that the correct answer is 120. However, almost everyone, when given this question, simply follows the left to right sequence of adding first then multiplying and obtains an answer of 300. Indeed, in every one of the sessions, the subjects gave an answer of 300. The leader simply explained the proper approach, corrected the participants in a straightforward manner, tried to show how the mistake was made, and assured the subjects that the error was a very common one.

Throughout the session, he was considerate, complimented subjects frequently, tried to explain errors, and avoided any kind of censure.

The bad guy entered the room whose chairs had been arranged in an informal semicircular pattern. After introducing himself as Mr. Hooks, he immediately asked that the chairs be placed in a classroom arrangement for a more "business-like" discussion. He acknowledged the ashtrays but announced that no smoking was allowed—no reason was given. He then passed out the list of problems and simply asked for answers row by row, ignoring the obvious gender or backgrounds differences among the group members. On several occasions, he asked the shill for answers that were predesigned to be erroneous, and, in each case, the leader responded with sarcasm or ridicule such as: "Didn't you learn that in school?" and so on.

Other subjects who gave wrong answers or impractical responses to questions were simply corrected or passed over. With one exception, the leader gave no verbal reward to those who gave correct answers or worthwhile suggestions. He did, however, single out one person in each group (usually a female), whose responses were acknowledged and complimented in a not-too-subtle attempt at favoritism. Throughout the session, he tried to respond to the rest of the group in a direct, impersonal manner and tried to exhibit many of the negative behaviors that had been pointed out in that plant's survey.

The Exercise Sequence

1. Each group worked at the assigned problems for exactly 35 minutes at which point each leader was interrupted and asked to answer an emergency phone call from headquarters. Each leader responded in exactly the same way, "I knew this might happen but thought it would come later. I'll have to take the call, but I'll be back in 5 minutes."
2. Five minutes later each leader returned and continued the discussion for 10 more minutes.
3. At the end of the sessions, both groups re-assembled in the original large room, and the original leader assured them that the whole exercise did involve real problems and that their input was appreciated but that the process was in part, something of a hoax. The subjects were also given an explanation of why the exercise had been carried out, that the actor/leaders had played special roles, and that the shill had been asked to cooperate by being the butt of most criticism.

The original leader then asked a spokesperson from each group to describe the way their group acted and reacted, especially when the leaders left to answer their phone calls. This discussion was usually quite long and as will be explained, produced some significant reactions and insights into leadership and its effects on subordinates.

The leader then went over a few of the questions and solutions the company was said to be interested in and, in closing, gave the traditional answer to the trick calculation problem, simply saying, "Well this one is so simple, we probably shouldn't have included it. The answer is obviously three hundred." This was intended to provoke a response from each group, and as explained below, was very successful in doing so. Because the groups had been seated on opposite sides of the room, it was easy to observe the reactions of each.

Reactions to the Exercise

The following reactions occurred in 11 of the 12 groups:

1. Once the leader left the room,
    a) Smokers in the bad guy group lit up cigarettes! (In one notable exception, no one smoked because all were nonsmokers.)

    b) In the good guy group, no smoker lit a cigarette. (In one ses-
    sion, a smoker attempted to so, but the group stopped him.)
    c) In the bad guy group, people simply spent the time engaged in
    negative comments regarding the leader.
    d) In the good guy group, members continued discussing the
    next problems on their list.

2.   When the re-assembled groups were given the traditional but incorrect answer to the "math" problem,

    a) People in the bad guy group applauded and expressed delight
    that their leader was shown to be wrong.
    b) People in the good guy group protested that the answer
    should be 120 because, as their leader had explained, one has
    to multiply first.
    c) In addition, some very insightful comments demonstrated the
    dynamics at work in each group.

- One management trainee: "When we sat down in our group, I was sitting next to Ted (the shill) who is a friend of mine, but as he kept getting into more and more trouble with Mr. Hooks, I found myself moving my chair as far away from him as I could."
- One female supervisor with 25 years of service: "I really started to hate Mr. Hooks. He reminded me so much of our Mr. X."
- A department manager: "I've got to admit, I do some of the things Hooks did (I mean Mr. Hooks)—not all, but some."
- An unidentified older supervisor: "I think this whole thing is silly," to which several group members responded sarcastically, "you would!"

Because the results were so consistent from group to group, it was possible to discuss their implications with some confidence. For example:

1.   The incident of "smoking behavior" when the leader left the room showed clearly the enduring effects of leader behavior on group discipline.

2. In the case of the good guy group, its members kept working even in the leader's absence. In the course of 35 minutes, he had created a group that functioned *independently* of his physical presence. In the bad guy group, work was done *only* while the leader was present. In his absence the group wasted time by simply complaining about his leadership. In 35 minutes, he had destroyed any sense of cooperation and turned it into resentment.

These implications led to a wide-open discussion and, for the most part, left subjects saying that they had really learned something about "good" and "bad" leadership.

Quantitative Results

Because one of the plants had been surveyed shortly before the training exercise had been conducted, an abbreviated follow-up was conducted to gauge any change. For economic reasons, only a relatively small random sample of employees was used in the follow-up.

The before-and-after IOR centile scores shown in Table 20.1 do show signs of improved attitudes toward supervision. These were statistically significant, although not overwhelming, in practical significance. Moreover, the absence of a control group lessened their interpretive value. At the same time, the fact that attitudes toward supervision did improve, whereas those toward all other IOR categories remained essentially constant, suggests that a small but real change did occur.

The statistical results were somewhat reinforced by plant managers, who were uncharacteristically vocal in their praise of the program, so much so that requests were made to conduct the exercise among new management trainees in each of the company's five territorial offices. Because the trainees represented a more sophisticated audience, there was some concern that

TABLE 20.1

Comparison of Survey Results Obtained Before
and Following Supervisory Training Exercise

| | Centiles | |
	Pre-training (all employees) ($N = 1,216$)	Post-training (sample) ($N = 271$)
IOR Category		
Leadership and Direction	27	38
Work Appeal	31	32
Work Demands	15	17
Physical Surroundings	35	31
Coworkers	45	47
Financial Rewards	40	40
Career Future	31	34

the hoax involved in the exercise would not be successful. The results, how-ever, were amazingly similar to those among plant supervisors.

The program did die, however, as word about the good guy–bad guy hoax spread. Without this surprise element, the exercise lost any impact. It might be added, the "bad guy" (Mr. Hooks) was really a "good guy" and went on to become a senior vice president where his acting skills were used construc-tively, or at least it has been so reported!

Although the evidence that this particular exercise had a lasting effect is only modest, it never-the-less did have a positive impact. Its inclusion here, however, was to demonstrate one novel way in which survey data can go be-yond assessment of training needs and can contribute to the development of training content that reflects very specific needs.

It might be added that the exercise reported here occurred some time ago (1963–1964) and may have foreshadowed later trends in realistic training in the management of human relations.

21

The Survey's Role
in a Federal Court Case

This chapter describes a special application of survey results. It involved the telling use of survey data in the longest discrimination case in federal court history. Because the survey data were collected almost a decade before the case finally came to trial, they served to document conditions in the company that were contemporaneous with the original charges of discrimination.

This summary may also be a lesson to managers who may one day be called to participate in a courtroom as a defendant or expert witness. To make those lessons as clear as possible, relevant parts of the court records are included.

In 1973, the Equal Opportunity Commissioner, on his last day in office, charged Sears and four other companies with every form of employment discrimination except religious discrimination. Sears alone, in view of its formidable equal employment efforts, decided to fight. Over a period of years, every charge but one was dropped, and *12 years* later, in 1985, Sears went to court to contest the one remaining charge: that it had discriminated against women in hiring or promoting them to high paying commission (big ticket) sales jobs.

Although at the time the author was no longer a Sears executive, he was called on as an expert witness in a long deposition and on even longer trial testimony and, later, rebuttals to present and explain the Sears survey program and its data from years of experience. Among other things, the data clearly showed a decided lack of interest among female employees in Big-Ticket selling—a high paying and highly competitive job that traditionally, but not exclusively, had been held by males. Although the EEOC argued with part of the survey testimony, almost all of it was uncontested, and

229

no evidence to the contrary was produced. This part of the case was more or less easy. The "fun" began when an earlier special study (conducted by the author) was actually presented as evidence against the Company.

THE SURVEY PROCEDURE

In 1976, as part of its defense, Sears requested a quick and informal study of noncommission saleswomen to determine their degree of interest in Big-Ticket selling. The purpose of the study was to give Sears an approximation of its likely back-pay liability in the improbable event that the case would go to trial and Sears might lose. Because the study was intended to give only an approximation, a series of structured group interviews seemed the best approach because this would allow for a probing of employee interest. To this end, a judgment sample of noncommission salespeople in approximately 24 stores was selected. (The decision to use a judgment sample was based on the fact that a quick response was needed and on the confident belief based on years of dealing with Sears employees that women throughout Sears had a decided distaste for "Big-Ticket" jobs.)

The study, referred to here as the Job Interest Survey or JIS, was simple in design but carefully executed by professionally trained territorial survey administrators. It involved a brief protocol and questionnaire, including an introduction and instructions that were read aloud by the administrators and then given to each subject to complete. In total, 502 noncommission salespeople (104 males and 398 females) in 27 stores were selected. This questionnaire included both a generalized and a tailored description of big-ticket selling. Because the Big-Ticket Job covered a broad array of assignments, the description first listed the characteristics common to all such assignments and was followed by a list of the special requirements, one or more of which might apply to some of the Big-Ticket Jobs, but not all. Employees were then asked to rate the accuracy of the description and to indicate their degree of interest in the job.

Because the study was intended only to give an estimate of the company's possible liability, it was felt that if it erred at all, it should be in overestimating that liability. As a result, the job description offered was intended to be accurate, as well as attractive, while at the same time recognizing that almost all Sears employees knew what a Big-Ticket Job was. In view of the attempt to make the description of the Big-Ticket Job as attractive as possible within the limits of accuracy, it came as a surprise to Sears, and later to the federal judge, that the EEOC attacked the job description as being strongly biased in the other direction, as discouraging female interest in the job.

After reading the description of Big-Ticket selling and agreeing that it was accurate (as 94% said it was), participants in the study were then asked about their interest in such a job assignment. The results clearly indicated that, at that time (1976), the overwhelming majority of women had little or no interest in such an assignment.

Because this was only one of scores of special studies the survey group had been asked to conduct on various subjects, the results were simply presented to management and were then more-or-less forgotten. It came as a great surprise when, 9 years later, this simple, small study became a very significant piece of evidence in the court case. (The moral here for clients is never throw away any data.) As it turned out, the EEOC had no evidence of its claimed female interest in Big-Ticket selling at the time of its original charge. In view of this, and the fact that the JIS study represented documented contemporary evidence of female lack of interest in Big-Ticket selling, its results took on heightened importance, and the EEOC spent a good deal of time and effort in attacking the study and its findings. In fact, in their zeal to attack the study, the EEOC resorted to a form of subterfuge.

(Some time ago, the comedian Don Adams acted out a skit in which he played an attorney addressing a jury. It went something like this: "Ladies and gentlemen of the jury: It's easy for my opponent the District Attorney to charge my client with all sorts of crimes—he's got proof! All I've got is trickery and deceit." At the time, this seemed a funny and innocent skit but it took on a less humorous tone when something very much like it was experienced in a Federal Courtroom!)

Excerpts from actual court testimony, tedious as they are at times, best show how this form of "subterfuge" proceeded. It centered on an EEOC effort to prove that the sample in the JIS study actually included people who were not noncommission salespeople in spite of Sears' insistence that they were. The "trap" was prepared in this way:

> MRS. B: *(attorney for EEOC)* Now, Dr. Smith, Sears, as you know, has indicated that there were twenty-two people who administered this survey who weren't non-commission salespeople.
> A. No, that's not correct.
> Q. It's not correct?
> A. Not in my book. As far as I'm concerned, all the people in the survey were non-commission salespeople or could be considered such.
> Q. And you're saying that anybody who was an assistant division manager you consider to be a non-commission salesperson.
> A. That's right.

Q.   Okay. Now, just a second, please. However, you don't con-
     sider division managers to be the same?
A.   No, I do not.
Q.   Wig consultants?
A.   I would think that a wig consultant would be classified as a
     non-commission salesperson, yes.
Q.   Okay. If it were demonstrated to you that there were people
     who took this survey who were other than non-commission
     salespeople even under your own definition, you would con-
     sider that to be error in the survey, would you not, in the
     administration of the survey?
A.   I'd really like to have some specifics before I answer. I think
     generally what you're saying is right.

Later, the following testimony occurred after numerous exchanges on
technical points between lawyers and the court:

Q.   Let me just say, the whole point, Dr. Smith, is not to have
     you admit that any of these individuals is anything at this
     time but rather to talk to you about what happens if sub-
     stantial number [sic] of people who were surveyed are not
     what they were supposed to be. And toward that end, if we
     could look at Plaintiff's Exhibit 7 ID.
     Basically, what I'm presenting these for is to say let's assume
     hypothetically that these represent persons who are not
     non-commission salespeople, okay.
     My first question to you is, speaking hypothetically, if there
     are 23 males out of 104 who were not non-commission
     salespeople, you divide 23 by 104 and obtain 22 percent of
     the males were not in the appropriate group.
     Now, speaking hypothetically, if 22 percent of those persons
     who you surveyed really weren't what they were supposed to
     be, does that affect the validity of your survey results at all?
A.   Yes, I think it would.
Q.   It would affect the confidence with which you could look at
     this survey as representative of the attitudes of the group
     that was supposed to be surveyed.

Thus the "trap" was set in having gotten agreement that "hypothetically"
should a significant portion of the sample consist of people who were misclassified—were something other than noncommission salespeople—the
results would have little validity.

Later in the trial, after pages of testimony on other survey data, the "trap"
turned from the hypothetical to the real, as the EEOC attorney presented an
exhibit taken from Sears own payroll tapes. It included the names and job titles of a large group of participants in the JIS study who were not noncommission people! What happened next is both instructive but frightening to a

witness—having been presented with information that seemingly showed significant misclassification of subjects and having already admitted that this would nullify the study.

Fortunately, during a long lunch break, a check of data processing records revealed the truth and exposed the subterfuge involved. Instead of using an August payroll tape, which would have shown the job titles of participants at the time of the study, the EEOC had used a later tape from December, which indicated that the named employees had been promoted or moved to other jobs in the interim. In other words, by using a later tape but implying that it covered the earlier period, the EEOC lawyer attempted to prove by trickery what she could not prove otherwise. Had those tapes not been properly identified, the trickery would have worked.

After the discovery of the false tape ruse, the Sears attorney could hardly contain herself, as she very professionally administered the "coup de grace." It proceeded as follows:

MS. EASTMAN: (attorney for Sears) Your Honor, I have here an exhibit, which is marked Sears Smith 6. It is a copy, a Xerox copy, of two pages provided to us by the EEOC and contains a list of the names that the EEOC provided to us the other night of people that they say were inappropriately included.

THE COURT: Okay.

MS. EASTMAN: Your Honor, if I may represent to you that Dr. Smith and I consulted with Washington in the interim since this subject came up and have been given certain information off of computer printouts. Dr. Smith, of course, cannot testify to his own knowledge about the content of the computer printouts, but if I may represent that our statistical witnesses will, if necessary, move the actual admission of this document and vouch for the information about which I'm going to question Dr. Smith and ask him to assume that it's true for the moment, if that's all right.

THE COURT: All right. You may proceed.

BY MS. EASTMAN: Now, Dr. Smith, turning your attention first to the first page of this exhibit. According to the EEOC, there are five people [listed here] who were erroneously included in the survey because they, in fact, were commission sales persons on the December year-end payroll tape; is that correct?

A.   Correct. Right.

Q.   Now, if I were to represent to you that all five of them (who she then named) had been promoted to commission sales according to the December tape after the date of the JIS survey, would you consider them to have been improperly included in the survey?

A.   Certainly not. They were full-time, non-commission salespeople at the time of the survey.

And so it went. In groups of five, the entire list of people who the EEOC claimed were misclassified were shown to have been properly classified *at the time of the study.*

So Much for Trickery and Deceit!

This case also demonstrated some other lessons that have nothing to do with "trickery." In fact, it demonstrated the opposite—the fate of a well-intended and thoroughly competent expert witness called by the EEOC who was simply ill prepared by the government attorneys. For those readers who may one day be called as an expert witness, the following account may underscore the need for extensive preparation.

> MRS. B: (attorney of EEOC) Now let's change topics for a moment, Dr. P. (the EEOC expert witness—unidentified in this account). In your written testimony, you discuss the 1976 Job Interest Survey conducted by Sears and reported by Dr. Frank Smith and Sandra Hagerty as a measurement of non-commission salespersons' interest in commission sales, correct?
>
> A. Yes.
>
> Q. Now, what is your professional opinion concerning use of the results from this survey?
>
> A. I believe that the results from the survey should not be relied on because the survey is untrustworthy in three major respects.
>
> Q. And what are those three major respects?
>
> A. They are the sample design, that is, the way the sample was drawn; the way the questionnaire was worded in certain respects; and the way the questionnaire was administered.

He then went on for some 30 pages of testimony, elaborating on each of his three objections to the study. It is interesting to note that almost everything he said would have been correct had his *assumptions* about the study and the *information* given him by the EEOC also been correct. They were not!

After a brief written rebuttal had been entered into the record explaining the actual facts of the case, all three of his objections to the study had to be retracted. Again, a sample of the actual, although tedious, process by which the retractions were obtained is presented here.

> MR. COHEN: (attorney for Sears) Dr. P., I'd like to hand you a document that's been marked Sears Smith Rebuttal Exhibit 1 and ask you to read the first two paragraphs. Have you had an opportunity to read the first two paragraphs, sir?
>
> A. Yes.
>
> Q. Have you read these two paragraphs before?
>
> A. Yes.

Q.   Now, I take it, Dr. P., that you would concede that had you understood Dr. Smith's testimony at trial to be the same as written in Paragraphs one and two, that you would not have called the procedure highly abnormal. Would you have, sir?

A.   What I was referring to as highly abnormal was what I read at trial.

Q.   Let me try to ask you more precisely, Dr. P. If Dr. Smith had stated the substance of what's in these two paragraphs at trial, you would not have called the procedure highly abnormal, would you have?

A.   That depends on whether or not he also would have said what he did say at trial.

Q.   Dr. P., I'd like you to assume that all Dr. Smith said about the administration of the survey in terms of how the respondents interacted with the administrators was what is written in the first two paragraphs of Sears' Smith Rebuttal Exhibit 1. Do you understand that?

THE COURT: As I understand the question, he is asking the witness to focus on this testimony and not consider anything else. And then he is going to ask questions about that testimony.

MR. COHEN: That's correct, your Honor.

BY MR. COHEN: Do you understand that, Dr. P?

A.   Under those circumstances, I would not have arrived at the judgment that the procedure was abnormal.

Q.   Thank you. Dr. P., I understand that you are familiar with Sears' morale survey program. Are you not?

A.   To a very limited extent.

Q.   You went to the library and looked up some of Dr. Smith's articles to try to find some material to use here at trial, did you not?

A.   That is correct.

Q.   And I take it you didn't find anything. Is that correct?

A.   That is correct.

Q.   Now, Dr. P., you understand that this survey, the Job Interest Survey, was conducted in a manner that was extremely similar to the way Sears had conducted other surveys, is that correct?

A.   That is not my understanding.

Q.   It's not your understanding. Now, you said that you were referring to one little qualification that you had with respect to your opinion that you wouldn't have called the procedure highly abnormal. And I take it that you're referring to Dr. Smith's rebuttal testimony where he says that the administrators read the first paragraph on the survey instrument. Is that correct?

A.   No. It's then read on the second page containing the definition of commission sales.

Q.   You understand that they didn't read the second page—or I'm asking you to assume that they didn't read the second page until they had the survey respondents have an opportunity to fill out the first.

A. I'm sorry. I misunderstood.
Q. So you were referring that it was unusual for the survey ad-
    ministrators to have read the description of big-ticket sell-
    ing that appears on page 2, is that what you mean?
A. I initially thought that what was being said here was that
    they read that before they filled out page 1.
Q. That's not what it says though.
A. That's my understanding.
Q. So you take back your former comments, is that correct?
A. Yes.

By this laborious process, all three objections to the study were retracted. It
gets worse.

This time, the same expert witness was simply wrong in his facts, so much
so that his testimony actually provoked a series of challenges from the court.
In this instance, the expert witness was very critical of the description of the
Big-Ticket Job that had been included in the Job Interest Survey. That description is presented here to make the subsequent interchange clear:

The following characteristics apply to all Big-Ticket jobs:

1. Opportunity for high earnings,
2. Professionally challenging work, requiring detailed product knowledge,
3. Some evening or weekend hours,
4. Aggressive selling—reaching out to customers.

Some of the following characteristics may apply to one or more Big-
Ticket jobs.

1. Customer in-home visits,
2. Peaks and valleys in earnings,
3. Specialized or technical knowledge of such things as:
       a) Credit policies
       b) Service schedules
       c) Proposal development
       d) Local building codes
       e) Preparation of cost estimates

After a fairly long discussion and critique of this definition, the EEOC attorney got to a question *of sorts*:

BY MS. B: Now, I want to ask you, how could somebody agree with
            [the] definition given of commission sales in question two
            of that survey and also be biased and affected in a response
            they give in question three as a result of question two.
            Could you explain that?

A.   Well, I can use an analogy that I used in the deposition that may be helpful in this case. If you are in the travel agent business and you want to assess interest in traveling to the Caribbean islands, let's say, you may provide a description of what Caribbean islands are to people in your market. And if you do that, it seems to me if you want to know about Caribbean islands in general, you would talk about features that all Caribbean islands have—a certain kind of climate, beaches, and so on. You could also say that some Caribbean islands have Marxist–Leninist government that is unfriendly to the United States, and others have lots of gambling. Not all have, but it is true that some do. If you did that, then I think it is likely that what you would be doing would be biasing people's responses. You would have a less good measure. As I say it to you—

THE COURT: You can only say positive things and not negative things.

THE WITNESS: No, not at all. Not the difference between positive and negative, but just something shared by all the islands. So you can say that all the islands have a lower standard of living than in the United States because it is true for all the islands. If you say some of them have casinos and then you asked them, now, would you [have] been interested in visiting a Caribbean island, there would be some people who likely would be affected by the presence of some characteristics that they would prefer not to have on a vacation. And so, if what you wanted to do is measure interest in going to the Caribbean, I think it would be a real mistake to mention characteristics that only some such islands have. It seems—

THE COURT: You don't want then to really know what the situation is because you are artificially limiting the knowledge that they are going to have. I don't understand your point at all.

THE WITNESS: Well, my point is that all Caribbean islands have a certain kind of climate, and presumably, it is important to communicate—

THE COURT: You are assuming that all the islands are exactly the same. They are not all the same. I don't see what your point is.

THE WITNESS: No, of course not. They all have swimming weather in the winter. Every single island in the Caribbean you can go swimming in the winter.

THE COURT: You are saying the temperature is roughly the same—

THE WITNESS: Exactly.

THE COURT: But the islands are not all the same.

THE WITNESS: Of course. If you want—

THE COURT: You don't want people to go to an island where they are furious once they get there because they didn't want to go to a place like that.

THE WITNESS: No, no.

THE COURT: That is not the way a travel agent would operate any more than a company would operate in dealing with its employees. I don't understand the point. If you want to go into it further.

BY MS. B: Let's break it up. If you wanted to find out who would be interested in going to an island that had casinos, how would you ask the question?

A.   You would describe the fact that there were casinos on the island.

Q.   If you wanted someone to go to an island that—if you wanted to find out how many people wanted to go to an island that had a Marxist–Leninist dictatorship, how would you ask?

A.   You would refer to the Marxist–Leninist dictatorship.

Q.   If you wanted to find out how many people wanted a warm place to go swimming in the winter, which is something all have in common, how would you ask that?

A.   You would refer simply to the warm climate and the swimming.

Q.   If you wanted to find out who wanted to go to a warm climate and go swimming on an island in the winter, would you ask here's a place where you can go in the winter, it has a warm climate and it also has gambling. Would that elicit the response, who wants to go swimming on an island?

THE COURT: I don't understand the whole point of all this. Why wouldn't you tell people exactly what they would expect or what they would experience if they go to these places. If you are talking about the method of giving information to people, that is one thing, but if you are talking about limiting the information you give to people, that is where you lose me, and that is the way it is coming across to me.

MS. B: Your Honor, that is not how it is intending to come across at all.

THE COURT: If you are talking about the form of the explanation, that is something I can understand, but I don't think your questions are getting to the form. And I don't think, by the way, gambling necessarily scares people away. It attracts some people and might repel others. It is true of almost everything, and I am just finding great difficulty in finding what is the argument or conclusion that you seek to draw from.

MS. B: Perhaps, Dr. P., we should leave aside the explanation—

THE COURT: I understand the point that he is making. I think that apart from the substance, which I have great difficulty with because I don't think it is fair to people to induce them to move into a job or it turns out that that job is not what they thought it was and they are not successful and it may either destroy their career or psyche or whatever, I really think people ought to know exactly where they are going before they are asked to go there. So, insofar as knowledge is concerned, if that is the substantive of the thing, that is a problem for me.

The testimony went on in this vein for another 10 pages and left the judge baffled.

SUMMARY

As to the entire 9-month-long court case, it should be noted that the survey data played a small but significant role. This seems clear in the judge's written opinion: "Sears presented detailed, un-contradicted evidence showing the company had actually recruited women to work as commission salespeople *despite surveys which showed that women were less interested than men in commission selling.*" Because the EEOC had no witnesses to testify to any kind of the alleged discrimination, the survey data was very important contemporary evidence and refuted what turned out to be EEOC guesses as to female job interests—guesses formulated long after the charge was made.

Sears won the case and, later, its appeal. At last count, Sears had been awarded over $22,000,000 in legal fees. Regardless of its outcome, however, the relevant lesson it has for expert witnesses on either side of an issue is to be prepared and speak only of what you know for certain. Any evidence presented will be questioned by other experts, and that is as it should be. Lawyers will present their side as strongly as they can and that, too, is as it should be. However, it is best to be prepared for "trickery," a la Don Adams, although that is not as it should be.

Appendix A

Technical Documentation: Steps in the Development of the *Index of Organizational Reactions* (IOR) Questionnaire

The scales of the IOR originated in the early 1960s and were initially encouraged by the then "landmark" factor analytic work of Wherry (1954). His factor analysis of the 14 scales of the Science Research Associates (SRA) Survey were particularly helpful in that these scales, in modified form, had been used in Sears for almost a decade (1950–1959).

In addition to a general satisfaction factor, Wherry identified four group factors: (a) Working conditions (b) Financial rewards (c) Supervision, and (d) Effective management and administration.

These four factors were taken as a base but were expanded for several reasons. First, Wherry's study was based only on the 14 categories rather than the 80 or so items of the SRA instrument. It was felt that his fourth factor could be better defined and perhaps expanded. Second, the SRA questionnaire did not cover topics such as work appeal, career futures, and company identification in the depth desired by Sears. As a result, additional potential scales were added to those clearly defined by Wherry. Given this base, several hundred items were selected or created to measure eight conditional scales.

Note: It should be noted that by the time the *core scales* had been reasonably developed, a highly reliable and well tested measure of job satisfaction:

(The Job Description Index [JDI], Smith, Kendall, & Hulin [1969]) had become available. Although some thought was given to adopting the JDI as an alternative to the Sears *core scales*, management opted to continue work on the IOR whose items were written in more explicit behavioral terms. At the same time, the excellent psychometric qualities of the JDI have been demonstrated over a long time span (see e.g., Kinicki et al., 2002). As such, it has been an important standard in the continued testing of the IOR.

Aside from numerous traditional item analyses, other reliability and validity studies were carried out internally and in cooperation with academic colleagues:

1. Reliability was estimated for each by traditional item-total scale correlations. Some of the early data were reported by Smith (1962) and later by Hulin (1966). Still later, reliability estimates were given by Dunham, Smith, and Blackburn (1977).

2. Factor analytic studies were also included in the work of Dunham et al. (1977). It involved five separate factor analyses among five diverse groups of employees ($N = 12,671$). It indicated that seven of the eight originally proposed scales represented stable factors. The exception, "Company Identification" scale proved factorially complex. The factorial structure of the IOR was also later examined by Goffin and Jackson (1988) using a completely different population. Their results strongly endorsed the factorial structure of all eight scales.

3. The convergent validity of the IOR was first noted by Hulin (1966) and both convergent and discriminant validities were determined by Dunham et al. (1977) and later confirmed by McCabe, Delessio, and Sasaki (1980). A modest extension of the IOR's discriminant validity was carried out among 120 employees who volunteered to complete the IOR scales along with eight scales of the Guilford-Martin Personality Inventory. Although two personalities did show significant correlations with total IOR scores, "Sociability and Cooperativeness" (.33 and .35 respectively), neither was taken as a challenge to the discriminant validity of the IOR. Recalled many years later, however, these correlations did seem to lend some support to the notion of a dispositional contribution to job satisfaction, most recently summarized by Judge and Larsen (2001).

4. The predictive validity of the IOR was shown in three separate studies. They involved the link between IOR results and: customer satisfaction, (chap. 5), employee absenteeism, Smith (1977) and in unionization (Hamner & Smith, 1978).

5. The foreign language adaptability of the IOR was established (that is, an equivalent Spanish language version was developed) in a study of

bilingual subjects by Katerburg, Smith, and Hoy (1977) and its results were confirmed by McCabe et al. (1980).

6. A brief and fairly favorable evaluation of the early research on the
   IOR and its applications can be seen in that by Cook, Hepworth,
   Wall, & Warr (1981).

Note: It is hoped that the 21st century reader will appreciate that some of
the early work on the IOR was limited by the use of very primitive data processing equipment (in some cases hand operated). That the aims and methods used are still in vogue, however, can perhaps be seen in an excellent and
comprehensive treatment of scale construction, in modern dress, by Stanton,
Balzer, Smith, Parra and Ironson (2001).

Appendix B

A Guide to Nondirective Interviewing

The following guide was originally designed as an informal instructional manual for employees who were selected to be members of a survey team. Because readers may be interested in this type as training, or may find an application for it in their own organization, the manual is presented in its original form. It should be noted, however, the techniques presented have very general applicability and can be readily transferred to almost any situation.

The type of interviewing discussed here is known as *employee-centered* or *nondirective*. It is based on the notion that interviewers do not know in advance what the employees being interviewed feel about their jobs or which facets of their work are seen as important. Interviewers obtain this information primarily by being listeners, and by accepting employee attitudes, feelings, and beliefs without judging their value or correctness. The following discussion is intended to equip you with a working knowledge of the employee-centered interviewing technique.

Each interview has three segments: the beginning, the body, and the ending. Each of these segments has its own purposes and should be handled in a special way. This manual describes the purposes and methods for each of these three phases of the interview.

THE BEGINNING OF THE INTERVIEW

Purpose

To start employees talking by:

- Putting them at ease. Interviewers accomplish this primarily by being friendly, interested, and sincere,
- Assuring them that what they say will be kept strictly confidential,
- Defining their role for them. That is, interviewers tell them that the interview is being held so that they can talk about whatever is important to them in their jobs.

The Introduction

People may come to an interview situation feeling a little tense and uneasy. It may be the first time they've participated and they may not know what to expect. The purpose of the introduction is to relieve whatever uncertainty and uneasiness employees may have.

On an intellectual level, a standard introduction is an attempt to inform employees of the interview's intent, who the interviewer is, and what ground rules it will follow. On an emotional level, the introduction is aimed at alleviating any anxiety that employees may feel in an unfamiliar situation. Relieving this kind of anxiety can be done in a variety of ways, but the quickest and easiest of these is to display genuine friendliness. That is, the interviewer should greet employees warmly and should invite them to sit down and be comfortable. Additionally, an interviewer should consistently introduce the session in a way that indicates a sincere interest in helping employees understand what the whole process is about. Despite the fact that the interviewer may have to repeat the introduction many times to many people, it is important to remember that individual employees will hear it only once. It is essential they receive the same orientation as that given to others.

These seemingly simple steps and gestures serve to let employees know that they are recognized as people whose opinions and attitudes have value and will be accepted for their own sake. These gestures also encourage employees to accept interviewers for what they are—representatives of the company who are sincerely interested in listening to their feelings and attitudes about their jobs.

One way of introducing the session is suggested here:

I'm ____ . As you probably were told, the questionnaire that was given here recently was the first part of a survey that's being conducted and this interview is the second part. The interview is really all yours and I'm interested in anything you would like to talk about. I don't have any questions to ask, and I will be happy to listen to anything you care to discuss. I want to assure you that whatever you say is strictly confidential. I'm not interested in identifying you personally. I merely add up all the comments I receive and make my report on the group as a whole.

THE BODY OF THE INTERVIEW

Purpose

1. To encourage employees to talk about their feelings, attitudes and opinions, about their jobs,
2. To help them express their thoughts fully and clearly,
3. To explore the solutions that employees propose to organizational problems.

Methods

I. *Behavioral stimulation*
    a. listening
    b. nodding the head & smiling
II. *Verbal stimulation*
    a. showing acceptance
    b. the repeat
    c. probing statements
    d. interpretive statements
    e. the pause

Behavioral Stimulation

The interviewer's own actions and behavior can encourage employees to express attitudes, ideas, and feelings.

Obvious Listening

Most people want to be taken seriously. Consequently, an interviewer should communicate a sincere interest in what an employee is saying. Employees who perceive that their comments are holding the attention of the interviewer will be prompted to freely express their thoughts.

Appearing to be interested is difficult when you don't feel this way! Consequently, the intent to listen is an essential precondition to effective interviewing. This is not always easy. After several interviews, the same topics may begin to appear in employee comments. It would be a mistake, however, to assume, "Oh, I've heard this before." Because some employees may present a new viewpoint on a familiar topic—they may see a subject from a different vantage point—it is best for an interviewer to assume an almost naïve attitude toward each interview, as if everything is being heard for the first time.

Employees should be allowed to talk without being interrupted. When a comment seems to call for an explanation or clarification, interviewers should wait for a thought to be completed before probing. It is essential to remember that interviewers who appear anxious to interject their views usually alienate employees and invariably limit the interview.

The Nod and the Smile

By displaying genuine interest in what is being said, a basic rapport can be established that will further encourage openness. Such encouragement, however, is usually required periodically throughout the interview. By nodding when an idea is expressed, an interviewer indicates that he or she understands the employee's comments.

By the same token, an occasional smile from interviewer is also reassuring. It is an indication of the sympathetic acceptance.

Verbal Stimulation

Because this type of interviewing is devoted to exploring employee opinions about their work and their organization, no attempt is made to force or direct their comments. Rather every attempt should be made to provide them with an opportunity to express their views freely and confidentially. The listening techniques can be thought of as a form of verbal "judo" in which employee comments are responded to only by way of encouraging their further elaboration.

Because some employees are inclined to talk freely, their interviews proceed smoothly with only occasional behavioral stimulation needed from interviewers. In most cases, however, verbal stimulation will aid the process and will help keep employees talking. These are statements that accept, repeat, probe, or interpret employees' comments.

Showing Acceptance

The following kinds of statements indicate the interviewer understands what has been said. These statements can be used in the natural flow of any exchange. They include comments such as "um-hum," or "That's interesting," or "I see." The use of such simple statements not only shows that an interviewer is listening and accepts what has been said, but encourages the individual to continue.

The Repeat

The repeat is probably the most frequently used verbal stimulation technique in employee-centered interviewing and generally requires a bit of practice to perfect. In this technique, the interviewer repeats the employee's words or phrase in a slightly questioning tone. The repeat can be used in many situations, but it is particularly helpful when the employee (a) shows strong feelings toward a subject but may appear reluctant to discuss it; (b) "rambles" about subjects unrelated to the work situation; or (c) asks what other people have said in their interviews.

- The employee shows strong feeling toward a subject. Employees sometimes mention topics and then drop them. Interviewers can encourage elaboration of these feelings by using the repeat. For example, after a very brief pause, interviewer repeats the employee's own words to them (or their exact meaning) with a slightly questioning, nonjudgmental tone.
  Caution: When using the repeat, do not misquote employees. If an employee says, "They should do a better job of handling pay here," do not interpret this to mean, "You say they don't pay well here?" Misquoting will be heard as an accusation or a rejection, and whatever rapport that has been established may be nullified.
- The employee rambles. The interviewer may also use the repeat with an employee who rambles. Rambling is very common in survey interviews for various reasons:

  1. People do not know what to say or how to start. As a result they say the first thing that comes to mind and just continue with it.
  2. Some people may not wish to discuss pertinent material until they are certain that the interviewer is a person they can trust. They may ramble in order to see how the interviewer will react.
  3. They are apprehensive. Some employees wish to avoid talking about critical situations because they fear that they may put their jobs in jeopardy. Instead, they may talk about a number of subjects, which may be unrelated to their work.
  4. They may simply be talkative people who naturally jump from one subject to another.

When an employee rambles, listen very carefully. In most cases, through the selective use of the "repeat" you will be able to focus attention on the most pertinent subjects. For example:

> Emp: ... and I came to work here about three years ago ... I've worked at a number of places but this is probably the best ... I always get along with everybody and I like all kinds of work ... I've done just about everything there is to do from driving a school bus to janitoring to selling, and as I say, I like them all.
>
> Int: I think I understand how you feel. You mentioned that you like all kinds of work but *this is probably the best?*
>
> Emp: Oh yes, it's more steady, the working conditions are better and it's cleaner.

In the above example, the employee rambles a bit but does comment about his present work. The interviewer waits until the employee pauses and then repeats the comment in a mildly questioning manner. This repeat usually brings an employee back to discussing his or her job situation.

- The employee asks what other people have said in their interviews. Occasionally, employees question interviewers about the comments that coworkers have made. Sometimes this is merely a way of trying to get the interviewers to assure them that they are not making inappropriate remarks. Or, employees may merely want to test interviewers to see whether the results of the survey are really confidential. On the other hand, they may only be making idle conversation. In the following example, the interviewer reassures the employee that survey results are confidential but uses the inquiry to direct the discussion back to those things that are important to the worker and relevant to the job situation.

> Emp: ... but our division needs to be reorganized. Mr. Werner isn't very efficient, although he does work hard. Haven't some of the others told you that?
>
> Int: I can understand why you'd want to know what the other employees have said, but as you know, these interviews are confidential and I really can't discuss them.
>
> Emp: Oh yes, I guess that's right.
>
> Int: (Pause) You were saying that although Mr. Werner works very hard, he's not very efficient. Could you tell me a little bit more about that?
>
> Emp: Well, mainly I meant the way he never seems to plan anything. Most of the time he makes a decision about what he wants or how he wants it done at the last minute. We never have time to get ready for anything.

- The repeat doesn't work. As you may be well aware, no technique is foolproof. Occasionally, the use of the repeat may backfire. Whenever this occurs, it is important to try again, as the following example illustrates.

>Emp: ... had the store just about 1 year so they've given us very nice working conditions.
>Int: Um-hum.
>Emp: This store pays as good as any place in town, but this area has a very low salary scale.
>Int: You say the store pays as good as any place in town, but that the area has a low salary scale?
>Emp: Well, that's what I said.
>Int: I'd be interested in your reasons for feeling this way.
>Emp: Well, I think it's because it's a resort town and lots of people ...

The Probing Statement

This technique is especially effective when used in an accepting manner that conveys an interest in having the conversation continue. It is frequently used when employees:

1. Generalize,
2. Express contradictory opinions,
3. Merely mention a topic, without giving any details,
4. Fail to identify the people or topic being discussed,
5. Question the value of the survey,
6. Ask if employees will be informed about the results of the survey,
7. Question the interviewer about the company policy or procedures,
8. Try to interview the interviewer,
9. Ask about the confidential nature of the survey,
10. Ask the interviewer for advice.

- The employee generalizes. Employees often are unaware that their comments may be completely new to the interviewer. As a result, they may refer to things metaphorically and only touch on very important points. Whenever this occurs, it is the interviewer's responsibility to use any of the techniques to obtain more specific information, which will clarify and "translate" metaphors into on-the-job behavioral terms.

>Emp: ... we had a Division Manager come in. He was new and during the first few days changes were really made. You should see how they affected the group. In my years here I've had several changes like that, but never with such an effect.

Int: I see. You say that during the first few days some changes
        were made?
Emp: They sure were. Things were really tough.
Int: Could you tell me about some of the changes, which took
        place?
Emp: Well, there were a lot of them. First of all, he rescheduled all of
        the passes and lunch hours and if that wasn't enough he …

In this example, the employee states that changes were made that affected
the work group. In order to understand what the changes were, the interviewer
uses the repeat and follows it up with a probing statement. The combination of
two techniques prompts the employee to clarify the initial statement.

- The employee makes contradictory statements. Whenever this happens, the interviewer should encourage the employee to discuss the
  comments that need clarification. The following example demonstrates
  how this might be done.

Emp: We've been so busy in our department that I even forget to
        take my pass sometimes. But I really like to work here be-
        cause I feel no one is particularly pushing me to get things
        done. Sometimes, though, you have to hunt for work and
        things to do when the big bosses walk through because
        we've been told to look busy.
Int: You say that you are so busy in your department that you
        sometimes forget to take your pass. Then later, I think you
        stated that you sometimes have to hunt for work and things
        to do. Did I understand you correctly?
Emp: That's right. When the mail comes in we have to break our
        backs, but then other times we worry that someone will
        come in and see us when there's a lull in the mail.

In probing and repeating, the interviewer should not risk antagonizing an
employee by appearing to challenge. Rather, a comment should be explored
in a way that accepts the contradiction as simply a natural misunderstanding on the part of the interviewer.

- The employee merely mentions a problem. Occasionally, an employee mentions a problem but gives no further information about it.
  In such cases, the interviewer should encourage further discussion or
  ask for examples. The kind of probing used in the following example
  is usually sufficient to encourage employees to discuss the subject in
  greater detail.

Emp: There are a lot of conflicting rumors around here. One day
        you hear one thing and the next day the opposite, so we
        need to know more about things.

Int: Would you care to give me an example?

Emp: Well, just last week there was a rumor that they were going to close this plant. This doesn't make much sense because we all know business has been good, but it still shook us up.

- The employee questions the value of the survey. In some cases, such a question is just a sign that the employee is uncomfortable in the interview situation, but regardless of the motivation, interviewers can use such questions to elicit further discussion of employee attitudes and opinions.

Emp: Do you think this will do any good?

Int: Well, after we have interviewed everyone in this department, a report of the findings is sent to management here. After this, a report will be made to your group and at that time if there are any problems you'll hear about what will be done to improve them. Since you brought it up, is there anything you think the survey should do?

As you can see, the interviewer factually explains what will be done with the survey results. More important, however, the interviewer uses the employee's question to accomplish a goal of the interview: to encourage the employee to express his or her feelings about various aspects of the job.

- Employees ask whether they will be informed of the survey results. People usually want to know the outcome of any venture in which they participate. Consequently, it's not unusual for employees to ask whether they will hear about the results of the survey. The following example suggests a way to handle these kinds of inquiries.

Emp: Tell me, will we ever hear about the results or is this just one of those things that you do and then never hear about again?

Int: Well, as I mentioned, we make our report of the overall findings to your manager. After she has a chance to read it over and digest it, she in turn will report back the results to all of you.

Emp: I see.

Int: How things are going for you these days?

Emp: Well, not too bad, I suppose. There are a couple of things ...

- The employee asks questions about policy and procedures. Employees may ask very direct questions about their compensation or their status in the organization. Interviewers should not even attempt to answer these questions. Instead, they should use the question to probe its source or reason—asking whether it has been discussed with management, for example.

> Emp: You know there is something that's been bugging me for a
>   while. You work in personnel, maybe you can tell me if it's
>   true that the company won't allow you to take 3 weeks of
>   vacation at one time.
> Int: You're wondering about a company policy is on this matter.
>   Have you talked to anyone here about this?
> Emp: Oh no. I've never brought it up.
> Int: You've never mentioned it?
> Emp: I've been meaning to talk to the manager, but every time I
>   try to see him his door is closed.

- The employee tries to interview the interviewer. When an interviewer becomes aware that the roles are being reversed, he or she
should gently return the discussion back to the employee and the
work situation.

> Emp: How long have you been at this company?
> Int: Eight years.
> Emp: You must have a very interesting job. How do you like it?
> Int: I enjoy it very much. You mentioned earlier that your job
>   was interesting. Could you tell me about the things that
>   make it interesting for you?

- The employee questions the confidentiality of the survey. Some employees do not understand how survey data are used. For example,
they may fear that what they say will be reported to their superiors.
So, when employees ask, "Is this interview really confidential?" they
may be requesting an assurance that their jobs will be protected if
they express their thoughts. Interviewers should respond emphati-
cally to this inquiry. Employees must be assured their comments will
be treated confidentially.

> Int: I certainly can assure you that it is. What we do is
>   this—when the survey is completed, we analyze all the re-
>   sults and summarize them in a general overall report for the
>   group as a whole—but in no case are the remarks of any
>   one employee *ever reported* or pinpointed.

- The employee asks the interviewer for advice. Employees may ask
the interviewer for direction or guidance. Whenever this happens,
it is important to remember that survey interviews are not intended
to be counseling sessions. As a matter of fact, to give advice to employees may do them and the survey program a disservice. Because
employees see you as a representative of management, they are
likely to take whatever you say quite seriously. As a result, although
you might be speaking quite generally, employees might feel that

any suggestions you make should be followed. This puts employees in the position of taking action or making a decision on the advice of someone who is quite removed from the situation—someone who has no formal responsibility for employees, who may not have all the facts, and who probably will not even be on the scene when the matter is handled. The following exchange shows how a request for advice is actually used to probe the reason underlying it:

Emp: Well, anyway, we're always running out of stock or else the merchandise isn't where we can get at it easily. Mr. Kane, our store manager, came down here the other day and he asked me why there weren't more socks on the counter. I really had no idea of what to say. I sure didn't want to say that the way my boss, Mr. Smart, orders merchandise leaves something to be desired, but, gee, I didn't feel I should be chewed out either.

Int: So, the upshot was you really felt on the spot?

Emp: Yes, I did. Luckily for me a customer walked up and asked me a question. So I excused myself and took care of the sale. By the time I finished, Mr. Kane had left.

Int: Um-hum.

Emp: Do you think the next time I see Mr. Kane I should talk to him about the matter since he brought it up in the first place?

Int: I really think you're in a better position than I am to answer that. What do you think is the best way to handle it?

Emp: Well, I'm not sure. If Mr. Smart didn't work so hard and wasn't so pleasant with us, it would be awfully hard to work here, but on the other hand ...

Interpreting the Employee's Comments

It is not always easy for people to express their feelings and ideas clearly. Often, they are touched on in very general terms. When put in the position of trying to describe and explain these feelings to a second party, employees may have difficulty being specific. For example, employees may be very dissatisfied with their boss, working conditions, or coworkers, but may be able to describe the problem only in a very roundabout way. Perhaps they have never really thought through the matter that they are discussing. When interviewers have a firm grasp of the ideas employees are struggling to communicate, they can help clarify these feelings by attempting to interpret them. This requires care and tact. It is often a matter of trying an interpretation "on for size" and should be attempted only when the interviewer is reasonably sure.

That the interviewer can sometimes help employees clarify their thoughts and feelings is shown here.

Emp: Well, the girl that I work with has been here—just like
       me—about 6 months. She told me, right when she started,
       that she's only interested in this job until she gets married
       in June … She stays on a break … sometimes half an hour,
       she doesn't care. And nobody says anything to her about it.
       She hardly ever helps with stock and then last week she got
       the same raise I did.
Int: Um-hum.
Emp: It just seems that hard work doesn't pay off … It isn't appre-
       ciated. It doesn't seem right, does it?
Int: Your raise seems to have little meaning to you … As a re-
       sult, you actually seem a little discouraged.
Emp: That's right. I thought my raise meant that they felt I was
       doing a good job. But she got the same raise … really for
       doing nothing. It just doesn't seem worth the effort.

The Pause

An employee may stop talking even when the interview is well underway
and an appropriate atmosphere has been established for it. When this happens, the interviewer should not be eager to fill the conversational void. Instead, the silence should continue to allow the employee to begin talking
again. This happens frequently. Employees may pause for a number of reasons, they may want to summon their courage or to collect their thoughts
before plunging into another topic, or they may have finished one subject
and may not know what to say next. In almost every case, the interviewer
should wait for employees to break the silence. The "pause" is frequently a
very potent conversational device and, if not broken by the interviewer, will
strongly encourage the employee to continue the discussion.

The silence, of course, can continue too long. When that happens, interviewers can repeat the employee's last statement or can refer back to any
point they wish to have clarified. An overly long pause may be a sign the interview is over. At this point, an interviewer may simply ask:

"Is there anything else you'd like to talk about?"

Exploring Solutions Expected by Employees

Because surveys are conducted to improve organizational effectiveness and job
satisfaction, it is often advisable to explore employee's suggestions for improvements. This can be done in several different ways. For example, if an employee
mentions a problem, an interviewer can ask any of the following questions:

"What do you think could be done to improve that situation?"

"Do you have a suggestion as to how this might be remedied?"

"If it were up to you, how would you go about handling that?"

"I wonder if you have any thoughts on how this situation could be corrected (solved, improved, changed, etc.)?"

This type of probing has very often led to meaningful improvements. When employees do have well-formed solutions and expectations, they should be covered as fully as possible because any management actions that are consistent with these suggestions may be especially successful, whereas those that run counter to them are likely to be difficult. Thus, in either case, knowledge of employee expectations can be extremely valuable.

Exploring employee solutions to problems serves a number of other useful purposes. Merely posing the question of possible solutions can help employees develop a certain degree of insight and can encourage them to analyze their feelings in greater depth. This kind of inner searching can also help interviewers obtain a better understanding of an organization's impact on employees.

Asking employees for possible solutions also acts as a triggering device because it often gets employees to think of other facets of an issue that may not have been mentioned. In addition, it forces employees to confront the problems that managers face in their attempts at corrective action. This realization may improve the relationship between managers and employees and can help bring about desired changes.

The success of this technique depends on the interviewer's ability to use it appropriately. The following hints may be helpful.

1. The technique should not be used in response to every problem mentioned in an interview.
2. Interviewers should not ask for likely solutions in a challenging or threatening way. Their tone of voice should simply convey an interest in exploring employee ideas and possible solutions.

THE END OF THE INTERVIEW

Most interviews end naturally. This usually is signaled when employees (a) start repeating previous statements; (b) make comments like "I guess that's about it"; or (c) move toward the edge of the chair or actually start to stand up.

It is the interviewer's responsibility to bring the interview to a close when employees seem to have nothing more to say. For example, the interviewer can summarize what has been said and ask, "Does that sum it up?" or "Is there anything else you would like to add?" If employees indicate that they have nothing more to say, the interviewer can conclude the interview: "Well, if there isn't anything else, I want to thank you. It was very nice talking with you."

Caution: Interviews can be terminated too rapidly. Sometimes employees must work up to what they want to say. Therefore, interviewers should use all the techniques at their disposal to insure that employees express everything on their minds. Some of the most insightful comments are made after an employee decides to continue an interview that has seemingly ended.

Note: When a nondirective interview has been properly conducted and not a single direct question has been asked, it is not at all uncommon for an employee to ask "Do you have anymore questions?" This is a compliment and almost always indicate you have been seen as actively engaged in the listening process.

Appendix C

An Evening With Leonardo

In many ways this is a memorial tribute to a very unusual man—W. W. Tudor. Wallie to all who knew him, contributed a great deal to the fun-like atmosphere that existed in Sears during his long tenure as Vice President of Personnel and as a member of its Board of Directors. The account that follows is an example of one such contribution. It is placed in the Appendix for it had nothing to do with survey work per se although it had much to do with morale and team building. It created a climate that encouraged the open sharing of information among a group of fairly sophisticated specialists who tended to center their attention on their own areas of responsibility. It is offered here as an example that other executives may wish to consider. Its effects did endure.

As a way of saying thank you to his staff for, as he put it, "making me look better than I was," Wallie hit on an idea of holding an annual department-wide dinner during and after which a selected member of his staff would make a presentation on a subject, selected by Wallie, that the member had studied and "mastered" during the year. The subjects were purposely chosen to be unrelated to Sears or business of any kind, and above all, to be outside the staff person's field of knowledge and experience. As a case in point: one staff person who had been baptized, confirmed, and married by successive Chicago archbishops and whose devotion to Catholicism was well known to all was assigned to study a religion—the Buddhist religion!

Over an 8-year period, the following topics were assigned:

> History of the Jewish people
> The history of wine
> The history of magic

Leonardo
The Buddhist religion
The occult
The life of Michelangelo

All of these subjects were to be explored on an extracurricular basis, but other than that, no guidance was given on what or how they were to be done or what expenses might be incurred. As might be expected, each presentation attempted to outdo its predecessor and the dinners quickly became black tie affairs and a social focus of the entire department.

The "History of the Jewish People" set the stage for all that followed. It was comprehensive and serious, yet very entertaining, and sprinkled with appropriate humor—some Jewish and some not. Above all, it was enlightening to all of us, not the least of whom were the Jewish members of the department. It could have and should have been published.

The next topic was indeed put into a book. The "History of Wine" covered the growth and cultivation of grapes around the world and resulted in a very entertaining talk on specific varieties of European wine as well as those in the Americas. This was followed by a very elaborate dinner during which several different wines were tasted along with a commentary on their qualities. All of this information was collected in book form and distributed to all members of the department.

"The History of Magic" was assigned to a staff member who had been an accomplished actor while in college. To our amusement, and often our consternation, he was still always "on stage." After it was discovered that magic was an area of show business completely unknown to him, it became his topic. He gave a brief, entertaining account of its history over dinner and then retreated only to reappear with top hat and cane to present a magic show. In the course of 1 year, he joined the magicians' union and learned enough to put on a first-rate performance. He sawed a woman in half, levitated one member of the department, did several card tricks, pulled pigeons out of a hat, and produced an endless stream of ribbons from what seemed like one small thimble. The whole presentation lasted about 90 minutes and worked like—well—like magic. His last trick was to pull out a rabbit with a card in its mouth. On the card was "Leonardo" and my name as the next presenter.

Now, one does not follow a magic act with any sense of assurance. I knew I couldn't compete with a trained actor, or even a rabbit for that matter, so I decided to "play it straight." At the same time, I thought it best to dress up the presentation with copies of Leonardo's works. Here my ignorance of his works came to the fore, and the condescending smile of the Art Institute librarian, when I asked to see Leonardo's paintings, still hurts. Not only were there none in Chicago, there were none in the entire Western Hemisphere! (That is no longer true. Sometime later the National Gallery did buy one of Leonardo's paintings, "Generva di Benci" from the Hermitage). After this encounter, I started reading and studying very seriously, but in view of the literally thousands of books, articles, and myths about Leonardo and his works, the real task was one of selectivity and verification. In this, I was helped enormously by a group of men, all experts in one or more areas of Leonardo's works who, as luck would have it, were invited to participate in a 2-week seminar at UCLA to dedicate the Elmer Belt Library of Avinciani. I spent 2 weeks of my vacation at that seminar and got to know most of the participants. They referred to themselves as the Avinciani and were extremely generous in sharing their knowledge. They were also inordinately patient in answering questions that must have seemed naïve to them. They not only answered questions, but invited me to visit them and, in some cases, we struck up a correspondence that lasted several years.

These special areas of interest in Leonardo are:

> Biography, Sir Kenneth Clark—Great Britain
> Biology & Anatomy, Dr. Kenneth Keele, F.A.C.A.—Great Britain
> Engineering, Dr. Ladislao Reti—Brazil
> Technology, Bern Dibner—USA
> Architecture, Prof. Ludwig Heydenreich—Germany
> Painting, Dr. Carlo Pedretti—USA
> Patrons, Prof. Andre Chastel—France
> Anatomy, Prof. Charles O'Malley—USA

I had additional good fortune when it came to Leonardo's inventions. IBM had commissioned an engineer to create working models of hundreds of Leonardo's designs for machines and other inventions. These were available to museums that had the 50,000 square feet of space needed to display them. Luckily, a chance conversation with a colleague in IBM led to a loan of a box car of working models for my presentation. Included were machine guns, file making machines, water moving devices, a one-piece automatic musical band, a parachute, helicopter, and several versions of airplanes. Thus was born a real IBM booster! I was now ready to at least compete with the rabbit. I also obtained a menu of a formal dinner once served to the Medici family. Because the Medicis were one of his patrons, it is likely that Leonardo may have sat down to this very meal or one like it. At least that was the claim I made at our dinner that evening. Its success is best attested by the fact that even our departmental controller enjoyed it even as he mentally figured its cost. In fact, it cost Wallie a small fortune but he, sometime later, forgave me.

What does all this have to do with team building and morale? Everything! That the successive annual dinners and presentations were extremely enjoyable and that they were greatly anticipated, goes without saying, but they did much more than that. They not only elevated luncheon conversations but created a whole new sense of camaraderie among people who had tended to center their attention and conversation on the specialized work of their own sections. The presentations also created a new sense of respect for the skills and abilities of those involved. Because the department was made up of distinct specializations, there was little need or opportunity for cross talk among its sections. We knew, for example, that the person in charge of Personnel policies was nationally recognized in that area, but until he presented the "History of the Jewish People," we had little awareness of his ability to grasp an unfamiliar subject and convey it so brilliantly and, although our devout Catholic member did not convert to Buddhism, he very credibly described a way of life that was beyond our awareness, and explained a creed that was not only foreign to him but actually contradicted some of his most cherished beliefs.

The magician, of course, not only carried the day but became something of a celebrity. What he mastered in 1 short year was truly amazing and clearly demonstrated the range of his talent, something that was not always apparent given his specialized role in the department and his constant on-stage façade. As an example of the growing team spirit in the department, he lent his new-found skills to several skits used in the Leonardo presentation.

In all of the presentations, a lot of very hard study and hours of preparation were involved. In the end, some of us became near experts on our assigned topics and have continued our studies to the present. As an example of this, some 10 years after my presentation, a Leonardo manuscript that had been lost for centuries was accidentally found in the Madrid Library. This forced me to revise much of the material I had collected on his works.

Above all, the projects were fun to do. If nothing else, the presentations broadened the interests of the whole department and led to the discussion of all sorts of historical and cultural subjects, which I think was Wallie's real intention. As a by-product, but an important one, the presentations improved inter-departmental communication among some 56 people who, for perhaps the first time, looked beyond their separate entities.

At Wallie's retirement, a final dinner was arranged at which a few of us gave updated reprises of our earlier presentations. I had to follow the rabbit bit again, and in keeping with the occasion, gave a brief lecture on, of course, "The Last Supper."

References

Allen, N., & Meyer, J. (1990). The measurement and antecedents of affective continuance and normative commitment to the organization. *Journal of Applied Psychology, 53,* 337–348.

Baker, H., & Jennings, K. (2001). Limitations on realistic recruiting and subsequent socialization effects. *Public Personnel Management, 29* (3), 367–378.

Baldwin, T., Magjuka, R., & Lother, B. (1991). The perils of participation: Effects of choice of training or trainee motivation and learning. *Personnel Psychology, 44,* 51–65.

Breaugh, J. (1983). Realistic job previews: A critical appraisal and future research directions. *Academy of Management Review, 8,* 612–619.

Brooke, P., Russel, D., & Price, J. (1988). Discriminant validation of measures of job satisfaction, job involvement, and organizational commitment. *Journal of Applied Psychology, 73,* 139–145.

Cook, J., Hepworth, S., Wall, T., & Warr, P. (1981). *The Experience of Work.* New York: Academic Press.

Dugoni, B., & Ilgen, D. (1981). Realistic job previews and adjustment of new employees. *Academy of Management Journal, 24,* 579–591.

Dunham, R. & Smith, F. (1979). *Organizational surveys: Internal assessment of organizational health.* Glenview, IL: Scott Foresman.

Dunham, R., Smith, F., & Blackburn, R. (1977). Validation of the index of organizational reactions (IOR) with JDI, MSQ and focus scales. *Academy of Management Journal, 20,* 420–432.

Dunnette, M., Campbell, J., & Hakel, M. (1967). Factors contributing to job satisfaction and job dissatisfaction in six occupational groups. *Organizational Behavior and Human Performance, 2,* 143–174.

Eby, L., Freeman, D., Rush, M., & Lance, D. (1999). Motivational basis of affective organizational commitment: A partial test of an integrated theoretical model. *Journal of Occupational and Organizational Psychology, 72,* 463–483.

Farkas, A., & Tetrick, L. (1989). Three-way organizational analysis of the causal ordering satisfaction and commitment on turnover decisions. *Journal of Applied Psychology, 74,* 855–868.

Fiedler, F. (1967). *A Theory of Leadership.* New York: McGraw Hill.

Fiedler, F. (1994). *Leadership experience and leadership performance*. Alexandria, VA: U.S. Army Research Institute.

Finegan, J. (2000). The impact of person and organizational values on organizational commitment. *Journal of Occupational and Organizational Psychology, 73,* 149–169.

Fleishman, E. (1953). Leadership climate, human relations training and supervision behavior. *Personnel Psychology, 6,* 205–222.

Fleishman E. (1998). Patterns of leadership behavior related to employee grievances and turnover: Some post hoc reflections. *Personnel Psychology, Winter,* 825–834.

Fleishman, E., & Harris, E. (1962). Patterns of leadership behavior related to employee grievances and turnover. *Personnel Psychology, 15,* 43–56.

Fleishman, E., Harris E., & Burt, H. (1955). Leadership and supervision in industry. *Bureau of Educational Research.* Columbus, OH: Monograph 33, Ohio State University Press.

Fleishman, E., & Peters, D. (1962). Interpersonal values, leadership attitudes and managerial success. *Personnel Psychology, 15,* 127–143.

Goffin, R., & Jackson, D. (1988). The structure and validation of the index of organizational reactions. *Multivariate Behavioral Research,* 327–347.

Grany, J., Smith, P., & Stone, E. (Eds.). (1992). *Job Satisfaction: How people feel about their jobs and how it affects their performance.* Lexington, MA: Lexington Books.

Hackett, R. (1989). Work attitudes and employee absenteeism: A synthesis of the literature. *Journal of Occupational Psychology, 62,* 235–248.

Hackman, J., & Oldham, G. (1975). Development of the job diagnostic survey. *Journal of Applied Psychology, 60,* 159–170.

Hamner, C., & Smith, F. (1978). Work attitudes as predictors of unionization activity. *Journal of Applied Psychology, 63,* 415–421.

Herman, J. (1973). Are situational contingencies limiting job attitude–job performance relationships? *Organizational Behavior and Human Performance, 10,* 208–224.

Herzberg, F. (1965). The motivation to work among finish supervisors. *Personnel Psychology, 18,* 393–402.

Herzberg, F. (1968). One more time: How to motivate employees? *Harvard Business Review, 46,* 53–62.

Herzberg, F., Mausner, B., & Snyderman, B. (1959). *The motivation to work.* New York: Wiley.

Higgs, A., & Ashworth, S. (1996). Organizational surveys: Tools for assessment and research. In A. I. Kraut (Ed.), *Organizational surveys: Tools for assessment and change* (pp. 19–40). San Francisco: Jossey Bass.

Hinrichs, J. (1996). Feedback, action planning, and follow-through. In A. I. Kraut (Ed.), *Organizational surveys: Tools for assessment and change* (pp. 255–279). San Francisco: Jossey Bass.

Hollenbeck, J., & Williams, C. (1986). A turnover functionally versus turnover frequency: A note on work attitudes and organizational effectiveness. *Journal of Applied Psychology, 71,* 606–611.

Hom, P., & Griffeth, R. (1995). *Employee turnover* Cincinnati, OH: South-Western.

Hom, P., Griffeth, R., Palich, L., & Bracker, J. (1999). Revisiting met expectations as a reason why realistic job previews work. *Personnel Psychology, 52,* 97–112.

Hom, P., and Kinicki, A. (2001). Toward a greater understanding of how dissatisfaction drives turnover. *Academy of Management Journal, 44 (5),* 975–987.

Hulin, C. (1966). The effects of community characteristics on measures of job satisfaction. *Journal of Applied Psychology, 50,* 185–192.

Hulin, C. (1971). Individual differences and job enrichment— The case against general treatments. In F. Maher (Ed.), *New perceptions of job enrichment* (pp. 41–55). Berkeley, CA: Von Norstrand and Reinhold.

Iococa, L., with William Novak. (1984). *An autobiography*. Toronto, Canada: Bantam Books.

Ivancovich, J. (1986). Predicting absenteeism from prior absence and work attitudes. *Academy of Managerial Journal, 28*, 219–228.

Jacoby, S. (1986). Employee attitude testing in Sears Roebuck and Co. (1938–1960). *Business History Review, 66*, 602–632.

Johnson, J. (1996). Linking employee perception of service climate to customer satisfaction. *Personnel Psychology, 49*, 831–851.

Johnson, S. (1996). Life in the consortium: The Mayflower Group. In A. I. Kraut (Ed.), Organizational surveys: Tools for assessment and change. *Organizational Surveys* (pp. 285–309). San Francisco: Jossey Press.

Jones, J. (1991). In search of excellent customer service. *Bank Management, 67*, 40–41.

Judge, T., & Larsen, R. (2001). Dispositional affect and job dissatisfaction: A review and theoretical extension. *Organizational Behavior and Human Decision Processes, 86*, 67–98.

Katerberg, R., Smith, F., & Hoy, S. (1977). Language, time and person effects on attitudes scale translations. *Journal of Applied Psychology, 62*, 385–391.

Katz, D. (1986). *The Big Store: Inside the crisis and revolution in Sears*. New York: Viking Press.

Kerr, S., Schriesheim, C., & Stogdill, R. (1974). Toward a theory of leadership based upon the consideration and initiation of structure literature. *Organizational Behavior Human Performance, 12*, 62–82.

Kinicki, A., McKee-Ryan, F., Schriesheim, C., & Carson, K. (2002). Assessing the construct validity of the job description index: A review and meta analysis. *Journal of Applied Psychology, 67*, 14–32.

Kraut, A. I. (Ed.). (1996). *Organizational surveys: Tools for assessment and change*. San Francisco: Jossey Bass.

Lee, T. (1988). How job dissatisfaction leads to employee turnover. *Journal of Business and Psychology, 2 (3)* 263–272.

Lee, T., & Mowday, R. (1987). Voluntary leaving an organization: An empirical investigation of Steers and Mowday's model of turnover. *Academy of Management Journal, 39 (4)*, 721–743.

Lee, T., & Mowday, R. (1990). Voluntary leaving an organization: An empirical investigation of Steers and Mowday's model of turnover. *Academy of Management Journal, 30 (4)*, 721–743.

Leonard, B. (2001, May). The CEO position has become a revolving door in U.S. corporation. How can HR help hire the right person for the top job? *HR Magazine*, 47–52.

Likert, R. (1967). *The human organization*. New York: McGraw Hill.

Marrow, A., Bowers, D., & Seashore, S. (1967). *Management by Participation*. New York: Harper & Row.

Maslow, A. (1943). A theory of human motivation. *Psychological Review, 50*, 370–396.

Maslow, A. (1958). *Motivational and personality*. New York: Harper and Row.

McCabe, D., Dalessio, A., & Sasaki, J. (1980). The convergent and discriminant validates between the IOR & JDI: English and Spanish versions. *Academy of Management Journal, 23 (4), 278–786.*

McGregor, D. (1944). Conditions of effective leadership. *Journal of Consulting Psychology, 8*, 55–63.

McGregor, D. (1960). *The human side of the enterprise*. New York: McGraw Hill.

Mobley, W. (1977). Intermediate linkages in the relationship between job satisfaction and employee turnover. *Journal of Applied Psychology, 62*, 237–240.

Mowday, A., Steers, R., & Porter, L. (1979). The measurement of organizational commitment. *Journal of Vocational Behavior, 14*, 224–247.

Mowday, R., Porter, L., and Steers, R. (1982). *Employee organizational linkages: The psychology of commitment, absenteeism and turnover*. New York: Academic Press.

Nadler, D. (1977). *Feedback and organizational development: Using data based methods*. Reading, MA: Addison Wesley.

Ondrach, O. (1974). Defense mechanisms and Herzberg theory. *Academy of Management Journal, 17*, 79–89.

Ostroff, C. (1992). The relationship between satisfaction, attitudes, and performance: An organizational level analysis. *Journal of Applied Psychology, 77*, 963–974.

Porter, L., Smith, F., & Crampton, W. (1976). Organizational commitment and managerial turnover: A longitudinal study. *Organizational Behavior and Human Performance, 15*, 87–98.

Rhoades, L., Eisenberger, R., & Armeli, S. (2001). Affective commitment to organization: The contribution of perceived organizational support. *Journal of Applied Psychology, 85*, 825–836.

Rhodes, S., & Steers, R. (1991). *Managing employee absenteeism*. Reading, MA: Addeson-Wesley.

Riordan, C., & Vandenberg, R. (1994). A central question in cross-cultural research: Do employees in different cultures interpret work-related measures in an equivalent manner? *Journal of Management Psychology, 20*, 643–671.

Rogers, C. (1951). *Client Centered Therapy*. Boston: Houghton Mifflin Press.

Rogg, K., Schmidt, D., Shul, C., & Schmitt, N. (2001). Human resource practices, organizational climate, and customer satisfaction. *Journal of Management, 27*, 431–449.

Rothlisberger, F., & Dickson, W. (1939). *Management and the Worker*. Cambridge, MA: Harvard University Press.

Rucci, A., Kirn, S., & Quinn R. (1998). The employee-customer-profit chain at Sears. *Harvard Business Review, 76*, 82–97.

Ryan, A., Chan, D., Ployhart, R., & Slade, L. (1999). Employee attitude surveys in a multinational organization: Considering language and culture in assessing measurement equivalence. *Personnel Psychology, 52*, 37–58.

Schein, E. (1993). How can organization learn faster? The challenge of entering the green room. *Sloan Management Review, 34*, 85–92.

Schmit, M., & Allscheid, S. (1995). Employee attitudes and customer satisfaction: Making theoretical and empirical connections. *Personnel Psychology, 48*, 521–536.

Schneider, B. (1980). The service organization: Climate is crucial. *Organization Dynamics, Autumn*, 52–69.

Schneider, B. (1990). The climate for service: Application of the construct. In B. Schneider (Ed.), *Organizational climate and culture*. San Francisco: Jossey Bass.

Schneider, B., & Bowen, D. (1985). Employee and customer perception of service in banks: A replication and extension. *Journal of Applied Psychology, 70*, 423–433.

Schneider, B., White, S., & Paul, M. (1998). Linking service climate and customer perception of service quality: Test of a casual model. *Journal of Applied Psychology, 83*, 150–163.

Scott, K., & Taylor, G. (1985). An examination of conflicting findings on the relationship between job satisfaction and absenteeism: A meta-analysis. *Academy of Management Journal, 28*, 599–612.

Senge, P. (1990). *The fifth discipline*. New York: Currency Doubleday.

Smith, F. (1962). *Problems and trends in operational use of employee attitude measurements*. Paper presented at annual meeting of American Psychological Association, St. Louis, MO.

Smith, F. (1976). The index of organizational reactions. *JSAS Catalog of Selected Documents, 6*: Ms. No. 1265.

Smith, F. (1977). Work attitudes as predictors of attendance on a specific day. *Journal of Applied Psychology, 62*, 16–19.

Smith, F., & Porter, L. (1977). What do executives really think about their organization? *Organizational Dynamics, Autumn*, 2–14.

Smith, P., Kendall, L., & Hulin, C. (1969). *The measurement of satisfaction in work and retirement: A strategy for the study of attitudes*. Chicago, IL: Rand McNally.

Somers, M., & Birnbaum, D. (2000). Exploring the relationship between commitment pro-files and work attitudes, employee withdrawal, and job performance. *Public Personnel Management, 29* (3), 353–364.

Stanton, J., Balzer, W., Smith P., Parra, L., & Ironson, G. (2001). A general measure of work stress: The stress in general scale. *Educational and Psychological Measurement, 61* (5), 866–888.

Stogdill, R., & Coons, A. (1957). *Leader behavior: Its description and measurement.* Columbus, OH: Ohio State University Press.

Terborg, J., Lee, T., Smith, F., Davis, G., & Turbin, M. (1982). Extension of the Schmidt and Hunter validity generalization procedure to the prediction of absenteeism behavior from knowledge of job satisfaction and organizational committal. *Journal of Applied Psychology, 67,* 440–449.

Tornow, W., & Wiley, J. (1991). Service quality and management practices: A look at employee attitudes, customer satisfaction and bottom-line consequences. *Human Resources Planning, 14,* 105–166.

Ulrich, D., Halbrook, R., Meder, D., Stuchlik, M., & Thorpe, S. (1991). Employee and customer attachments: Synergies for competitive advantage. *Human Resource Planning, 14,* 89–104.

Vitelies, M. (1953). *Motivation and morale in industry.* New York: Norton.

Vroom, V. (1964). *Work and motivation.* New York: John Wiley.

Wherry, R. (1954). An orthogonal re-rotation of the Baer and Ash studies of the SRA inventory. *Personnel Psychology, 7,* 365–380.

Wiley, J. (1996). Linking survey results to customer satisfaction and business results. In A. I. Kraut (Ed.), *Organizational surveys: Tools for assessment and change* (pp. 330–359). San Francisco: Jossey Bass.

Williams, L., & Hazer, J. (1986). Antecedents and consequences of satisfaction on commitment in turnover models: A reanalysis using talent variable structure equation methods. *Journal of Applied Psychology, 71,* 219–231.

SUGGESTED READINGS

In addition to articles noted in the text, the following are some of the known research studies, which have used the Index of Organizational Reactions (IOR) since its publication.

Adams, E. F. (1976). *The effect of minority supervisors on subordinate attitudes and perceptions.* Unpublished doctoral dissertation, University of Illinois, Champaign-Urbana.

Adams, E. F. (1980). *An investigation of an organization accommodating managerial changes.* Unpublished doctoral dissertation, University of Illinois at Champaign-Urbana.

Brown, R. R.(1986). *Individual, situational, and demographic factors predicting faculty commitment to the university.* Unpublished doctoral dissertation, University of Oregon

Butler, B. B. (1987). *Factors associated with job satisfaction among social workers.* Unpublished doctoral dissertation, Virginia Commonwealth University.

Castaneda, M., & Nahauandi, A. (1991). Link of manager behavior to supervisory performance rating and subordinate satisfaction. *Group and Organizational Studies, 16* (4), 357–366.

Deckard, G. J. (1985). *Work, stress, mood, and ecological dysfunction in health and social service settings.* Unpublished doctoral dissertation, University of Missouri, Kansas City.

Dunham, R. (1977). Reactions to job characteristics: Moderating effects of organization. *Academy of Management Journal, 20* (1), 42–65.

Evans, D., Pellizzari, J., Culbert, J., & Metzen, M. (1993). Personality, marital, and occupational factors associated with quality of life. *Journal of Clinical Psychology, 49* (4), 477–485.

Ferratt, T., Dunham, R., & Pierce, J. (1981). Self report measures of job characteristics and affective responses: An examination of discriminant validity. *Academy of Management Journal, 24* (4), 780–794.

Furnham, A., Toop, A., Lewis, C. & Fisher, A. (1995). P-E fit and job satisfaction: A failure to support Holland's theory in three British samples. *Personality and Individual Differences, 19* (5), 677–690.

Golenbiewski, R., & Roundtree, B. (1986). Phases of burnout and properties of work environments: Replicating and extending of covariants. *Organizational Development Journal, 4* (2), 25–30.

McCabe, D. J. (1977). *The relationship of organizational structure, job characteristics, and background variables with work satisfaction.* Unpublished doctoral dissertation, Illinois Institute of Technology, Chicago.

Merwin, C. M. (1981). *An examination of a leadership theory: Correlates of leadership in schools of nursing.* The University of Texas at Austin. (1981)

Motowidlo, S., & Borman, W. (1978). Relationship between military morale, motivation, satisfaction and unit effectiveness. *Journal of Applied Psychology, 63* (1), 47–52.

Moyers, P. A. (1992). Engagement in professional updating by occupational therapists. Unpublished doctoral dissertation, Ball State University.

Navas Luque, M. (1988). Innovacion technologia, factors psicosociales y estres en puesto de trabado: Un estudio empirico. *ReVista De Psicologia Social, 3* (2), 181–191.

Pierce, J. (1979). Employee affective responses to work unit structure and job design: A test of an interviewing variable. *Journal of Management, 5* (2), 193–211.

Pierce, J., McTavish, D., & Knudsen, K. (1986). The measurement of job characteristics: A content and contextual analytic look at scale validity. *Journal of Occupational Behavior, 74* (4), 299–313.

Smith, F., Roberts, K., & Hulin, C. (1976). Ten-year job satisfaction trends in a stable organization. *Academy Management Journal, 19* (3), 462–469.

Smith, F., Roberts, K., & Hulin, C. (1977). Trends in job-related attitudes of managerial and professional employees. *Academy of Management Journal, 10* (3), 454–460.

Wimberley, D. L. (1991). *Work satisfaction, work-related stress, marital/family stress, and spousal support of married veterinarians.* Unpublished doctoral dissertation, Oklahoma State University.

Author Index

Subject Index